Rediscovering Empathy

Rediscovering Empathy

Agency, Folk Psychology, and the Human Sciences

Karsten R. Stueber

A Bradford Book
The MIT Press
Cambridge, Massachusetts
London, England

MIT Press books may be purchased at special quantity discounts for business or sales promotional use. For information, please email special_sales@mitpress.mit.edu or write to Special Sales Department, The MIT Press, 55 Hayward Street, Cambridge, MA 02142.

This book was set in Stone Serif and Stone Sans on 3B2 by Asco Typesetters, Hong Kong, and was printed and bound in the United States of America.

Library of Congress Cataloging-in-Publication Data

Stueber, Karsten R.
Rediscovering empathy : agency, folk psychology, and the human sciences / Karsten R. Stueber.
    p. cm.
"A Bradford book."
Includes bibliographical references and index.
ISBN-13: 978-0-262-19550-8 (hc : alk. paper)
ISBN-10: 0-262-19550-X (hc : alk. paper)
1. Psychology—Philosophy. 2. Science and psychology. 3. Empathy. I. Title.
BF64.S78 2006
152.4'1—dc22   2005058414

10 9 8 7 6 5 4 3 2 1

In memory of my father, Kurt Stüber

Contents

Preface

This book constitutes a systematic and historically informed defense of the controversial thesis that empathy is epistemically central to our folk-psychological ability to understand other agents. I will develop the argument for empathy in the context of current philosophy of mind and the interdisciplinary debate about the nature of our mindreading abilities, a debate that involves a multitude of disciplines ranging from philosophy to neuroscience. As I will explain in the introduction, one can defend empathy successfully in the current context only if one is also aware of the historical origins of, the critical debate surrounding, and the eventual rejection of the viability of the concept of empathy in the philosophy of social science. A systematic defense of empathy has to be able to address the prima facie plausible objections raised within the philosophy of social science. According to the prevalent view in the philosophy of the social sciences, to conceive of empathy as epistemically central to our ability to understand other agents is an expression of epistemic naiveté, a proposal tainted by its association with an objectionable Cartesian conception of the mind. By countering these objections this book attempts philosophically to rehabilitate the empathy thesis that was popular at the beginning of the twentieth century.

Having found my philosophical bearing in an environment that was skeptical about empathy, I was rather prejudiced against the claims of simulation theorists—today's equivalent of empathy theorists—when I first encountered them. Yet at the same time I was intrigued by the ongoing debate about our mindreading abilities. My book is the culmination of my thinking about empathy in the current context and the outcome of a process of overcoming my own philosophical doubts about empathy's epistemic relevance, a process that took six to seven years. I started to write the manuscript in the academic year 2003–2004 during my sabbatical granted by the College of the Holy Cross. As with any philosophical endeavor, my own thinking has been helped by conversations about relevant topics in a variety of contexts. I found particularly conducive in this respect the discussions with audiences at my presentations at the Society for Philosophy and Psychology, the European Society for Philosophy and Psychology, the Social Science Roundtable, and my participation at the NEH Institute organized by Paul Roth and Jim Bohman at St. Louis in 1998. I have greatly benefited from discussions about relevant issues that I had with Bob Gordon, Paul Roth, Dan Hutto, Chris Gaucker, Joe Cruz, Jim Bohman, Mark Risjord, Kristin Andrews, and Bert Kögler, with whom I also cooperated in editing an anthology about related topics a few years ago. Most of these colleagues are also owed thanks for providing useful comments on drafts on some of my earlier work that can be seen as stepping stones for this book manuscript. I should not forget to mention David Henderson in this regard. Not only did his talk introduce me to the current debate between simulation theory and theory theory, but conversations with him have proven to be particularly valuable for my project. Jeff Bloechl deserves special thanks for reading parts of the manuscript and providing editorial suggestions, a task that is even more appreciated as it required him to step outside of his own area of philosophical expertise. Similarly, Ralph Hertwig has read and provided useful comments on the chapter on the notion of bounded rationality. My student Andrew Cameron must be acknowledged for his work on the index of this book. His work has been supported by a small grant from the College of the Holy Cross. Finally, I would like to express my gratitude to the reviewers of the manuscript for their valuable comments and to Tom Stone, philosophy and cognitive science editor at MIT Press, for supporting this project from the very beginning.

Curiously, writing a book about empathy does not always increase one's empathetic abilities. For nevertheless being supportive of my project, I am very grateful to my longtime intellectual companion and wife Manisha Sinha and our seven-year-old son Sheel. Manisha's proofreading of the whole manuscript and her insightful editorial suggestions have been especially significant in the final phase of completing the manuscript. Even Sheel took an ardent interest in reading drafts of the manuscript and urged me to curtail my Germanic tendency for writing run-on sentences. I have tried my best in this regard. The three of us are happy to welcome the newest member of our family, Shiv—"little dude," according to Sheel—whose arrival made the final phase of publishing this manuscript a joyous challenge. This book is dedicated to the memory of my father, who unexpectedly and sadly passed away in the summer of 2003 after I started my final research on this book, two weeks after our final meeting.

Introduction

After all, empathy is a varied, yet unavoidable and natural affair.
—Theodor Lipps (1912–1913)

Typical adult human beings have developed the ability to understand other persons as minded creatures, to recognize others' states of mind, and to make sense of their behavior in light of their mind's causal powers. We understand that our fellow beings are creatures who can see what is in front of them, remember things that happened to them in the past, deliberate about what to do in the future; they can feel pain, be happy, feel depressed, guilty, ashamed, or proud. We also grasp that other persons act the way they do because of their state of mind and that their state of mind is causally influenced by their interactions with the environment and with other human beings. We predict that another person will probably not climb the Eiffel Tower because he is afraid of heights, or explain that he does not work well with a colleague by pointing out that he is jealous of him. Similarly, we assume that somebody knows what is in a box if he has looked into it, and that he will be disappointed if he does not achieve what he wanted to achieve, as for instance when he fails a test he wanted to pass. Without doubt, our ability to understand other people as minded creatures in this way has to be conceived of as the psychological foundation of our ability to be social animals and to become full members of society. The inability to read the minds of others would put us at a distinct disadvantage to pursue our individual interests in any social context where the success of our action depends in large part on the cooperation and reaction of other people. More importantly, severe deficiencies in our ability to read others' minds such as is exemplified in autism not only diminish our ability to pursue our individual interests in a social context; they also have been shown to be associated with fundamental restrictions in our ability to form basic social bonds and to be initiated into social practices such as the speaking of a common language.

The abilities and the repertoire of mental concepts such as beliefs, desires, and emotions that ordinary people without any specific psychological training possess and use for understanding other people as minded creatures are referred to collectively by contemporary philosophers and psychologists as folk psychology. At the moment, these abilities are the topic of intense psychological and neurobiological research that is trying to characterize their underlying causal mechanisms. Yet even though the term "folk psychology" is a recent one,[1] the central issues debated today have their specific philosophical ancestry in traditional philosophy of the social sciences. In particular, the issue of how we understand other minds was one of the central philosophical concerns in the late nineteenth and early twentieth centuries, when it was seen as the foundational issue one had to address in order to properly determine the scientific status of disciplines such as history, psychology, and sociology—that is, disciplines that have to do with the exploration of human agency and that to some extent use the same conceptual framework that ordinary folk do. The controversial point within both contexts has always been whether our epistemic access to other minds proceeds in a manner radically different from that by which we acquire knowledge about other domains of investigation, or whether it is structurally similar to such methods. The former view is taken by traditional proponents of the empathy view and by current simulation theorists. The latter view has been argued for by so-called naturalists in traditional philosophy of social science and by theory theorists in the context of current philosophy of mind.

The reason that defenders of the empathy viewpoint have felt that our understanding of other minds is special has to do with the fact that we not only attribute mental states to other persons from a third-person perspective but also conceive of ourselves as minded creatures from a first-person perspective. We assume that our access to our own mind is more direct and in some way epistemically privileged than our access to the mind of another. We not only recognize the other person as a minded creature, but we recognize each other as same-minded and as persons who have access to their minds from a first-person perspective. Accordingly, it has been assumed that our judgment of same-mindedness and the recognition of another person's mental states have to fundamentally take note of the peculiarity of the subjective and the first-person element involved in mental matters. In contrast to our grasp of other domains of investigations, understanding other minds has been seen as proceeding from an egocentric perspective.

The following simple example illustrates the debate about the egocentricity of our folk-psychological abilities to read other minds. Consider the judgment that another person is the same height as myself. There are in principle two ways of establishing this fact. On the one hand, we can measure each of us using a measuring tape attached to the wall. We are then the same height if such measurement comes up with the same value for both of us. This evidently involves use of an external, or what one also might call a theoretical/universal, standard in order to establish that we are the same height. I would like to call this the *detached* or *theoretical* method of measurement. Our judgment that we wear the same shirt or, to take a more complicated case, our judgment that we belong to the same biological class as whales seems to follow the same model. We know the criteria according to which various classes are defined by our biological theory, and we appeal to those criteria in classifying both humans and whales as mammals. In proceeding in the detached manner we utilize prior knowledge of a scale of measurement or knowledge of a theory—in this case, a biological theory—that we can also apply to ourselves. My knowledge of the other person and my knowledge of his height are cognitively mediated by a standard or theory under which both of us can be subsumed.

There is another way of establishing that I am the same height as another person. In this case I do not use an external standard as a measuring tool, but instead use myself as the standard. According to this method of measurement, we are the same height if it turns out that the head of the other person is at exactly the same level as my head when we are standing back to back. I establish that we are the same height because I recognize that another person is my height; that is, I find out that we are of the same height not by using a neutral or theoretical standard but by using an *egocentric* standard. Empathy theorists claim analogously that there is something epistemically special in our access to other minds: in learning of other minds we proceed essentially in an egocentric manner, similar to the manner in which we determine the height of another person. My finding out about another person's mind depends on using myself and my own mind as a standard or model for the other person's mind. In particular, proponents of the empathy view claim that I gain knowledge of other minds primarily because I can simulate or imitate others' mental processes in my own mind. I do not rely on knowledge of a psychological theory of other human beings for that purpose. Yet in claiming that our folk-psychological capacities primarily make use of such egocentric methods, proponents of the empathy view do not merely claim that we at times can use the egocentric method instead of a psychological theory. None of the participants in this debate will deny that, in contrast to our situation in other domains of investigation, we indeed have the ability to empathize with another person in the above sense and that we can use empathy as a way to determine what is in another person's mind. Similarly, none of the proponents should be understood as claiming that we never use a theoretical approach to other minds. I can obviously use both the egocentric and the detached method of measurement to find out whether or not I and someone else are the same height. The debate, as I will understand it in this book, is rather about whether or not empathy as an egocentric and less theory-dependent strategy has to be conceived of as the *epistemically central* way in which we find out about other minds, as something that we cannot do without in order to gain knowledge of other minds.

Originally hailed as the fundamental method of gaining knowledge of other minds and as the unique method of the human sciences at the turn from the nineteenth to the twentieth century, empathy has long lost its past glory, even among philosophers who are still inclined to maintain a methodological distinction between the social and the natural sciences. For the last century, philosophers of social science from very different philosophical traditions—with a few notable exceptions—have tended to regard the above view of empathy as epistemically naive and incapable of providing an epistemically sanctioned method of folk-psychological interpretation and explanation. Only recently, after a century of philosophical neglect and widespread philosophical disdain for the claim that empathy is the epistemically central method for our understanding of other agents, is empathy again being taken seriously by philosophers, psychologists, and neuroscientists and is being defended in a variety of forms by so-called simulation theorists. Their newfound interest in empathy mirrors the enthusiasm of past philosophers of history and the social sciences who considered empathy to be the primary method for acquiring objective knowledge of other agents. In light of this new enthusiasm for empathy from such diverse disciplines, and given these opposing evaluations of the role of empathy in philosophy of social science and philosophy of mind, it is time to take a second and in-depth look at the question of empathy, its role, and its limitations for understanding other agents and other minds in the conceptual framework of folk psychology.

I will argue in this book that the renewed attention to empathy as the primary method for understanding other minds is indeed well deserved and that empathy must be regarded as the epistemically central, default method for understanding other agents within the folk-psychological framework. I will proceed systematically by focusing my discussion primarily within the context of the current discussion about folk psychology, since I do think that this discussion allows us to define a much more precise and more articulate conception of the exact structure of empathy and of our folk-psychological practices. Nevertheless, such a systematic defense of empathy ultimately can be successful only if it is also able to address the prima facie rather plausible philosophical misgivings about empathy that have been responsible for its failure to gain widespread acceptance in the philosophical community over the last century—a fact of which participants in today's debate are often insufficiently aware.

1 Empathy and Knowledge of Other Minds: A Historical Perspective

A few brief historical reflections on the concept of empathy are in order, since they will allow us to get a better understanding of the central issues in the philosophy of social science that need to be addressed in order to defend empathy's central epistemic role in folk-psychological contexts. It will also provide the reader with a better sense of my motivation for the organization of this book. Empathy's emergence as one of the primary concepts for solving the problem of other minds and as a central concept in the discussion about the foundation of the human sciences is best understood as the convergence of two rather independent philosophical traditions or discourses at the beginning of the twentieth century: the hermeneutic tradition of the "philological sciences" (Boeckh 1886), which focused predominantly on the concept of understanding (*Verstehen*), and the discussion within philosophical aesthetics, which was responsible for introducing the concept of empathy (*Einfühlung*). Here the work of Theodor

Lipps is particularly important since for him the aesthetic problem and the problem of other minds are essentially linked. Since both traditions took themselves to be addressing the peculiarity of our grasp of phenomena whose external appearance "expresses" in some sense an inner mental or "spiritual" reality in bodily acts, artifacts, texts, or social institutions,[2] it is perhaps not surprising that at times understanding and empathy have been seen as nearly identical.

As some readers might know, the term "empathy" was introduced into English as the translation that Titchener choose for the German term *"Einfühlung"* (Titchner 1909a, 21; see also Wispe 1987), a term that quickly became a central and technical term in aesthetics after Robert Vischer introduced it in his 1873 "On the Optical Sense of Form: A Contribution to Aesthetics," together with a rather bewildering array of related terms such as *Anfühlung, Zufühlung, Zusammenfühlung, Nachfühlung* (whose exact translation is of no interest in this context). Vischer himself acknowledges his use of the term "empathy" as having been inspired by Karl Sterner's explication of dreams, according to which one projects one's own bodily form unconsciously—"and with this also the soul—into the form of the object" (Vischer 1873, 92).

Vischer has to be credited with introducing the term *"Einfühlung"* as a noun and as a technical concept in the context of philosophical aesthetics. Yet the verb *"einfühlen"* had been used earlier in a less technical fashion. His famous father, Friedrich Theodor Vischer, and Hermann Lotze, for example, had used it in the context of aesthetics. Its use seems to go back at least to pantheistically inclined romantic thinkers such as Herder, Novalis, and others.[3] In his "Vom Erkennen und Empfinden der menschlichen Seele" (1774/1964), Herder, for example, speaks of the ability of humankind "to feel into everything, to feel everything out of himself" (1774 [1964], 7–8, my translation) and of humankind's ability to recognize everything in nature in analogy to oneself. For Herder, such empathy is understood as a quasi-perceptual act that has to be strictly distinguished from a mere inferential process such as that used with a syllogism. He sees it as in the end justified because of his trust in God who has given humans such empathetic ability as the "key" to recognize "the interior of things." Novalis (1981), in his essay "Die Lehrlinge zu Sais," exhorts humankind to leave or at least to complement the dissecting and analytic attitude of science that has deadened "friendly nature" (101). Instead, humankind should adopt a more poetic attitude that would allow us to grasp nature as what one might call a "spiritual totality." For Novalis, such a poetic attitude is ultimately grounded in our natural capacity to feel what nature feels (123).

Within romanticism, our ability to empathize with nature was closely tied to a pantheistic metaphysics and to a critique of modern society organized according to purely rational principles of science. For the romantic, nature is properly understood only if it is seen as an outward symbol of some inner spiritual reality. From the perspective of modern science, however, such a metaphysical stance is seen as an arbitrary projection or "introjection."[4] Yet even after one disavows the metaphysical perspective of romanticism and recognizes the detached attitude of science as appropriate for investigating nature, our aesthetic experiences and judgments about the beauty of natural objects and human artifacts have to be recognized as naturally occurring phenomena that must be psychologically accounted for. Phenomenologically, our aesthetic experiences are characterized by a similar directness and an associated phenomenal quality as the perceptual recognition of an object as blue or red, square or triangular, that form the basis of scientific theorizing according to a positivist conception of science. Mechanisms of empathy, as explicated by Lipps in his aesthetics, are intended to fill this explanatory vacuum and are used explain the noninferential and quasi-perceptual character of aesthetic experiences. Aesthetic experiences are understood as specific perceptual encounters with external states of affairs that cause certain internal resonance phenomena that are projected into and felt as a quality of the perceived object.[5] They are understood as a form of "objectified self-enjoyment" (Lipps 1906, 100). Interestingly, Lipps links our recognition of the mindedness of other people directly to our aesthetic appreciation of the beauty of external objects, since for him the paradigm of beauty for humans is the form, movement, and expressivity of the human body itself (Lipps 1903a, 102). Our aesthetic appreciation of objects is in the end grounded in seeing their form in analogy to the expressive quality of human vitality in the body. Their form initiates the same response as the expressions of the human body. For this reason Lipps conceives of empathy not merely as an important aesthetic concept but as a basic sociological and psychological category (Lipps 1903b).

For Lipps, the projective mechanisms of empathy are based on an innate, instinctual and, beyond that, ultimately inexplicable human tendency to motor mimicry, already noticed by Smith (1853 [1966], 4). We feel like yawning in the company of other yawners and tend to move our own legs in a room full of dancers. Most of the time, such external imitations of bodily movement are inhibited either through external circumstances or as part of our natural and cultural maturation. Lipps speculates that this "inhibited imitation" is still present as an inner tendency for imitation with specific associated kinesthetic experience in the mere observation of another person's movement and in the aesthetic contemplation of an object. Since we are not aware of "inner imitation" as imitation, we experience and project the associated phenomenal quality into the observed object (Lipps 1903b, 120; 1903a, 191).

It is in this context worthwhile to clear up a common misconception due to an uncharitable reading of Lipps by Edith Stein (1917 [1980]). Stein accuses Lipps of confusing empathy (*Einfühlung*) with a more mystical feeling of oneness (*Einsfühlung*) with the other person or object.[6] Admittedly Lipps says that empathy, especially aesthetic empathy, leads to a complete identification between the observer and the movement of the observed persons or objects (1903b, 191, 121–126). But this does not imply that empathy leads to losing oneself in a different reality or, still less, to acting according to that perspective on reality. In an important sense, I know perfectly well that the anger that I experience in observing another angry person or in contemplating an artistic sculpture is not my anger—it is not me that is angry. In short, the anger I experience in empathy lacks all of its motivating force (Lipps 1906, 112–113; 1903b/1905, 46–48). Similarly, in identifying with the movements of an acrobat on a rope high above the ground—one of Lipps's favorite examples—I "know" that I myself am not high above the ground (1903b, 123).[7] Lipps's use of the identification terminology in order to explicate the phenomenon of empathy does not signify advocacy of a complete loss of the self in its object. Instead he wants to emphasize that empathy must be strictly distinguished from a more theoretical and inferential stance toward another person's mind, particularly in the form of the inference from analogy that was suggested by John Stuart Mill. According to the inference from analogy, we infer that the other person is in a particular mental state by observing his physical behavior and by knowing that such behavior is in our own case associated with a particular mental state, while assuming that the other person is in relevant aspects like me. Empathy, as Lipps conceived of it, "is not the name for any inference; rather it is the name for an original and not further derivable, at the same time most wonderful fact, which is different from an inference, indeed absolutely incompatible [with it]" (1907, 713, my translation).[8]

Lipps's work popularized empathy as a central category for philosophical thinking about understanding other minds at the beginning of the twentieth century. Edmund Husserl and his student Edith Stein used and developed the category of empathy as a key concept in their explication of reciprocal intersubjectivity between minded individuals. Empathy not only allows me to solve the basic problem of other minds; that is, it not only allows me to recognize another person as being minded. It also enables me to develop myself more fully as a reflective and self-critical individual, since it enables me to recognize the opinions of others about myself.[9] Moreover, and more important for our purposes, this opened the way for the concept of empathy to merge in the general philosophical consciousness with concept of understanding so central to the hermeneutic tradition of philosophy.

Hermeneutics is best understood as the theory of interpretation and understanding, a theory that tries to determine the manner in which we grasp and explicate the meaning of another person's utterances, written or otherwise, and try to understand those utterances as expressions of inner thoughts.[10] More or less systematic theoretical reflections on the nature and proper procedure of interpreting another person's expressions were rather widespread in intellectual history. (For a survey see Grondin 1994.) They tended to be particularly important in times when the interpretation of familiar texts became contested territory, or when a particular interpretive practice dealing with a certain array of texts became newly established.[11] One finds a variety of hermeneutical considerations outlining methodological prescriptions closely tied to various interpretive practices such as theology, jurisprudence, and philology. However, particularly in the seventeenth and eighteenth centuries one also finds serious attempts to provide descriptions of general rules for the "good interpreter" (Dannhauser 1630) to find the intended meaning of various texts and "reasonable speeches and writings" (Chladenius 1742). Such methodological considerations were understood to be part of the logical organon for every researcher since in order to determine the validity of an argument or the truth of a sentence one first has to correctly grasp its intended meaning. Hermeneutics was considered to provide tools of reasoning for all of the sciences, and in this manner it was understood as supplementing the organon of Aristotle and Bacon (Beetz 1981).

Nineteenth-century hermeneutics, however, tended to see itself less in the tradition of specifying rules of interpretation. In the aftermath of the cult of the aesthetic genius, who in the production of the work of art does not follow rules but rather creates his own, Schleiermacher's influential hermeneutical considerations emphasized that interpretation requires understanding the individual style of a particular author. Interpreting a text requires congenially grasping the individuality of a specific author by understanding how his use of a common language governed by traditional linguistic conventions of his time reflects his own unique first-person point of view, which is expressed in a particular style of writing. For Schleiermacher (1998), understanding therefore depends on knowledge of the social linguistic conventions and knowledge of the thoughts and specific intentions of each individual author. The art of understanding consists in two complementary and mutually supportive parts, that is, grammatical and psychological interpretation (1998, 9, 229).[12] Yet even for Schleiermacher and his student, Boeckh, hermeneutics does not concern itself merely with a methodology of the human sciences. Boeckh, for example, describes understanding, which is philology's essential method, in more general terms as being concerned with "the knowing of the known" that for him minimally requires reconstructing another person's thoughts as thoughts in our own mind (Boeckh 1886, 19).[13] Grasping the thoughts of another person in this manner is a task that is relevant for all the sciences insofar as they depend on the social interaction of individual scientists. (Boeckh 1886, 11, 33). For Boeckh hermeneutics as the essential methodology of philology is still part of a general organon. Only with Droysen and Dilthey does understanding become identified as a separate methodology of the historical and human sciences and defined in contrast to the explanatory enterprise of the natural sciences.[14]

Nevertheless, in establishing psychological interpretation as at least one of the essential aspects of interpretation, Schleiermacher linked our ability to understand other minds with our capacity to transform ourselves imaginatively into an occupant of the other person's point of view. Such imaginative transformation was for him an essential ingredient of any interpretive process (Schleiermacher 1998, 92). Indeed, for hermeneutic thinkers of this time, such transformation is considered possible only because of the basic structural and psychological similarity between the interpreter and the object of interpretation. To quote Droysen, a representative of this tradition:

> The possibility of understanding arises from the—for us congenial—manner of expressions that lie before us as historical material. A further condition of this possibility is the fact that man's nature, at once sensuous and spiritual, expresses every one of its inner processes in some form apprehensible by the senses, mirrors these inner processes, indeed in every expression. On being perceived, an expression, by projecting itself into the inner experience of the percipient, calls forth the same inner process. Thus, *on hearing the cry of anguish we feel the anguish of the person who cries* and so on. (Droysen 1893, 12–13; 1977, 423; my emphasis and translation)[15]

Following Schleiermacher, Droysen does not reduce historical interpretation to a version of psychological interpretation. For Droysen, psychological interpretation is still merely a moment in historical interpretation since historical interpretation proceeds by situating the historical agent, in a quasi-Hegelian manner, in the context of ethical ideas and the play of ethical forces of which the individual agent might not always be aware. The task of the historian is in the end the construction of a synthetic narrative that integrates all of the relevant aspects of human agency into a lively painting of the chosen time period. Only the early Dilthey regards psychological interpretation and a particular conception of psychology as the primary basis of all of the human sciences. For him, the coherence of cultural systems such as law, art, and religion is nothing but the psychic coherence constitutive of a human being.[16] It was Dilthey's psychological turn or complete "psychologization" of the interpretive process that made possible the common identification of the concept of understanding and empathy that we find at the beginning of the twentieth century. Even though the above thinkers in the hermeneutic tradition tended not to use the terms *"Einfühlung"* or *"einfühlen,"* they used similar enough terminology—such as *"mitfühlen"* (feeling with), *"nacherleben"* (reexperiencing), *"nachbilden"* (reconstructing), *"hineinversetzen"* (putting oneself into), or *"Transposition."* Once empathy was established as a central means to understanding other minds, it became quite natural to think of understanding as a form of empathy.[17]

In contrast to Lipps, philosophers in the hermeneutic tradition were not interested primarily in the question of how one can find out whether or not there are other minds, or whether some other person is a minded creature.

Their primary interpretive problems were not of how one recognizes the emotional state of another based on his facial expressions, which is precisely the sort of question that was central for Lipps. Thinkers in the hermeneutic tradition were more interested in determining the epistemic means for justifying the interpretation of utterances, written texts, and actions of others. They were also interested in explicating the manner in which we evaluate the significance of these acts in the context of larger historical narratives. Instead of appealing to underlying psychological mechanisms such as inner imitation in the perception of the bodily movements, hermeneutic thinkers focused on two very different aspects of the interpretive process, which they saw as justifying a strict distinction between the human and the natural sciences. Specifically, it was emphasized that the structures of significance and meaning that we encounter in the folk-psychological and social scientific contexts are constituted according to principles that have no equivalent in our investigation of nature by the natural sciences. It was pointed out that structures of meaning and significance are holistically constituted and that they are normatively structured (as I would like to call it), since they are teleologically organized in light of human purposes and values.[18] Consequently, one should not expect, or so it was felt, that the explication of human affairs proceeds in subsuming observed events under same general lawlike regularities as is required for the explanatory project in the natural sciences. Rather, the holistic structure of meaning and significance demands a radically different method of devising and epistemically justifying a particular interpretation. In order to grasp the significance of a particular act, a particular utterance, or a particular text passage one must integrate it into its larger context. A specific passage needs to be seen in the context of the whole text of which it is a part, and a particular action of a person has to be seen in the context of the whole life of an individual or in the larger social or historical context.

Interpretation therefore cannot escape what has come to be called the *hermeneutic circle*. One can determine the significance of a specific text passage only if one understands its contribution to the significance of the larger whole. Yet one cannot justify the interpretation of a whole except in light of the overall consistency of its parts. Likewise, in order to understand the significance of a particular act of an individual I must inherently grasp the context to which that act belongs, as well as how it fits into this context and vice versa.[19] For this reason, the model of scientific explanations according to which nature is analyzed in terms of its most basic atomic elements and then explained with the help of strict lawful regularities between these elements came to be regarded as inappropriate for the human sciences. Accordingly, the early Dilthey rejects a conception of psychology in analogy to the natural sciences, which he also calls analytic (*zergliedernde*) or explanatory psychology, and argues for a descriptive psychology—or what one might also call a psychology of understanding—as the basis of the human sciences. For him the context into which we have to integrate elements of meaning is primarily a mental one. It is a context that presents itself to us through "inner experience" and introspection.[20] One can grasp the significance of a text or even of a social institution only if it can be related to this primary mental context of significance. Understanding an object as possessing meaning or a person as expressing a thought is based on an act of mental transposition that allows the subject to integrate them into a lived unity of cohering and interrelated mental states.[21]

Dilthey is certainly right to insist, against an associationist and empiricist psychology, that I am from a first-person point of view not merely aware of my mental states as unrelated sensory data. I am also aware of them as being related to my prior experiences or thoughts. I experience a face primarily not as having a certain shape, but as being familiar or unfamiliar. Similarly, in entertaining a thought I am also aware of it cohering (or not) with other thoughts, even though this does not exclude the possibility that I might be mistaken about such judgments. Yet in emphasizing the "lived totality" of the mental as the primary context of significance, Dilthey undermines his own project of psychologically grounding the human sciences, since the interpretive task in the human sciences is not limited to contexts that are experienced by one individual (Gadamer 1960 [1989]; Danto 1965). As today's philosophers of history and historians agree, in explicating the particular historical significance of an event or act the historian has to integrate this event into a larger historical context. Such analysis is not necessarily bound by the conceptual categories of agents but proceeds retrospectively, by taking into account their long-range and at times unintended consequences. To say that the shots in Sarajevo were the start of the First World War does integrate the action of one assassin within a larger context, but it is not a context that is accessible introspectively from the first-person perspective. Even the significance of an individual's action is not necessarily directly experienced. More often it is revealed only retrospectively when later aspects of a person's biography have been recognized.

Subsequently, Dilthey himself has recognized the shortcoming of his attempt to ground the human sciences psychologically, emphasizing a direct and inner access to the realm of mental phenomena.[22] In his work *Der Aufbau der Geschichtlichen Welt in den Geisteswissenschaften* (1981), he gives up on the idea that introspective access to a totality of lived experience provides us with the primary unit of significance. He considers individuals as having access to the meaning and grasping the significance of particular practices—religious rituals, marriage ceremonies, elections, and so on—only because they are embedded in a specific cultural and social context that is normatively structured (162–163). Using Hegelian terminology, Dilthey refers to this normatively structured social realm as "objective spirit." Dilthey insists that conceiving of understanding as presupposing the integration of an individual into this normatively structured realm can no longer be conceived in a psychological manner as he had argued earlier on (96). On the other hand, Dilthey retains categories that are reminiscent of his earlier ideas and still speaks of "reexperiencing" (*Nacherleben*), "reconstructing" (*nachbilden*), or "putting oneself into" (*hineinversetzen*). Yet he does not fully justify the appropriateness of this terminology in his later work.[23] He rather hints at a position that retains a commitment to the claim that we understand each other as individual agents only because we are psychologically similar without implying that each of us is introspectively aware of the totality of life experiences. We are psychologically similar because each of us can participate in a normatively structured social realm. Even if we are members of differently structured social realms, we still are able to understand each other because we can be responsive to a variety of norms and are able to reorient ourselves in contexts where different norms rule.

Within the philosophy of social science, particularly philosophy of history, it has been Collingwood (1946) and not Dilthey who has developed this line of thought most explicitly in suggesting that the inner imitation of thoughts, or what he calls the reenactment of thoughts, is a central epistemic tool for understanding other agents since it is only in this manner that we are able to understand agents as rational agents. In Dilthey, it is difficult to ascertain whether or not empathy as an egocentric form of mental imitation is seen as having any special role to play in our understanding of other agents.[24] At times it appears as if the role of empathy in the understanding of individual agency is replaced by more theory-laden interpretive procedures. The reexperiencing (*Nacherleben*) of Dilthey's later phase is certainly not a simple resonance phenomenon due to the observation of the gesture or facial expression of another person, as Lipps described it. Rather, the reexperiencing that Dilthey has in mind is methodologically guided by our interpretation of a variety of historical sources and by our knowledge of the general political, economic, social, and psychological states of affairs relevant for an adequate grasp of a particular historical time. We will understand an agent like Bismarck only if we understand him at the same time as, for example, the representative of the psychological category of a man of action and a representative of the landowning class of Prussian nobility (Dilthey 1981, 172; see also 175–177, 266). For that reason it becomes questionable whether empathy can serve any genuine epistemic function in this context. Interpretation of other agents appears to be completely dependent on theoretical knowledge, since such knowledge seems to do the primary explanatory work. After having taken what the hermeneutic tradition after Schleiermacher has called psychological interpretation as the all-encompassing basis for the human sciences, the later Dilthey fails to determine the proper status of the so-called psychological interpretation for our understanding of agency in the social realm.[25]

Let us summarize our historical survey so far. Empathy as a form of *inner imitation* has been regarded as central in the realm of the human sciences dealing with human agency and human institutions because it was felt that only in this manner can one understand specific phenomena as expressions of an underlying mental reality. So far we also have encountered two basic argumentative strategies for this claim. Lipps argues for the centrality of empathy by inferring the existence of certain resonance phenomena on the neurobiological level, whereas hermeneutic thinkers appealed primarily to the necessity of inner imitation because they thought that the principles constitutive of the mental realm do not fit the analytic and explanatory approach of the natural sciences. Yet despite the fact that hermeneutic thinkers would like to maintain a methodological distinction between the human and the natural sciences—because only the human sciences deal with phenomena that are inherently meaningful (Giddens 1976)—philosophers of social science, with the exception of a few adherents of Collingwood's doctrine of reenactment, tend to be rather dismissive of empathy's epistemic role in the human sciences. Hermeneutic philosophers, even if they do champion understanding (*Verstehen*), are nowadays rather careful to distinguish understanding from empathy. Indeed most philosophers of social science would regard betting on empathy as central to gaining knowledge of other minds as the equivalent of betting on a dead horse.

Within the hermeneutic context, rejecting the identification of the concepts of empathy and understanding is certainly to be explained partly by the early Dilthey's overemphasis on psychological interpretation. Yet this complete and implausible psychologization of the interpretive process in the human sciences cannot fully explain empathy's decline as a central method for understanding human affairs, especially individual agency in folk-psychological terms. It is one thing to realize that empathy cannot be regarded as the only method of the human sciences; it is quite another to assert that empathy plays no central role in our understanding of individual agency in the folk-psychological realm, as I would like to argue in this book. To understand the wholesale rejection of empathy as playing any significant epistemic role in interpreting agency, it is important to realize that the empathy position was understood as being essentially tied to a problematic Cartesian conception of the mind of which philosophers from all traditions became rather wary in the twentieth century. More specifically, it was viewed as being dependent on a view according to which we are primarily acquainted with our own mental states from a first-person perspective and according to which we define our mental concepts privately in reference to those inner experiences. For that reason, Cartesianism was considered to be in principle incapable of answering the question of how we can be justified in using our knowledge of our own mind to gain knowledge of other minds. In becoming associated with Cartesianism, the empathy view was seen as advocating an epistemically naive and mysterious conception of a theoretically unmediated meeting between two minds.

The precarious epistemic status of the empathy proposal is also evident in Lipps's justification of empathy as a form of inner imitation. Even though Lipps's proposal is certainly an interesting hypothesis about how we can have knowledge of other minds—particularly knowledge of the other person's emotional states based on our perception of their facial expression—as articulated by him it stands in need of further elaboration for two specific reasons. First, Lipps's position includes specific empirical theses about underlying psychological mechanisms for recognizing mental states in other persons. Given the state of psychological research at his time, his hypothesis certainly cannot be regarded to be sufficiently justified by empirical evidence. Other accounts that postulate mechanisms of complex yet unconscious inferential procedures are certainly equally plausible to a certain degree. Prandtl (1910, 82ff., 109ff.), for example, has suggested that our recognition of the emotional states of another person is based on inferences determined by psychological laws of reproduction and association. According to this line of thought we attribute a particular mental state to another person in the following manner: When we see the facial outlines of another person's angry face we associate the visual representation of his face with a visual representation of our own facial expressions. However, this visual representation of our own facial expression is in some way causally connected with a particular feeling or at least with some form of representation of such feeling. Yet since the "felt" state does not otherwise correspond to my outlook on the world or does not fit in with my own inner mental life or actual bodily expressions, I infer that it must be the other person who is in this particular mental state. Notice that pointing to the fact that our recognition of another person's emotion based on his facial expression appears to be a noninferential perceptual act does not constitute a sufficient basis to adjudicate this dispute, since everybody acknowledges that such inferences are unconscious and happen on the subpersonal level. Phenomenology cannot be understood as being an infallible guide to the structure of underlying psychological mechanisms.

Equally important, phenomenology also cannot be understood as providing direct answers to normative epistemological questions. Phenomenological first impressions can be epistemically very deceiving. This brings us to the second problem for Lipps. To address the question of how we gain knowledge of other minds, it is not sufficient merely to address the question of underlying causal mechanisms; one also has to address the question of whether we can reasonably expect that the use of such a mechanism leads to *justified true beliefs* about the mental states of other people. Lipps merely points out that projective empathy should be understood as a "most wonderful fact" of nature and that it cannot be conceived of as an inference. He thus does not address the question of why using empathy in this manner can be seen to be more than a mere projection, that is, he does not sufficiently address the question of *quid iuris*. Even if we use empathy in this manner to project our own feelings onto the other person, with what right can we expect that such a method will provide us with genuine knowledge of the other person's mental states?

The above epistemic questions become even more pronounced in a context where empathy is not seen merely as enabling us to attribute specific mental states to other people, but where mental imitation supposedly also enables us to *explain* and *predict* the complex behavior of others using folk-psychological terminology. To suggest that historians, for example, merely explain the action of historical agents because their minds resonate with the mind of the person under investigation seems to misdescribe the manner in which historians painstakingly argue for their interpretation in light of various evidential sources. At most, philosophers of social science were willing to grant empathy a very limited role in the context of discovery for proposing certain interpretive hypotheses about the behavior of other people. (See for example Hempel 1965.) They saw its role as similar to the epistemically limited function that one grants the egocentric method in measuring a person's height. To depend for measurements of heights on comparison with my own height is prima facie not a very reliable method. It is very difficult to compare different egocentric scales of measurements unless one already has a detached standard. It also seems that using my own height as standard lacks sufficient longevity and objectivity. My own height tends to change with age, and even within the frame of a day it seems to fluctuate a bit. Normal adults tend to be an inch taller after a night of rest than in the evening.

For similar reasons, using the egocentric method was regarded as a rather imperfect manner of gaining knowledge of other minds. Whereas it was thought possibly to provide us with some insight into the minds of other people from the same cultural contexts, empathy was judged to fall short in bridging deeply engrained cultural differences between agents. Moreover, even within this limited sphere it was felt that empathy could never provide us with sufficient epistemic justification for explanatory hypotheses about another person's behavior. Pointing out that I would have acted in a certain manner if I would have had certain mental states does not seem a sufficient basis for explaining why you would have acted in that manner unless one presupposes the validity of certain general principles—that is, unless one presupposes some theoretical knowledge of general explanatory principles. From this perspective, the ability for mental simulation and imitation can certainly be regarded as an additional heuristic tool for finding explanatory hypotheses. Still, it alone will never be able to provide us with knowledge of another person's mind or an adequate psychological account of his or her behavior. Among philosophers willing to grant empathy any role for understanding other agents—and a variety of them have been doubtful even of that claim—most have viewed it as playing a rather marginal epistemic role. The heavy epistemic work is fulfilled solely by theoretical knowledge ranging from folk psychology to specific sociological and historical theories.

2 Arguing for Empathy Systematically

Bearing all of the above in mind, I will argue in the following that the orthodox consensus against empathy in the philosophy of social science got it wrong. Empathy should be seen as the epistemically central, even if at times limited, default method of gaining knowledge of the minds of other individual agents. It will be shown that all of the standard objections against empathy as the central epistemic method for understanding other minds can be met, even if this means that one has to grant that our folk-psychological practice also depends on theoretical knowledge in a sense to be more precisely defined. Yet to grant the relevance of some theoretical knowledge to folk psychology is not to grant that empathy is epistemically superfluous or negligible.

The prior historical survey has revealed that the debate about empathy was interested simultaneously in investigating the psychological processes of our mindreading abilities—that is, questions of "descriptive epistemology"—and in addressing the nature of the epistemic justification of our beliefs about other minds—issues of "normative epistemology" (Goldman 2002). It has involved empirical considerations about underlying causal mechanisms and more a priori reflections about the structure of significance and the nature of rational agency and thought processes. I understand both aspects of the traditional debate as playing important roles for my conception of empathy. I am rather doubtful that the question of empathy's role in our folk-psychological practice can be decided only through empirical research, as it is sometimes claimed by participants of the contemporary debate of folk psychology. They see the discussion driven primarily by results of scientific studies in developmental child psychology, psychopathology, and cognitive neuroscience, to name a few. The ultimate aim of such research is to provide psychologically realistic accounts of our mentalizing abilities in terms of their underlying causal mechanisms, and in this way to account for their scope and possible short-comings. At times one gets the impression that traditional arm chair philosophizing that has been so central for conceiving of the problem of other minds is looked down upon even by philosophers who participate in this debate. I think that the exclusive emphasis on empirical considerations about underlying psychological mechanism alone is a mistake. No analysis of our folk-psychological practices can be sufficiently justified if it does not take into account the central conceptual issues and normative epistemic issues that have been responsible for the generally negative evaluation of the empathy view in the last century.

This stance should not be taken to imply that I recommend that a philosophical reflection about folk psychology proceeds without taking into account relevant results of psychological research in this domain. As a naturalistically minded philosopher I consider it unacceptable for philosophical considerations about mental matters to proceed wholly without knowledge of the pertinent results of psychological investigations. Indeed I will argue that such empirical research—particularly recent neurobiological findings—is philosophically relevant as it will help us to overcome and finally lay to rest the ghosts of Cartesianism and behaviorism that still have undue influence in contemporary philosophy of mind. Neurobiological considerations will support Lipps's conception of empathy as mechanisms of inner imitations. Such mechanisms should be regarded as a form of empathy that I will call *basic empathy*. Mechanisms of basic empathy have to be understood as mechanisms that underlie our theoretically unmediated quasi-perceptual ability to recognize other creatures directly as minded creatures and to recognize them implicitly as creatures that are fundamentally like us. Yet my argument for these claims will not depend only on empirical research about underlying causal mechanisms. It will also include considerations about the nature of our grasp of folk-psychological concepts.

Moreover, accepting basic empathy in this manner does not wholeheartedly support the claim that empathy is the central method for understanding other agents, since I am prepared to argue that even a theory-theory position could accommodate itself to the above insights. Basic empathy, as I understand it, allows us to recognize, for example, *that* another person is angry, or *that* he intends to grasp a cup. Yet we also have to be able to explain a person's subsequent behavior in complex social situations. We need to understand why that person is angry, or why he responded to a particular situation in a certain manner. For this reason, additional arguments are required showing that such complex understanding of another person's behavior depends essentially on empathy and that it cannot be conceived of as proceeding solely on the basis of knowledge of a psychological theory. I will thus distinguish between basic and reenactive empathy and will argue that only through *reenactive empathy*—that is, only by using our cognitive and deliberative capacities in order to reenact or imitate in our own mind the thought processes of the other person—are we able to conceive of another person's more complex social behavior as the behavior of a rational agent who acts for a reason.

My defense of reenactive empathy as playing a central epistemic role in understanding other agents will be closely tied to the fundamental fact that within folk psychology we view each other as rational creatures who act for reasons. In contrast to the argument for basic empathy, considerations about neurobiological mechanisms or results of psychological experiments will not play the decisive role here. Rather, questions about the centrality of reenactive empathy require philosophical reflection from the armchair regarding the nature of rational agency—concerns that have played a central role in Collingwood's defense of reenactment and, more recently, in Jane Heal's defense of simulation. As I will explain, thinking about the nature of rational agency allows us to develop arguments that suggest that it is very implausible to conceive of our folk-psychological practices as being implemented by mechanisms of theoretical inferences.

Finally, even if one could grant that the empathy view could prevail based on empirical considerations about underlying causal mechanisms alone, we still would need to address the pertinent normative objections to empathy raised explicitly within the context of philosophy of social science. Otherwise, traditional critics of the empathy view could always respond that their concerns have not been addressed. From their perspective, showing that empathy is as a matter of fact the method that we most naturally apply in the folk-psychological context is compatible with the claim that in doing so we are being epistemically naive. Moreover, they would claim that this epistemic naiveté can be overcome only by applying folk-psychological categories in a more disciplined and theoretical manner. I, for one, would find it a rather shallow victory for empathy if we could show only that empathy is an often-used causal heuristic that nonetheless has no role to play in a normative context where the epistemic justification of our beliefs about other minds is at issue. In this book I intend to do better.

The book consists of six chapters. Given that my defense of empathy—particularly reenactive empathy—depends on the claim that within the folk-psychological context we view each other as rational agents, and given the fact that this assumption is rather contested in contemporary philosophy of mind, I will spend the first two chapters defending the view according to which rational agency is a central category of folk psychology. In the first chapter I will focus on what I regard as the dominant conception of folk psychology in the philosophy of mind and explain why I consider it to fall short of accounting for our folk-psychological practices. More specifically, the dominant view wrongly conceives of folk psychology as a theory adopted from a detached perspective; that is, it views it as a theory that even alien minds with a completely different psychology could adopt for the purpose of explaining human behavior. Consequently, beliefs and desires are conceived of as mere internal causes of behavior. Agents, however, do not understand their beliefs and desires merely as internal events but as reasons for their actions. In this manner they take ownership of their behavior by situating it in a world as it appears from their perspective. I will suggest that the conceptual scheme of folk psychology is best viewed as being adopted from the point of view of agents who in experiencing their agency view themselves as acting for reasons and who use folk-psychological terminology in order to view other persons as acting for reasons like themselves. I will call this view of folk psychology the *engaged conception*.

Moreover, I will defend this view against the claim that the concept of rational agency cannot be regarded as important for our folk-psychological practices because psychological experiments have shown that our natural inferential strategies systematically violate norms of reasoning or norms of rationality. I will suggest that the rationality debate in contemporary philosophy and psychology is confused about the nature of the traditional claim that humans are rational animals. Traditionally, this claim has not been taken to imply that our best normative theories of rationality also have to be understood as articulating the structure of an inner program of human minds. Conceiving of human beings as rational animals implies only that the thoughts and actions of persons are situated within a normative dimension that allows us to critically evaluate their actions as rational or irrational, as their having good or bad reasons for their actions. Indeed, I will suggest that modern psychological research does not only leave unchallenged the traditional conception of rationality. Rather, in using such experimental results to prove the irrational nature of humankind, one already presupposes the traditional conception according to which human beings are in some sense responsive to the norms of reasoning.

In the second chapter I will continue my defense of the claim that the rationality assumption is central to folk psychology. The puzzlement about rationality in contemporary philosophy of mind is also due to a misunderstanding of the exact nature of the principle of charity as a constitutive principle of folk-psychological interpretation. As my defense of the global principle of charity will show, associating charity with an ideal conception of rationality is the equivalent of having a local conception of charity. Charity is more plausibly conceived of as constraining the interpretive process in a global manner and as implying that agents have the ability to maintain the consistency of sufficiently large subsets of their overall belief set. Yet in contrast to a widespread tendency among contemporary philosophers and psychologists, I want to resist the temptation to downsize our norms of rationality as articulated by our best theories of decision making and logical and probabilistic reasoning to fit our finite human capacities. My discussion of Gigerenzer's notion of bounded rationality will show that this tendency is reinforced by failing to sufficiently notice that our judgments about the rationality of an action are highly contextualized judgments that have to take into account a multitude of normative standards and facts of the situation, including the limits of an agent's cognitive abilities. Accordingly, abstract norms of logical reasoning have to be conceived of as norms of rationality that are relevant to evaluating whether an agent acted rationally in certain situations. Yet one's action in a particular context does not necessarily have to be judged to be irrational merely because it does not conform to one of the relevant norms.

Having outlined my understanding of the rationality assumption within the folk-psychological context, I will then systematically defend my claim

for the epistemic centrality of empathy in the next two chapters by critically discussing the contemporary debate between simulation theorists
and theory-theorists. In the third chapter, I situate and characterize the
simulation proposal within the context of the empirical debate about the
theory of mind in contemporary psychology. Whether one views the simulation proposal primarily as a thesis about underlying subpersonal mechanisms or instead as a thesis about personal-level phenomena, it is best to
regard the simulation proposal as suggesting that folk-psychological understanding consists of three distinct phases. Consequently, the empathy
proposal is best understood as arguing for the epistemic centrality of the
second phase, that is, the simulation phase or the phase of mental imitation. As I will show, the centrality of empathy or simulation for our folk-
psychological practices can be defended even if various forms of theoretical
knowledge will have to be admitted in the first and the third phase, as long
as such knowledge does not infect the central simulation phase and as long
as such knowledge does not make the simulation phase epistemically superfluous. It is particularly in this context (chapter 4) that the distinction
between basic and reenactive empathy will be argued for and questions
about our grasp of folk-psychological concepts will have to be addressed.
Both first-personal and third-personal accounts favored by some contemporary theorists show significant blind spots in this regard. Reference to
mechanisms of inner imitation as revealed by contemporary neuroscientific research—to what I call basic empathy—will allow us to overcome
the limits of the traditional accounts of both first-personal and third-
personal accounts of mental concepts. It will also allow us to understand
how an intersubjective conceptual framework for understanding other
agents could be established without falling into the traps of the traditional
accounts.

In contrast to some simulation theorists, I am nonetheless willing to accept that our grasp of folk-psychological concepts depends on implicitly
grasping how various kinds of mental states interact. I am willing to grant
that our grasp of folk-psychological concepts involves theoretical knowledge in a minimal sense, but without admitting a theory-theory account
of how we understand another agent's more complex behavior in a folk-
psychological context. Rather, reenactive empathy will be shown to be
central to understanding other agents in this respect. I will articulate two
arguments for the importance of reenactive empathy, both of which are

suggested in rudimentary form by Collingwood: what I would like to call the *argument from the essential contextuality of thoughts as reasons* and the *argument from the essential indexicality of thoughts as reasons*. In addition I will suggest that it is implausible to think that a theory-theorist could counter the above argument based solely on empirical considerations. For that very reason, empirical research into our mindreading abilities is most plausibly seen as not deciding the issue between simulation theory and theory-theory. It has to be viewed as investigating the underlying mechanisms implementing our folk-psychological abilities to view other agents as acting for a reason. Yet such abilities have to be thought of as essentially involving empathy.

In the final two chapters I will address the pertinent epistemic objections to empathy that have been raised by philosophers of social science and that have not been sufficiently discussed in the contemporary context. In chapter 5, I address Carl Hempel's claim that empathy is epistemically unable to sanction predictions or explanations of behavior. Given that Hempel's orthodox model of explanation is no longer accepted, a discussion of Hempel's objections has to distinguish strictly between the question of the epistemic justification of prediction and that of explanation. Only explanations require implicit reference to folk-psychological generalizations. Using Woodward's conception of explanation, I will suggest that the proper explanatory domain for folk-psychological generalizations is the domain of rational agency. Accordingly, reference to an agent's beliefs and desires has explanatory force for accounting for his behavior only if we can also understand them as reasons for their actions. Folk-psychological explanations are indeed dependent on folk-psychological generalizations. Yet they are able to back up explanatory accounts of behavior only as long as we are not in doubt that we are in the proper domain of folk psychology. It is exactly for this reason that empathy, *pace* Hempel, plays a central role in the epistemic justification of our explanatory accounts of individual behavior.

Finally, in the last chapter of the book I will address the specific objections raised from the hermeneutic and Wittgensteinian traditions in the philosophy of social science. What unifies these objections against empathy is the recognition that the social and cultural embeddedness of an agent plays a central role in the constitution of his mind and his habits of thoughts. From this perspective, the empathy view is part of a Cartesian

conception of the mind that insufficiently recognizes the social constitution of the mind. Given the social and cultural embeddedness of our
minds, it is also naive to think that we are able easily to abstract from our
own well-entrenched habits of thought in an attempt to simulate another
person's thoughts. I will carefully analyze the most significant version of
these objections. I do not consider these objections to be able to dislodge
my arguments for the epistemic centrality of empathy for understanding
agency, since the empathy view is not in fact committed to an implausible
Cartesian view of the mind. But I do regard the above considerations as
requiring an important qualification from the empathy theorist. Empathy
theorists should be prepared to admit certain limitations in our ability to
make sense of other agents using empathy alone. Furthermore, they should
recognize supplemental and theoretical strategies available to overcome
these limitations. Yet recognizing such limitations of empathy is not to
deny that empathy must be regarded as the central default mode of understanding other agents in terms of their reasons. It is only in light of our
empathetic capacities that we can identify certain interpretive problems
that need to be overcome with the help of supplemental strategies.

Despite the fact that the empathy theorist has to admit the importance
of theoretical knowledge in the folk-psychological context—particularly
when epistemically normative concerns are raised—empathy is still of central epistemic importance to our folk-psychological understanding of other
agents. As the book will show, the central question for deciding whether or
not the egocentric method of empathy is epistemically central to understanding other agents is not whether it proceeds independently of all
theoretical knowledge. Rather the question is whether the appeal to theoretical knowledge makes empathy as a form of mental simulation or imitation epistemically superfluous. And if I am right, this question has to
be answered negatively. Expressed more positively, empathy has to be
regarded as the central epistemic default strategy in our folk-psychological
practices.

3   Brief Excursus: Empathy, Sympathy, and Social Psychology

Before we get into *media res*, a few words about the difference between empathy and sympathy and the role of empathy research in social psychology
are in order. Frankly admitted, the title of the book, "Rediscovering Em-

pathy," can be properly understood only when viewed from the perspective of philosophy, particularly philosophy of social science. Social psychologists are likely to be astonished about the title, given the extensive and important research on empathy in their specific domain of investigation. Whereas recent dictionaries in philosophy tend not to say much about empathy, no major dictionary or handbook in psychology is without an at times lengthy entry on empathy.

Yet one has to be very careful in this context. Social psychologists are not primarily interested in empathy as a specific cognitive mechanism of inner imitation for gaining knowledge of other minds. Instead, they tend to be interested in empathy as the psychological foundation for social relations and altruistic behavior. In my opinion, it is for this very reason that social psychologists, as they have themselves noted (Davis 1994; Hoffman 2000; Eisenberg and Strayer 1984), did not always have a well-defined concept of empathy within their research tradition. Under the heading of empathy, social psychologists have investigated whatever they have tended to regard as the psychological basis of social cohesion and as the basis of genuine altruistic behavior. In describing the multiple conception of empathy, one psychologist, for example, distinguishes between "cognitive and participatory empathy," between "affective empathy," "empathetic joining," and "parallel and reactive empathy" (Staub in Eisenberg and Strayer 1984, 104ff). As can been seen from Davis's attempt to provide a "multidimensional measure" of empathy as a dispositional trait of various individuals—thereby trying to unify various research traditions in social psychology—empathy seems to refer to a bundle of sometimes quite different capacities and attitudes of one person toward the states of mind and situations of another. It ranges from the cognitive ability to have knowledge of the other person's mental states—in whatever manner one arrives at such judgments—to the ability to take the perspective of another person and to respond emotionally to the state of mind and situation of the observed target. Davis's Interpersonal Reactivity Index (IRI) is a questionnaire that tries to scale one's empathetic responses on a variety of dimensions such as "perspective taking" or "the tendency to spontaneously adopt the psychological view of others in everyday life"; "empathetic concern" or "the tendency to experience feelings of sympathy or compassion for unfortunate others"; "personal distress" or "the tendency to experience distress or discomfort in response to extreme distress in others"; and "fantasy" or "the tendency to imaginatively transpose oneself into fictional situations" (Davis 1994, 55–57).

Whereas Davis has tried to clarify the domain of empirical empathy re-search by explicitly acknowledging its multidimensionality, others have tried to limit its scope. In the last twenty to thirty years social psychologists have also tried to focus research on particular aspects of empathy, either (i) by investigating what they call empathetic accuracy or (ii) by trying to sharpen empathy research in mainly defining it as a phenomenon of the "vicariously sharing of an affect" of one individual with another (Eisenberg and Strayer 1984, 3) or as involving a "psychological process that makes a person have feelings that are more congruent with another person's situa-tion than with his own situation" (Hoffman 2000, 30). For our purposes, research on empathetic accuracy would seem prima facie to be particularly relevant. Yet empathetic accuracy has been defined as the accuracy of our "everyday mindreading" capacity;[26] that is, it has been defined by what cognitive psychologists call the accuracy of our "theory of mind" capacity and what I would prefer to call the accuracy of our folk-psychological abili-ties. It is thus research that is neutral regarding the question of whether our cognition of another person's mind proceeds in an egocentric or detached and at least implicitly theoretical manner.

I do not object to defining empathy research as primarily concerned with an affective phenomenon, if that suits the purposes of social psychologist. I am not interested in mere verbal squabbles. Yet I would object to the claim that empathy as the vicarious sharing of an emotional state should be un-derstood as the only right way of defining and explicating the concept of empathy, as is sometimes asserted in this context.[27] Empathy as under-stood within the original philosophical context is best seen as a form of *inner or mental imitation for the purpose of gaining knowledge of other minds.* Even if Lipps is especially interested in the recognition of emotions based on the perception of facial expressions, it has to be stressed that even for him empathy as inner imitation applies to the whole range of mental phe-nomena. It is in this sense that I will understand the concept of empathy in this book.

In contrast to the cognitive concerns that characterize the concept of empathy in its original philosophical context, empathy research in social psychology is best understood as merging the concept of empathy and its primarily cognitive concerns with the concept of sympathy within moral psychology dating back at least to David Hume and Adam Smith. David Hume in his *Treatise* (1739–40) and *An Enquiry Concerning the Principle of Morals* (1751), and Adam Smith in *The Theory of Moral Sentiments* (1759, 42–51), appealed to the capacity of sympathy to explain how human beings who are motivated by egoistic interests could form a moral perspective and could be motivated to act because of the pain and pleasure of other human beings.[28] For Hume, such capacity for sympathy is based on the fact that human beings are psychologically structured in the same manner (1739–40, 318): "The minds of men are mirrors to one another" (365). What is happening in the mind of one person can therefore easily resonate in the mind of another. Yet in Hume the concept of sympathy shows a multidimensionality similar to that of the concept of empathy in social psychology. Our ability to sympathize with our fellow creatures refers to a rather diverse capacity to be influenced, to fully grasp, and to be concerned with and moved by the mental states—passions and opinions—of other agents. In particular, sympathy is associated with three different psychological processes.[29] It is (i) understood as a process of *psychological contagion* both in an affective and in a cognitive sense: affective contagion consists in automatic emotional transference. A person starts feeling happy because the rest of the people in the room are happy, or a person starts feeling panic because everyone else in the room starts to panic. In this case, your emotional state is caused by your association with people in a similar emotional state. Nevertheless even though you share the emotional state of people around you, you experience your mental state primarily as your own (Scheler 1923, 22). Hume does not limit contagion to affective mental states, but explicitly includes cognitive states such as opinions and beliefs. Here he seems to think of psychological processes that are responsible for the formation of certain cultural and cognitive traditions,[30] a process that has also been recognized by Max Scheler. In contrast to a situation of explicit learning in which I am aware of the fact that the other person has a certain opinion that he tries to communicate, as far as intellectual contagion is concerned, I "merely judge that A is B because the other judges so and without knowing that the other judges so" (Scheler 1923, 48).

Sympathy is also (ii) associated with a process of allowing us to know the mental states of another person. Yet Hume himself never identifies sympathy as the basic or primary means of recognizing the mental states of other people or recognizing that other people have mental states. Rather, sympathy plays a role as a second step of fully understanding the mind of another person:

> 'Tis indeed evident, that when we sympathize with the passions and sentiments of others, these movements appear at first in *our* mind as mere ideas, and are conceiv'd to belong to another person, as we conceive any other matter of fact.... No passion of another discovers itself immediately to the mind. We are only sensible to its causes or effects. From *these* we infer the passion: and consequently *these* give rise to our sympathy. (Hume 1739–40, 319, 576)

Thus, for Hume, the process of sympathy seems to be initiated only after we have already inferred that the other person is in a mental state, particularly an emotion, based on our observation of his behavior. Such an inference convinces us, for example, of the "reality of the passion" in the other person. Hume does not say much about the underlying mechanisms that are responsible for such a transformation from idea to impression. He merely mentions that this process is somehow assisted through the relation of contiguity and resemblance (ibid., 320). One could say that sympathy functions as a means of fully recognizing that the other person is in a conscious mental state with an associated rich phenomenal quality and with important existential significance for him. Sympathy is an important second step in the understanding of another person because it allows us to understand another person's mental state as a phenomenon that is equivalent to our own. Sympathy thus plays the role of transforming a mental-state attribution to another person from a detached theoretical perspective into a phenomenon that has practical significance for us (Hume 1739–40, 319, 576; Wispe 1991).[31]

Sympathy is also (iii) identified as an emotion *sui generis*. Sympathy in this sense refers to a specific emotional reaction that has the situation and state of mind of another person as its object, such as when I sympathize with someone else's pain or grief. Indeed, in ordinary parlance, sympathizing (and even empathizing) with another person is often used in this sense of the term.[32]

Here is not the place to lament the insufficient conceptual distinctions of philosophers in moral psychology. I agree with Max Scheler that the above three senses of sympathy are very different psychological phenomena that are only contingently related. I would also follow him in his suggestion of defining sympathy proper as an emotion *sui generis*, that is, as sympathy in the third sense. I am more interested in a diagnosis of why philosophers such as Hume and Smith did not sufficiently distinguish between these very different psychological phenomena. It could be a result of either conceptual sloppiness or perhaps a failure to have fully grasped the Humean distinction between the cause and the object of an emotion (Hume 1739–40, 278). More importantly, one has to remember the explanatory context in which the concept of sympathy functions. Sympathy is introduced to explain why individuals driven by their own self-interest show any concern for others and the society they live in. For that purpose, it is not that important to distinguish conceptually between the different senses of sympathy. Sympathy in all of these senses contributes psychologically to the integration of the individual into a community, a group of people who think and feel similarly to other members and are concerned for each other. Sympathy is not introduced as a notion intended to solve the other mind problem in an epistemic sense. It was not knowledge of other minds, but concern for other minds and other persons that was the primary philosophical problem philosophers tried to address with the notion of sympathy. For that very reason one should also not be surprised that psychologists replicate the multidimensionality of the concept of sympathy in their definition of empathy, since empathy research in social psychology is to a large extent focused on describing various stages of moral development and explaining social emotions and altruistic behavior. This book, however, is not interested in empathy in this sense. Rather, it situates empathy as a method of mental imitation in the original epistemic context in which empathy was discussed by philosophers. Given its original context it should be clear that understanding empathy in this manner is legitimate. My hope is furthermore that this book has the effect of reminding social psychologists of empathy's original philosophical context.

1 Folk Psychology and Rational Agency

Any investigation into our folk-psychological capacities to interpret, predict, and explain the behavior of other people is best conducted by first gaining a preliminary understanding of the central features of the conceptual framework that is used for such purposes. Philosophers and psychologists are not only divided about empathy's epistemic role within this context; they are also fundamentally at odds about how to characterize the essential features of our folk-psychological practices. In particular, they disagree vehemently about whether folk-psychological interpretations of other agents are constrained by the assumption of rationality, an assumption that will be central to my defense of the empathy position later on. Even contemporary defenders of the empathy position are not in agreement in this respect. Critics of the rationality model of folk psychology tend to point to empirical findings in cognitive psychology purported to show that agents' reasoning deviates systematically from normatively sanctioned inferential standards without their actions being thereby completely unintelligible and uninterpretable. For that very reason, the above critics assert, rationality cannot be regarded as a psychologically realistic constraint on the interpretation of other agents.

As I will show, the rationality debate has been to a large extent hindered by conceptual confusions on both sides. More significantly, the idea that we view each other primarily as rational agents within the folk-psychological context has come under attack owing to the influence and allure of the interpretive framework that has been philosophically dominant for a long time. According to this view, folk psychology is a theoretical, quasi-scientific praxis adopted from a third-person perspective, more specifically from a perspective where the "researchers" and their "subjects" do not necessarily have similarly structured minds. Only within this context do the insights about the inferential shortcomings of human beings become outright challenges to the rationality model of folk psychology. Moreover, this view has also been responsible for the fact that the eliminativist challenge to folk psychology has been given such sustained yet ultimately undeserved attention within recent discussion in philosophy of mind. It is thus important to understand why the dominant philosophical perspective on interpretation falls fundamentally short of accounting for our folk-psychological conceptions of other persons and how it leads to a distortion of our folk-psychological practices by mischaracterizing the context within which folk psychology is situated as an explanatory practice.

1.1   Eliminativism and the Allure of the Detached Conception of Folk Psychology

The theoretical conception of folk psychology was popularized by Sellars (1963) through his famous myth of genius Jones. Jones is a scientist who does not think of himself as having beliefs, desires, or any other mental states, but who nonetheless articulates a folk-psychological theory that postulates the existence of inner mental states in order to provide an explanatory account of the observed behavior of other persons. For the purpose of the myth, it seems inessential that Jones is a creature like the ones whose behavior he tries to account for; even Martians who would never conceive of themselves in folk-psychological terms could have adopted the same explanatory stance (Churchland 1989a, 3). Accordingly, so the argument goes, it is inessential to folk psychology that it has been developed primarily as a theory to account for human behavior. It could also be applied to the complex behavior of any biological species as long as such application is judged to be fruitful according to criteria used to judge the validity of any other conceptual framework, that is, "its explanatory, predictive, and manipulative success" (Churchland 1989b.) I will call the above conception of folk psychology, according to which it is a theory that even alien minds with a completely different psychology could adopt for explanatory purposes, the *detached conception of folk psychology*.

Philosophers have been attracted to the detached conception of folk psychology independent from considerations about underlying psychological mechanisms. For them it seems decisive that—in comparison to some of its alternatives such as Cartesianism and behaviorism—the detached conception provides a vastly superior account of folk psychology as an intersubjectively accessible practice in which various members use the same concepts to explain, predict, and talk about the behavior of other people. Particularly Cartesianism, which takes mental concepts to be defined in reference to mental states that are accessible only from the first-person perspective, is seen as unable to account for this feature of our folk-psychological practice, since it cannot explicate how we can even conceive of the other person as being same-minded, that is, as having a mind with the same kinds of mental states as we do.[1] Logical behaviorism, on the other hand, does address the intersubjective nature of our folk-psychological practice. Nevertheless, it was soon realized that its attempt to define mental concepts reductively in terms of input–output relations, using only nonmental terminology, was doomed to failure. In response to this failure, with the ascent of functionalism, it has become popular for contemporary philosophers to think of folk psychology not as a conceptual framework in which each term is defined in isolation but as a framework in which the meaning of each term is, as Quine has suggested, holistically constituted by its inferential relations with other terms. Moreover, to make epistemic and logical sense of the explanatory character of our folk-psychological practice—given a Humean view of causation and a Hempelian conception of explanation (Churchland 1970, 1989a)—folk psychology has come to be thought of as a conceptual practice with the structure of a theory. Like a scientific theory, such a theory is also thought of as containing lawlike psychological generalizations, such as, for example, the *central action principle of folk psychology* (CAP), according to which a person who wants x and believes that A-ing is a means of achieving x and believes that there is no preferable way of bringing about x will, ceteris paribus, do A.[2] Psychological concepts are treated in this context as theoretical concepts whose content is defined by their role in a theory, particularly their contribution in the formulation of lawlike generalizations describing relations between various theoretical entities.

Given these primarily epistemic and conceptual concerns, it should come as no surprise that a position advocating the egocentric method of empathy as the foundation of our folk-psychological practices has not been seen as a serious philosophical alternative—particularly since proponents of the empathy view did not address the issue of folk-psychological concepts and seemed prima facie to lack a suitable and non-Cartesian account of them. Thinking of psychological concepts as theoretical concepts requires us to consider the attribution of mental states to other people as an inference based on available evidence grounded in observations of the other person's physical behavior, with theoretical principles linking the existence of these mental states in a complex fashion to such evidence. Yet such a *theoretical inference* has to be clearly distinguished from the traditional inference from analogy, which presupposes a Cartesian conception of a mind and takes the first-person perspective on the mind to be primary. An additional attractive feature of the detached perspective on folk psychology is that it is, in contrast to behaviorism, not without the conceptual resources to say something interesting about the privileged epistemic status that we grant self-reports within the folk-psychological context. The special status of first-person authority and the phenomenological fact that knowledge of our own mental states does not appear to be based on inferential processes can be acknowledged, but it no longer has to be understood in terms of special cognitive mechanisms such as introspection. It can be reinterpreted as a special feature of our language game that is explained in light of linguistic conditioning (Rorty 1970; Sellars 1963) or understood in analogy to the direct reporting use of theoretical terms by an expert of a theory who has become practically very familiar with a particular theoretical framework (Gopnik 1993; Churchland 1989b).

The appeal of the detached conception of folk psychology is based mainly on its promise of being able to retire the hindrances philosophers had encountered in thinking about folk psychology from the Cartesian and behaviorist perspectives. For such a theoretical conception of folk psychology to be completely persuasive, its broad outline as presented above would certainly need to be filled in with more detail. Given that ordinary folks do not explicitly formulate generalizations like CAP, one wonders exactly how, for example, to understand the claim that such theoretical principles are somehow implicit in our folk-psychological practices. Does this need to be read in a psychologically realistic sense as requiring that such principles are somehow internally represented by each person who is competent in our folk-psychological practice? Or does it merely mean that the structure of our folk-psychological practices and our explicit knowledge of these practices is made transparent in a systematic fashion only if viewed as embodying a psychological theory (Stich and Ravenscroft 1996)?[3]

In this chapter I am not interested in entering into the debate about the finer details of how best to formulate the commitments of the detached conception of folk psychology. Rather, I want to argue that however one decides these questions, the detached conception of folk psychology encourages a rather impoverished view of human agency as long as it regards mental states like beliefs and desires merely as internal causes of behavior and as long as it conceives of our ability to describe ourselves in folk-psychological terminology as inessential to the phenomena that folk-psychological practices are interested in explaining and predicting. In adopting a detached conception of folk psychology, we fundamentally dislocate the primary context of our folk-psychological discourse. It is this philosophical distortion of the focus of our folk-psychological practices that is also responsible for the central place that the eliminativist challenge has had in recent discussions of folk psychology.

Accepting the detached conception implies that conceiving of other agents and ourselves in folk-psychological terms is optional. It furthermore allows for entertaining the possibility that folk psychology could be a "radically false" theory representing a "degenerating research program" (Churchland 1989a, 1, 8) that has been deplorably stagnant over a long period of time and is explanatorily impotent in providing a satisfactory account of central psychological phenomena like visual illusions or the mechanisms of the learning process. On such a conception, folk psychology is seen as one among many possible conceptual frameworks of accounting for human agency. For this reason, it is in competition with a neurobiological account of human behavior. Given that folk-psychological categories like beliefs and desires are not easily reducible to the categories of the advancing neurosciences that promise to provide us with a more comprehensive and complete explanation of the intricacies of human behavior, Churchland (1989a,b) famously concludes that it is very likely that folk psychology will be replaced by a completed neuroscience.[4] Mental states like beliefs and desires assumed to exist within the realm of folk psychology are compared to entities like demons, witches, and phlogiston—entities that were once appealed to in specific explanatory contexts, but which have since been shown to be nonexistent by the advancing sciences, thrown into the dustbin of history and marked as mere fancies of the human imagination.

There are various ways in which one can respond to the eliminativist challenge. One can doubt the empirical adequacy of Churchland's claims about the pitiful status of folk-psychological theory. Claiming that folk psychology is a degenerating research program presupposes that the practices of ordinary folks should be judged in the same manner as the theoretical practices of natural scientists. Yet ordinary folks do not seem to be interested in articulating a general theory and in refining lawlike generalizations, and perhaps are better conceived of in analogy to historians who use general knowledge of the world in order to explain specific events (Horgan and Woodward 1991). Instead of interpreting the unchanging nature of folk psychology in a negative manner as "stagnation," one could also take it as a sign that the ancient Greeks were already brilliant psychologists (Wilkes 1984, 356). Furthermore, even though ordinary folks are not necessarily interested in developing psychological theories, those who have become professional psychologists did indeed enhance our psychological understanding of humankind while making use of the central terminology of folk psychology (Horgan and Woodward 1991; Wilkes 1984). In this context one might think of the recent research in developmental child psychology, which we will survey briefly later on, or the research on the fallacies of ordinary reasoning (Nisbett and Ross 1980). Even within the context of the detached conception of folk psychology, therefore, the eliminativist challenge is not overwhelming. How important a challenge one takes it to be depends at least in part on whether or not one shares Churchland's enthusiasm and hopes for the developing neurosciences.

Yet I find the above response in the end to be philosophically unsatisfactory. Conceiving of the fate of folk psychology as being solely decided by future developments in neurobiology creates a certain philosophical uneasiness because of the central place that folk-psychological categories play in our practical life. The suggestion that folk psychology could be wrong and that beliefs and desires do not really exist directly challenges our self-conception as responsible agents that constitutes the foundation of our practical life. If my belief and desires do not play any role in bringing about my actions then it seems that thinking of myself as the author of my actions, who is to be legitimately praised or blamed for them, is nothing but a grand illusion. And it is for this reason that Fodor, in his usual hyperbolic style, identifies the possibility that folk psychology could be false with "the end of the world" (1990, 156). Some philosophers have therefore chosen a second path to combat the threat of eliminativism, expressing the above uneasiness typically by challenging the eliminativist premise that folk psychology is a theory.[5] If folk psychology is not a theory, a fortiori it cannot be a false theory or a theory that can be replaced by neurobiological theories of human behavior. For example, it has been claimed that folk psychology is not a theory because it is also used "to blame and praise; to warn, threaten, prohibit," and so on (Wilkes 1984, 347). This is taken as an indication that folk psychology does not primarily delineate natural kinds. Its main function is rather to serve human interests, and its ability to do so insulates it to a large extent from eliminativist pressures. Lynn Rudder Baker has elaborated these intuitions more systematically by contrasting what she calls the practical realist picture with the physicalist picture (Baker 1995). For the practical realist, folk psychology is not a theory (what she calls a proto-science) because

> it is a nondetachable part of the whole commonsense conception of reality, which makes possible the activities of everyday life from getting a job to paying off our debt to sending in absentee ballots. As long as people are the kinds of beings who seek to survive and flourish, and have the capacity to make and discuss long-range strategies for survival and flourishing ... the commonsense conception of reality (and with it commonsense psychology) will be indispensable. (Baker 1999, 14)

Although I have great sympathies with the above sentiments that have led philosophers to deny that our folk-psychological vocabulary constitutes a theory, I regard the argumentative strategy unable to counter the eliminativist challenge and to silence the above philosophical worries. First, Baker seems to have an implausibly strict notion of what constitutes a theory. She admits that folk psychology is a conceptual framework that is revisable and refinable in light of empirical findings by cognitive psychology, which uses the very same folk-psychological notions (Baker 1995, 79). The only reason why she does not count it as a theory (or proto-science) has to do with the fact that we cannot imagine its wholesale falsifiability or replaceability. But according to this criterion, it is unclear that biological theories should count as scientific theories since it is very difficult to imagine at the moment how they could be replaced by any lower-level science. I am inclined to count more liberally any body of information as a theory if it includes some general statements and if it is revisable—counting abandonment or full replacement as limited notions of revisability—in response to a confrontation with empirical data. More importantly, Baker fails to show that folk psychology is not replaceable by another very different conceptual framework that could develop in light of new neuroscientific findings, even if it is not wholly replaceable by the neurosciences as we now know them. Nothing Baker says shows that such a successor theory would not be able to facilitate human flourishing and serve human needs. Perhaps in such a new conceptual system we would not be able to make sense of activities such as paying off debts or getting a job, but it is not clear that such activities are nonoptional human needs. Marx, for one, thought that such activities are an expression of a social system that is in fact detrimental to human flourishing.

In the end, Baker's argument against eliminativism comes down to the claim that "the descriptions of human behavior that figure in folk psychological explanations and predictions are descriptions that *already* imply perception, intelligence and personhood on the part of the agent" (Churchland 1989a, 17–18). Yet, as Churchland quite correctly points out, merely showing that the domain of the explanandum cannot be identified independently of theoretical notions does not prove that the theory is irrefutable or that it is not a genuine theory. It is standard scientific practice to conceive of the explanandum in terms of the theory that is also used to explain it. Certainly witches cannot be identified without the concept of mysterious supernatural powers that one also appeals to in order to explain the actions of witches. But that merely proves that the old familiar categorization of the domain of the explanandum can be shown to be unjustified in light of a superior theory that reveals the old theory to be outdated. Baker might be quite right in asserting that the categorization of folk-psychological explananda ordinarily presupposes other folk-psychological notions. Nonetheless, she fails to explain why such categorization is inescapable and essential for human flourishing as she claims it to be. For that very reason, the Churchlands are always able to dismiss these arguments as typical intuitions indicative of the fact that folk psychology is a very *entrenched* theory adopted from the detached perspective that cannot look beyond its basic assumptions.

I will use a different strategy against eliminativism. My target is not the assumption that folk psychology is a theory. Instead my target is the claim that folk psychology is a theory adopted from the detached perspective, since it is only in the context of this specific aspect that entertaining the option of replacing our folk-psychological notions becomes intelligible. According to the detached perspective, beliefs and desires are conceived of as merely internal states whose occurrences allow me to predict with a certain probability what a certain person will do. That the agent is also able to think of his behavior in this manner is irrelevant for the phenomenon to be explained as it is only the observed physical behavior of other human beings that create the explanatory need that is addressed by folk psychology. I would like to suggest that the detached conception of folk psychology gets it to a certain extent backward and is fundamentally mistaken in conceiving of folk psychology as a practice in which self-reports are regarded to be an optional feature of a theoretical framework that has in fact nothing to do with the phenomenon that needs to be explained. More appropriately, we should think of our experience as agents who act for reasons as a primary phenomenal fact that is on equal footing with the observation of the behavior of other agents.

For that purpose it is useful to consider for a moment how we conceive of responsible agency within the folk-psychological realm. The anxiety that eliminativism has caused certainly has to do with our fear that if we lose our concepts of belief and desire we will no longer be able to conceive of ourselves as responsible agents. Yet the discussion in contemporary philosophy of mind has tended to focus merely on the challenge to the causal explanatory potential of our notions of belief and desire in light of the challenge from the advancement of neurobiology. It has only partly realized that the assumption that actions are caused by beliefs and desires is only a necessary but not a sufficient condition for responsible agency.[6] As Harry Frankfurt's subtle considerations about the nature of moral responsibility and about the possibility of alienation from one's self have made amply clear, responsible agency does not merely require the existence of beliefs and desires that internally cause a certain behavior (Frankfurt 1988).[7] To characterize agency in this manner allows for the possibility that I might be a mere spectator toward the mental states that cause my behavior, as in the case of the wanton, a creature who does not care about which desire should determine his will. Such a creature is the psychological equivalent of the drifter who takes whatever car will give him a ride, wherever that might take him. We certainly can say that his actions are caused by his thoughts and his desires. He also might be said to act perfectly rationally insofar as his actions satisfy the demands of instrumental rationality; that is, they are rationally appropriate given his beliefs and desires. Yet in a way we are inclined to say that such a human being is not a full agent since he does not take ownership of his actions in light of his beliefs and desires. For that very reason he can not be regarded as the "author" of his actions. The actions belong to him only because something in him is the cause of that action.

Let me illustrate the metaphor of authorship in a bit more detail. If I am writing on the computer, my recognizing that I am typing is not sufficient to make me the author of the text I am writing. I could just be following the dictation of somebody else, whose elaboration I might even vehemently disagree with. For my typing to count as the typing of my text of which I am in the full sense the author, I have to be aware of certain beliefs and desires, and I have to be aware of them in the right manner as making sense of the type of action I am engaged in. Recognizing, for example, that I would like to buy an expensive car that I believe is way beyond my budget would not be relevant for making my typing the writing of this text. It is also required that I regard certain of my beliefs and desires as my reasons for my typing. They make it *for me* in some sense intelligible and appropriate that I am doing the typing. I am thus typing not only in order to achieve a certain objective without being aware of it as the aim of my action. Insofar as I am aware of my beliefs and desires as my reasons, I am also aware that I am acting in order to achieve a certain goal. In this particular case, for example, one could say that I am typing because I want to show that the detached conception provides an inadequate account of folk psychology.

To be a responsible agent who can be seen as the author of his actions it is thus required not only that the action is caused by a particular set of beliefs and desires. It is also not sufficient that the agent knows that he has various beliefs and desires or that these beliefs and desires cause his actions. Instead it is necessary that the agent sees these beliefs and desires in some sense as appropriately related to what he is doing and that he acknowledges them as his reasons for his action. Reasons are thus "elements of a possible story line along which to make up what we are doing" (Velleman 2000, 28). It allows us to take ownership of our behavior by situating it in a world as it appears from our perspective. Agents should be understood as acting not only because of their beliefs and desires; agents act in a full sense only because they are also able to recognize their individual perspective on the world as their reason for their actions. In this manner agents act, to use Kantian terminology, not only *according* to reason but *for the sake of reason*.[8] Following the terminology of Pettit one could say that agents are not mere intentional systems whose behavior is caused by a complex interaction of various mental states, but that they are also "thinking intentional systems" (Pettit 1993, 57) that are reflectively aware of their reasons for their actions.

The above remarks should not be taken to imply that agents need to deliberate intensively about their choices and possible alternatives for every action. Conscious deliberation is only one method for recognizing certain beliefs and desires as the reasons for my actions. Most of our activities are not the outcome of active deliberation, but are caused by processes of routines and habits. I do not need to deliberate about how and when to drive to work, or how to walk to the lecture hall from my office. Indeed, if I needed to deliberate about every action I perform I would be hopelessly overwhelmed. Yet as part of my routine I tend to know what my reasons are for engaging in activities—driving to school, walking to the class room, reading the newspaper, brushing my teeth, coaching my son's soccer team—and normally would be able to explain my action in these terms if prompted to do so.

Even though action does not require me to deliberate actively each time I act, the above conception of action as an activity that agents perform for their reasons implicitly allows for the possibility of a critical stance that other agents take toward me or that I can take toward myself. It implies the possibility of taking the deliberative perspective in which the appropriateness or particular relevance of my beliefs and desires as my reasons for actions are at issue. It is indeed for this very reason that folk-psychological notions are used to blame and praise since in acting we are committed to viewing our beliefs and desires as reasons for actions. In this manner our behavior becomes praiseworthy or blameworthy by the standards according to which beliefs and desires can function as reasons for actions. We are not merely viewing them as "motivating reasons" (Smith 1994) from a spectator's point of view, as beliefs and desires that cause us to act; we also have to see them as somehow making sense of our actions by some standard of intelligibility. Prima facie plausible criticism of my reasons for acting has the potential to alienate me from my actions by making me recognize that my beliefs and desires fall short of being appropriate reasons for them. An example might be helpful in this respect. Suppose that somebody is by nature a traditionalist who desires that marriage should be only between a man and a woman and who would feel uncomfortable allowing homosexuals to get married. He prefers civil unions for homosexuals. In the current American context, I assume a lot of people do indeed feel this way. Let's further assume that the person feels also inclined to vote for a constitutional amendment that would explicitly define marriage as being only between one man and one woman but would allow for same-sex civil unions. As a committed secularist, this person also realizes, however, that he does not have much of a justification for the claim that marriage is an institution that should be reserved for unions between men and women, or for the claim that a secular state should reserve the institution of marriage in this manner. In this case his ability to criticize his vote without resolving this inner conflict does alienate him from his very own action of voting for the amendment. As we ordinarily say, he is voting only half-heartedly.

At the moment we do not have to decide which standards are relevant for such evaluation; indeed, whether a standard is appropriate for such evaluation is a question that could be itself challenged. Prima facie, standards of theoretical and practical rationality, moral norms, and social conventions are relevant for such purposes. Viewing agency in the above manner implies regarding agents in Korsgaard's terms as "normative animals," "who are capable of reflection about what we ought to believe and to do" (Korsgaard 1996, 46–47),[9] because their own conceptions of themselves as agents requires them to be responsive to criticism of their beliefs and desires as reasons. We have to view agents in Burge's terms as "critical reasoners" who have the capacity

> to recognize and effectively employ reasonable criticism or support for reasons and reasoning.... As critical reasoner, one not only reasons. One recognizes reasons as reasons. One evaluates, checks, weighs, criticizes, supplements one's reasoning and reasoning. (Burge 1996, 98)

In the context of the discussion of the detached conception of folk psychology, it is important to recognize that the above considerations cannot be easily dismissed as a philosophical elaboration of the notion of responsible agency from the perspective of an entrenched yet merely optional framework of folk-psychological notions. These abstract philosophical considerations are linked to and grounded in the manner in which we experience ourselves as agents. As a matter of fact, an inability to acknowledge our mental states as reasons for our actions has to be seen as a serious mental deficiency. If we had no access to the reasons for our actions from a first-person perspective, we could not maintain a coherent conception of ourselves as agents interacting with the world. Had I no reasons for my actions, I would not only be unable to explain why I did what I did, I would also be inherently alienated from my actions since I could not understand them as *my actions*. At most my actions would be similar to my bodily reflexes, the blinking of my eyes or my sneezing. Such behavior is behavior I can recognize as my own in an immediate sense only if I recognize it as involving my body. Imagine signing a sheet of paper without recognizing any reasons for doing so, such as wanting to buy a house and recognizing that this signature will enable you to acquire the necessary mortgage. Without being able to recognize your reasons for your actions, you would also have no knowledge about what you are doing in this particular circumstance. You would still recognize that your body is doing something, writing something on a paper, yet you would not be able to take immediate ownership of this behavior as far as its wider environment is concerned; that is, you could not understand it as a signing of a contract. Your action in this particular environment would be a complete mystery to you.

This point is brought home by a pertinent description that Thomas DeBaggio provides in his reflection on his struggle with Alzheimer's and the slow deterioration of his mind due to this terrible disease:

Sometimes I go into the kitchen for a drink of water. By the time I get there I can't remember why I am there, but my body ends up at the ice machine. I stand in front of the ice machine and stare at it. From somewhere inside my head comes the message "You are in front of the ice machine because you wanted a glass of water."

At other times I can't remember why I went into the room and my body and mind are of no help to me. Sometime later my mind flashes a message and I remember but it is so long ago I am no longer interested. (DeBaggio 2002, 66)[10]

Based on this short passage, Debaggio's difficulty seems to be twofold. He is not only unable to recognize or remember the beliefs and desires that are relevant for the action at hand, but he also finds it difficult to recognize their relevance as reasons if his mind flashes them as a message. Such experiences seem to be similar to the experiences of schizophrenics, who think of some their thoughts as being inserted in their mind but who are unable to integrate them coherently into the context of their other thoughts.

Consequently, the above considerations are not easily countered by Paul and Patricia Churchland's (1981, 1989) standard move against the supposedly self-refuting nature of the eliminativist position. According to this objection, eliminativism is self-refuting or pragmatically contradictory because if it is true one cannot think or believe that it is true. The Churchlands tend to dismiss such worries as another indication of the entrenched nature of our folk-psychological notions and their centrality for our practical lives, worries indicative of a situation in which such entrenched notions are challenged without a successor theory being fully developed. Once such a theory is developed, they claim, such worries would disappear as being unfounded. But if the above observations are correct, having a conception of oneself as somebody who strives to satisfy his desires and acts in order to achieve a goal is not part of a theory from a detached perspective. It is part of the phenomenon of human behavior itself that would need to be accounted for even from the perspective of neurobiology, if it is to be a comprehensive account of human behavior. In fact, not being able to conceive of oneself in folk-psychological terms is indicative of a serious mental deficiency that leads to an inability to interact with one's environment in a "normal" manner. Such considerations are further supported by the fact that thinking about oneself in folk-psychological terminology seems to be invariant among various cultures (Gopnik and Meltzoff 1997). It is therefore very unlikely that our folk-psychological concepts, which enable us to conceive of ourselves as having a conception of an external world with which we interact, will be replaced by an advanced neurobiological theory without the central terms of such a successor theory finding any equivalent among our ordinary folk-psychological notions.

Yet it is crucial to understand the precise scope of the above argument. So far I have not addressed the central epistemic question of this book, namely, of how we accomplish epistemically to apply folk-psychological categories to other agents and whether such accomplishment depends on a theory or proceeds more egocentrically relying on empathy. I have only argued against the detached conception of folk psychology and argued for the claim that our conception of agency and our experience of ourselves as agents do not allow us to understand the application of folk theory to other human agents as a theory—if it is a theory—adopted by creatures who do not think of themselves as agents who act for reasons. I also do not want to be understood as having shown that it is conceptually impossible to adopt a folk-psychological theory from such a detached perspective. Indeed, we seem to do it ourselves when we apply our folk-psychological notions to artificial systems and animals. My aim has been more modest. I have argued that the detached conception of folk psychology has distorted our understanding of the *primary domain of folk psychology*, that is, its use for the interpretation of conspecifics. In its primary domain, folk psychology cannot be understood as a theory that is adopted from the view from nowhere, to use Nagel's phrase, but rather has to be minimally understood as being adopted from *the engaged perspective*. It is adopted from the point of view of agents who in experiencing their agenthood have to view themselves in folk-psychological terms and who use the same terminology to explain and predict the behavior of other human beings whom they conceive of as agents like themselves. I will call my conception the *engaged conception of folk psychology*. I intend this conception as a corrective to the principal distortion of the contemporary discussion about folk psychology that I see exemplified in the attention that has been given to the eliminativist challenge. My argument is aimed at releasing the eliminativist pressure from our folk-psychological categories by providing an explication of the deeply held intuition that folk-psychological notions cannot be conceived of as merely optional tools for describing ourselves and other agents. In this manner I hope to allow us to conduct the debate about the status of folk psychology without being side-tracked by implausible claims about the merely optional character of its conceptual framework.

Nevertheless, it has to be admitted that my case for an engaged conception of folk psychology has not fully addressed the metaphysical question of whether folk-psychological explanations of behavior should be granted an explanatory autonomy from neurobiological and physical explanations of behavior. Specifically, I have not countered the claim that folk-psychological notions do not describe any causally efficacious properties because the possibility of a sufficient and complete physical explanation for any physical event preempts the objectivity of mental explanations (Kim 1993, 1998b). Here I only want to point out that such metaphysical issues are largely independent from the epistemic questions addressed in this book. Even if we could not view folk psychology as a genuinely explanatory practice, such a conclusion would not have any outright eliminativist consequences, given my interpretation of folk psychology. Instead it would force us to reinterpret our folk-psychological practices in a more Wittgensteinian manner. According to this view, folk-psychological interpretation would not explicate another person's action by situating it in the causal structure of the world (Kim 1984, 1998a; Stueber 2003), at least not in the causal structure of the world as described by the other sciences. It would only enable us to understand the significance of another person's action from his own point of view in terms of his struggles to gain a consistent understanding of himself as author of his activities. Yet even then, it would remain an epistemologically interesting question of how we apply folk-psychological categories to other persons conceived of as rational agents. For this reason, the metaphysical issue of mental causation will not be discussed in this book. Since I tend to think that the philosophical challenges to the explanatory autonomy of folk psychology can be met and I have argued so elsewhere (Stueber 2005), I will proceed on the assumption that folk psychology is a genuinely explanatory practice.

1.2 Humans as Rational Animals: Clearing Up a Confusion in the Rationality Debate

If my argument for an engaged conception of folk psychology is persuasive so far, one has to conceive of the notion of rational agents, who act for reasons, as being central to our folk-psychological framework.[11] In this case, folk-psychological explanations are best viewed as "rationalizing explanations." They attempt to explain an agent's behavior in terms of mental states that causally motivate the agent to act and that also provide the agent with reasons for his actions from the first-person perspective. As has often been noted, in folk psychology the first-person and third-person perspectives—the justificatory or rational normative and the causal explanatory perspective—are interestingly intertwined. In this sense they seem to reveal the agent, as Davidson expresses it, "in his role as a Rational Animal," since "from the agent's point of view there was, when he acted, something to be said for his action" (Davidson 1980, 8–9). From this perspective, which also seems to have the weight of 2000 years of philosophical tradition behind it, it is surprising to read in a recent book that "mindreading does *not* depend on an assumption of rationality, on any reasonable construal of rationality" (Nichols and Stich 2003, 144). Even more astounding is the fact that this view is rather widespread among philosophers and psychologists alike.

I will refer to the above denial of the centrality of the concept of rationality to our folk-psychological understanding of other agents the *nonrationality conception of folk psychology*. As I will try to illustrate, the fundamental denial of the rationality assumption is another indication of the pervasive influence of the detached conception of folk psychology. In that context, the question of (i) whether humans are rational animals has been identified, by proponents of both sides of the debate, with the question of (ii) whether or not all of our actions conform to or approximate to a large extent normative standards that have been articulated by what we regard as the best theories of rationality. Proponents of the rationality assumption, for instance, articulate their position by claiming that action explanations represent not only the agent as rational; they also represent each and every action not only as "the thing generally done" but as the "appropriate thing to have done" (Dray 1957, 128). In this manner, such explanations make actions intelligible by revealing them "to be or to approximate to being, as they rationally ought to be" (McDowell 1985, 389; see also Heal 1995a, 52). On this reading of the rationality assumption, a negative answer to (ii) would imply a negative answer to (i).

Before we look closely at the arguments that have been used against the rationality approach to interpretation, it is vital to get a better grasp of the exact notion of rationality that is the focus of the debate. One has to be mindful of the fact that our commonsense notion of rationality is ambiguous. First, we judge an action to be rational in a *subjective* sense, judging its rationality merely from the point of the cognitive and conative perspective of the agent. Second, we also evaluate rationality of an action in an *objective* sense, judging it in terms of its ability to objectively achieve the *intended goal* of the agent (see Perner 2004). If I try to walk over an icy lake in order to reach the other side, believing that it will hold my weight, but I fall through the ice, my action has to be judged to be perfectly rational from a subjective point of view. It is an action that every rational agent having such beliefs and desires can be expected to take. Yet we also can regard the same action as objectively irrational regardless of whether the agent himself could have cognitively apprehended that the ice was not strong enough to hold him. Objectively speaking, it was not the thing that he ought to have done in order to reach the intended goal. More importantly, characterizing an action as rational or irrational from an objective point of view would not contribute anything to causally explaining why the agent acted the way he did, since objective reasons cannot necessarily be understood as reasons that motivated him to act. Defenders of the rationality assumption are therefore most plausibly read—and they also intend to be read in this manner—as referring to rationality in a subjective sense. They regard folk-psychological explanations as revealing human beings as rational animals and as showing their actions as the rationally appropriate ones given an agent's cognitive understanding of his situation.

Similarly, proponents of the nonrationality view have to be careful of how exactly they formulate their position according to which mindreading is independent of any notion of rationality. First, such a claim is straightforwardly empirically false if it is taken to suggest that evaluating an action as rational or irrational in either the objective or subjective sense is not a central folk-psychological practice. In contrast to events such as the falling of a stone, human actions are events that are generally recognized as scoring somewhere between perfect rationality and complete irrationality. Second, the claim that rationality is not important for mindreading is most plausibly restricted to the notion of subjective rationality. Recent psychological experiments suggest that the notion of objective rationality is involved in the interpretation of other agents from a very young age onward. The result of habituation experiments conducted by Gegerly and others are best interpreted as showing that already at twelve months infants conceive of certain actions as being goal directed and as objectively rational means for achieving those goals in a particular situation (Gegerly et al. 1995; Perner 2004).[12] In these experiments, children were first habituated to view a sequence of events such as certain movements of geometric figures. Adults interpret such movements naturally as goal-directed ations, as one "person" trying to reach another. Children seem to understand them similarly. After the habituation phase, they show less surprise viewing a physically different behavior if it can be understood as an action having the same goal of reaching another person than if they view physically identical behavior that in a new surrounding can only implausibly be interpreted in this manner. More concretely, children who view a sequence of events such as a person "intentionally" jumping over a wall (represented by a movement of a circle) to reach another person (another circle) expect a very different physical behavior in a situation in which the wall is removed and jumping is no longer required for reaching the other person. They look longer at a sequence of events where a "person" jumps but where such action is not necessary for achieving that person's objective. These longer looking times are interpreted as indicating that, from the perspective of the infant, the same physical movement is unexpected and surprising. It does not conform to the interpretive framework adopted in the habituation phase. Infants in the control group that are habituated to view a sequence of events as a mere causal sequence, however, do not seem to differ in how they process the observed movements. These results and the differences between children in these two groups can be accounted for only if one grants that children not only perceive another person's behavior as physical movement but also are able to understand it as a goal-directed action.

Interestingly, the above results also find confirmation in imitation studies with slightly older infants (Gegerly, Bekkering, and Király 2002). Infants of around fourteen months tend to imitate the exact physical movement of another person if and only if they interpret this action as the most effective and rational means for reaching a specific goal. Children, for example, will only use their head to activate a light button if they have seen adults do so while having their hands free. Their tendency to imitate such movement significantly drops, however, if they see the adult perform the same action while her hand is occupied with other things such as holding a scarf. They therefore seem to interpret the movement of the head as an effective and necessary means for the end if and only if other more obvious means such as the hands could also have been used.

If the interpretation of the experimental results by Gegerly and others holds up, then the denial of the rationality assumption cannot be understood as implying that a notion of rationality does not play any causal role in the development of our adult folk-psychological abilities. To be charitable and philosophically more productive, the nonrationality conception of folk psychology should be seen as being mainly concerned with the subjective notion of rationality. I take it to assert that our practice of interpreting, predicting, or explaining the behavior of an agent in folk-psychological terminology does not logically depend on the assumption that his action was rational *or* that he is a rational agent even if one conceives of rationality in a subjective sense. Even though we can certainly inquire whether a particular action was rational or irrational, this is an additional evaluative question. It does not play any role in identifying the behavior as an action or the person as an agent. It merely serves the pragmatic function of expressing our approval or disapproval of an action or agent in order to influence his behavior.[13]

Ordinarily, proponents of the nonrationality conception of folk psychology argue for their claim by pointing to empirical evidence accumulated by psychological research over the last thirty years demonstrating that human inferences systematically deviate from the norms of the "standard model of rationality." According to that model, inferences are rational only if they proceed "in accordance with principles of reasoning that are based on rules of logic, probability theory, and so forth" (Stein 1996, 4). Countless experiments have shown that human subjects do rather poorly in recognizing the validity of certain logical inferences; that they are not very good at judging correlation of events; and that they show a confirmation bias. They are also insufficiently open-minded in testing their hypotheses; they tend to persist and persevere in their beliefs despite evidence to the contrary; they are prone to inconsistent decisions; and they are severely probability-challenged—showing, for example, a systematic base rate neglect in judging the probability of a certain event or the truth of a particular proposition (for a survey see Nisbett and Ross 1980; Stein 1996; and Baron 2000).[14]

Two of the most well-known experimental results demonstrating such severe shortcomings of our logical reasoning capacities are Peter Wason's (1968) and Amos Tversky and Daniel Kahneman's (1983) demonstrations that subjects have an insufficient logical understanding of what is required for the testing of certain conditionals and that they have the tendency to commit the so-called conjunction fallacy in probabilistic judgments. Wason showed subjects the open face of four cards displaying a vowel, a consonant, an even number, and an odd number, and asked them how they would test the truth of a rule such as "If a card has a vowel on one side, then it has an even number on the other." Subjects were specifically requested to indicate the minimum number of cards necessary to determine whether the above conditional is true. Given that a conditional is false only if the antecedent is true and the consequent is false, subjects needed to check what is on the other side of two cards, namely, the one with the vowel and the one with the odd number. Most subjects, however, indicated that it would be necessary either to turn only the card with a vowel or to turn a combination of this card and the card showing the even number.

Kahneman and Tversky illustrated a similar lack of logical understanding within the context of probabilistic reasoning. Subjects were asked to estimate the probability of various scenarios about Linda, more specifically what jobs and hobbies she most likely would have. Linda was described to them as thirty-one years old, single, outspoken, very bright, and a former philosophy major in her student years who was deeply concerned with issues of discrimination and social justice. It was even revealed that Linda participated in antinuclear demonstrations. Most surprisingly from the perspective of probability theory, thinking about Linda so described seems to have a very negative effect on our probabilistic capacities. Subjects tend to judge the probability of Linda being a bank teller *and* being active in the feminist movement to be higher than the probability of Linda being merely a bank teller. Yet according to probability theory the probability of the conjunction of two otherwise independent events cannot be higher than the probability of one of the events occurring on its own. As Kahneman and Tversky point out, this probabilistic rule is grounded in the basic logical fact that for a conjunction to be true, both conjuncts have to be true. Yet the converse does not hold (Kahneman and Tversky 1996, 586). The truth of a conjunct does not presuppose the truth of the conjunction.

Kahneman and Tversky account for this deviation from our normative conception of probabilistic reasoning by suggesting that we do not follow normative rules of probability theory. Instead our reasoning is guided by various heuristics, most prominently the availability heuristics and the representative heuristic that interfere with recognizing the relevant criteria for correct probabilistic reasoning. According to the availability heuristic, we judge the probability of types of events in terms of how easy it is for an individual to recall a particular token. This leads us, for example, to systematically overestimate low-frequency events and underestimate the probability of unknown or unfamiliar factors. In the Linda case we seem to be following the representative heuristic. We judge the probability of Linda's being a bank teller or being a feminist bank teller according to the degree of similarity between our conception of bank tellers and feminists on the one side and Linda's description on the other. It is quite obvious that Linda's characterization corresponds much better to our stereotypical conception of a feminist rather than a bank teller.

As has been pointed out by various psychologists, the use of the above heuristics can certainly lead to adequate results in our everyday dealings with the world. However, researchers in the psychological and philosophical communities have tended to be mainly impressed by the fact that the use of such heuristics leads to serious inferential shortcomings and cognitive illusions in other contexts taken to be particularly relevant for the well-being of modern society. If even highly trained doctors (Tversky and Kahneman 1983) were unable to process probabilistic information appropriately, then one could indeed surmise that modern society, contrary to its self-image, is not built on rational foundations, at least not on the foundation of a rational mind. No wonder, then, that those researchers became "increasingly more impressed with the evidence of people's departures from normative standards of inference and less impressed with the evidence of their adherence to them" (Nisbett and Ross 1980, 6). At the minimum, the results were seen as requiring educational reforms to bring our inferential practices more in compliance with our normative theories of rationality. Others interpreted the results even more strongly as having a "bleak implication for human rationality" (Nisbett and Borgida 1975, 8). They were seen as directly repudiating our self-conception as a rational animal, since we "lack the correct program for many important judgmental tasks" (Slovic, Fischhoff, and Lichtenstein 1976, 174). Thus "pace Aristotle, it can be argued that irrational behavior is the norm not the exception" (Sutherland 1994, vii).[15] Naturalistically inclined philosophers such as Stephen Stich declared that traditional conception of man as a rational animal has been seriously undermined by this research (Stich 1994, 337). In his opinion it conclusively repudiates the idea that folk psychology depends on the rationality assumption, since we are able to interpret and understand the subjects of these psychological experiments in a folk-psychological framework despite the irrationality of the reasoning. Instead, he claims it is not the rationality assumption but mere parochial similarity to our practices that should be understood as primarily constraining our folk psychology. At most, this implies reasonableness-like-us as a standard for interpretation. Unfortunately, if the conclusions drawn from the results of the psychological experiments hold up scrutiny, this might not be much rationality at all. Unsurprisingly, Stich has tended to find such a parochial notion of reasonableness uninteresting for the scientific study of cognitive processes (Stich 1994 and 1990, chap. 2).[16]

I am not interested in challenging the results of the psychological experiments. I am more than happy to concede that human beings *at times* and *in certain contexts* deviate systematically from the standard model of rationality. Yet I am not willing to grant that the nonrationality conception of folk psychology follows or that human beings cannot any longer be conceived of as rational animals. It is important to realize that in drawing this conclusion, philosophers and psychologists make very specific assumptions. They presuppose (i) that our best theories of logic, probability, and decision making articulate the appropriate standards for the evaluation of behavior as rational or irrational, and they tend to require (ii) that in order for a person to be called rational his mind has to be programmed according to rational principles so conceived. More explicitly, the argument for human irrationality has the following structure:

1. Our best theories of logic, probability, and decision making articulate the appropriate standards for the evaluation of behavior as rational or irrational.

2. Humans are rational animals if and only if their minds are rationally organized; that is, they are rational if and only if they are programmed according to the principles of our best normative theories of rationality.

3. If our minds are rationally programmed, then our behavior (including our reasoning) would conform sufficiently to the principles of our best normative theories.

4. The psychological experiments cited above show that our behavior does not sufficiently conform to the principles of our best normative theories.

It thus follows that humans are not rational animals.

The furor over human rationality that the psychological experiments have ignited is best understood as the result of what I would like to call the *cognitive model of rationality*, that is, the framework created by the marriage of the standard model of rationality (premise 1) and the cognitive model of the mind (premise 2). Within the detached conception of folk psychology such a marriage is prima facie quite plausible, since it seems to allow us to understand from the detached third-person perspective how our beliefs and desires could be internal causes of and also reasons for our action. According to the cognitive model, beliefs and desires can be understood as reasons for and causes of behavior because they are internally processed and because they internally cause behavior according to the very principles that we use to judge whether they are rationally linked to other mental states and to behavior.

Within the context of the cognitive conception of rationality there are two obvious ways to respond to the above argument in order to save humankind from the charge of irrationality. First, one can challenge its third premise by arguing that the human mind can be regarded to be programmed according to our ideal theories of rationality, despite the fact that this is not always manifested behaviorally. Within the cognitive framework, such discrepancy between underlying program and behavioral manifestation can be accounted for in terms of the distinction between competence and performance. According to Chomskian linguistic theory, for example, all speakers possess ideal grammatical competence in the form of an internally represented set of linguistic rules. Yet in processing linguistic expressions according to these rules we also have to rely on other cognitive systems, such as short-term memory or systems for focusing our attention. Certain failures to process grammatical information correctly can be understood as a result not of a failure in our competence but a failure of applying these rules correctly because of limitations in other cognitive systems. Along these lines, Cohen (1981) has argued that the above failures in reasoning should be understood as performance errors and not as fundamental shortcomings of our reasoning competence. More importantly, he argues that we are forced to conceive of our reasoning competence as structured according to the standard conception of rationality. The articulation of our normative standards of rationality and the descriptive task of explicating the principles of our reasoning are nothing but an attempt to provide a coherent and systematic account of the same intuitive judgments about what inferences are normatively appropriate. The "contribution to the psychology of cognition" is "a by-product of the logical or philosophical analysis of norms rather than something that experimentally oriented psychologists need to devote effort to constructing" (Cohen 1981, 321).

I do not regard this strategy of defending human rationality to be very persuasive. As has been pointed out (Stein 1996; Stich 1990), it is rather doubtful that a normative theory of reasoning can be conceived of as providing a systematization of all untutored and naive intuitions about what forms of reasoning is normatively appropriate. As the above reasoning experiments have revealed, those intuitions also sanction normatively inappropriate forms of reasoning. And Stein has emphasized (1996, 161ff.), it is inherently implausible that a psychologically realistic description of our reasoning competence can avoid taking into account considerations from neurobiology or evolutionary theory. Since we are creatures with limited cognitive resources it is unlikely that evolution selected a reasoning competence that a creature with our limitations could never implement. In addition, a theory that maintains that the principles of our normative theories of rationality are part of our natural reasoning competence would also have to give an account of the fact that normative theories of probability are rather recent. According to Gigerenzer, the "acceptance of the metaphor of the mind as an intuitive statistician" is closely linked to the "institutionalization of inferential statistics in the 1950s" (2000, 13). If this suggestion is right, ancient Greeks have had no intuitions about the probability of Linda being a bank teller. That we have such intuitions would not be a result of our natural reasoning competence. It would be a result of the fact that we live in a certain cultural environment where certain probabilistic theories are normatively accepted and where we are daily bombarded with ever-changing statistical information ranging from the likelihood of putting on weight if eating a certain kind of food, to the probability of the next terrorist attack, or of rainfall the next day. I am therefore prepared to grant that we are not creatures that are programmed according to all of the norms of the standard conception of rationality.[17]

Another popular response to the argument denying humans the status of rational animals has been to doubt the appropriateness of the standard conception of human rationality as presupposed in its first premise. According to this line of reasoning, we should be skeptical about the assertion that our best theories of logical inference and probability theory are also the best normative theories for the evaluation of the rationality of agents and their actions. Such theories can at most be considered to articulate a notion of ideal rationality relevant for nonhuman creatures without our limits in cognitive resources. In articulating a normative theory of human rationality, it is more plausible to follow the general principle that "ought" implies "can." The reasoning capacity of human agents has to be evaluated in respect to how well it enables agents with limited resources to succeed in satisfying their desires in the real world. Given our restricted memory capacities, for example, it is impossible for us to maintain a deductively closed or ideally consistent belief system and still go on with the normal routine of life. An individual without limited mental resources could be expected to maintain absolute logical consistency among his beliefs, and he could be expected to draw all possible inferences from those beliefs. Creatures like us, on the other hand, would irrationally waste their time and clutter their mind trying to accomplish such a logical feast (Harman 1999). From this perspective, the principle to maintain a completely consistent and a deductively closed belief system can be regarded as normatively obligatory only for ideally rational agents but not for human beings with finite cognitive resources. Instead of accepting the standard conception of rationality, we have been tempted to downsize our norms of rationality as articulated by our best theories of decision making and logical and probabilistic reasoning in order to make them correspond to our finite human capacities. To mark the distinction, philosophers and psychologists have started to talk about models of "minimal rationality" (Cherniak 1986) or "bounded and ecological rationality" (Gigerenzer et al. 1999; Gigerenzer 2000).

To a certain extent, I am favorably disposed to reject the standard conception of rationality as I have articulated it in the first premise of the irrationality argument. Yet I want to resist the temptation to downsize our norms of rationality as articulated by our best theories of decision making and logical and probabilistic reasoning. I continue to believe that our best theories of logic, probability, and scientific method do articulate standards that are relevant for the evaluation of human reasoning and decision making, and that it is indeed normatively appropriate to attempt to improve our behavior in light of them. In particular I think that the conjunction rule of probability theory can be defended as an appropriate normative standard for the evaluation of the rationality of our probabilistic inferences. As has been pointed out, not following the conjunction rule makes us "dutch-bookable"; that is, it leads us, contrary to what we desire and value, to accept a set of bets that necessarily will result in a loss. Furthermore, improper evaluation of the evidence for a particular belief can be a serious problem in everyday affairs since it can lead to the formation of irrational prejudices. As I will explain in more detail in the next chapter, the mistake of the standard conception does not consist in taking those principles as being relevant for the evaluation of the rationality of specific actions. Rather, both the standard conception and its critics take insufficient note of the fact that our judgments about the rationality of an action are highly contextualized judgments that have to consider a multitude of normative standards and facets of the situation, including the limits of an agent's cognitive abilities.

More importantly, the question of whether our theories of logic, probability, and decision making also provide the best normative theories of rationality is in the end not central to deciding whether the irrationality argument succeeds in denying human beings the status of rational animals in the traditional sense. However we conceive of the normative standards for the evaluation of the rationality of specific actions and inferences, the question of whether or not human behavior conforms to them should not be seen as implying an answer to the question of whether human beings have to be conceived of as rational animals. The traditional conception of humans as rational animals never presupposed the cognitive model of human rationality that today's thinkers often assume. The current debate about the question of whether or not human beings can be recognized as rational animals within the cognitive model is therefore fundamentally at odds with the traditional picture of human rationality.

It has to be admitted that proponents of the nonrationality conception of folk psychology are not the only ones to be held responsible for this muddled state of affairs. Proponents of the rationality assumption are also to blame, owing to a fundamental ambiguity in their formulation of the rationality conception of folk psychology. As we have seen, they identify the claim that folk-psychological explanations reveal agents in "their role as rational animals" with the claim that folk-psychological practices interpret each individual action as the way it "ought rationally to be." Since such normative evaluation of individual actions most plausibly proceeds in light of our best normative theories of rationality, the current debate assumes that we can be given the honor of being called rational if and only if our best normative theories of rationality are descriptively adequate of our behavior or describe our inner mental program.[18] But the traditional conception of human beings as rational animals presupposes neither the cognitive model of rationality nor that rational animals mostly act as they rationally ought to act according to our best normative standards. To be a rational animal requires that one has reasons for one's actions and that one acts because of these reasons. Acting for a reason implies only that one's beliefs and desires are suitable objects for an evaluation according to our normative theories of rationality. It does not mean that one also has a good reason that conforms to our best normative theories of rationality. Colling-wood, in his recently published *The Principles of History*, rightly points out that "actions done by reasonable agents in pursuit of ends determined by their reason ... include—is it necessary to add?—acts done by an unreason-able agent in pursuit of ends (or in the adoption of means) determined by his unreason," for, he continues,

> what is meant by unreason, in the context of this kind, is not the absence of reasons but the presence of bad ones; and *a bad reason is still a reason* [my emphasis]. A brute that wants discourse of reason does not make a fool of itself.... The old belief that man is the only "rational animal" may well be mistaken, not so much because it implied too much rationality in man; it never did that, for it never implied that man was more than feebly, intermittently, and precariously rational, as because it implied too little in non-human animals. (Collingwood 1999, 46–47)

As Tversky and Kahneman themselves admit in their interpretation of the conjunction fallacy, although the subjects' reasoning can be faulted in light of probability theory, this does not show that they did not have any reasons for their judgments. Rather, in following the representative heuris-tics subjects do have such reasons, because "the representative heuristic generally favors the outcomes that make good stories or good hypotheses" and "the conjunction feminist bank teller is a better hypothesis about Linda than bank teller" (Tversky and Kahneman 1983, 311). It is a com-pletely different issue whether such reasons are also normatively sufficient for justifying the subjects' judgments.

The traditional conception of rationality is neutral about the underlying cognitive mechanism of human capacities and human rationality. It con-ceives of rationality primarily in a normative manner. It implies merely that the thoughts and actions of such an animal are situated within a nor-mative dimension that allows us to critically evaluate its actions as rational or irrational, and to evaluate it as having good or bad reasons for such actions. Rationality in this broader sense is not defined in contrast to irra-tionality, and it does not logically imply that a rational animal satisfies a great majority of the principles of our best theories of rationality. Rather, it implies a difference between organisms that are plausibly seen as being capable of responding to the norms of rationality and as being evaluable accordingly and organisms like plants that are not so evaluable. The con-trast with rationality in this broader sense is with *nonrationality* or *arational-ity*. The concept of being a rational animal is analogous to the concept of being a citizen or being a colleague. Being a citizen or being a colleague implies that one is normatively evaluable and that one is in principle able to grasp the norms of good citizenship or the norms of appropriate behavior for colleagues. But even bad citizens or bad colleagues are still citizens and colleagues and have to be reprimanded according to the appropriate norms. To put it differently, the concept of being a rational animal is not analogous to the concept of being a true statement or even being a rational action. Instead, it is analogous to the concept of being a statement in that it is characterized by a certain bipolar dimension of evaluation. Similar to a statement's being capable of being true or false, a rational animal is capable of acting rationally or irrationally. A rational animal is an animal that acts for a reason, understands beliefs and desires as reasons for his actions, and whose actions are evaluable in terms of degrees of rationality.

It is for this very reason that Aristotle, who is generally regarded as having inspired the definition of man as rational animal, does not speak of the program of the rational soul. Rather he speaks of various virtues of the rational part of the soul (*Nicomachean Ethics*, book VI) and defines life according to such virtues as the most appropriate life for a human being. This does not imply that human beings are by nature programmed to live in the most rational fashion as the cognitive model suggests. By nature we are to be judged according to certain normative standards of reason, because human beings have the potential to live up to such norms and realize rational virtues. Aristotle is quite aware of the fact that such virtues might not be realized. To be able to live up to our normative ideals requires the right kind of habituation and emotional attunement to the world and it requires the proper theoretical instruction and philosophical reflection. It is exactly for this reason that Aristotle spends so much time articulating the principles of valid and sound logical reasoning in the various works of his *Organon*. Such reflections can be understood as supporting rational animals in their struggle to realize the theoretical virtues in the same way that ethical reflections help us to realize our practical virtues since "if, like archers, we have a target to aim at, we are more likely to hit the right mark" (NE 1094a25).

In the context of our current conception of logical and probabilistic reasoning, we certainly differ from Aristotle in respect to what we regard as the appropriate norms of rationality. Since the Enlightenment and particularly through recent psychological research we also have become much more aware of the cultural and social structures and the natural habits of the human mind that systematically impede the realization of our rational potential. Both Bacon and Descartes understood the scientific method as a discipline that needs to be individually adopted and socially institutionalized in order for humans to realize their rational potential and to overcome the mind's natural shortcomings, which Descartes diagnosed to be due mainly to an imbalance between our unlimited power of will and our finite cognitive capacities, and which Bacon describes in his doctrine of idols. Only in this manner does the Enlightenment deem it to be appropriate for humans "to dare to use their own reason." Despite their specific disagreement with Aristotle about how to conceive of the norms of reasons, the thinkers of the Enlightenment assumed with Aristotle that human beings are to be evaluable according to such norms however they are conceived. It is thus an unfortunate exaggeration that the recent empirical findings about the shortcomings of our inferential strategies "would appall Aristotle" (Stich 1994, 337) because they supposedly repudiate his conception of human beings as rational animals.

Thus, recognizing the systematic difficulties of humans in following specific norms of reasoning does not challenge the traditional conception of human beings as rational animals. That it has taken to do so is in my opinion a result of the influence of the detached conception of folk psychology, which encourages the conception of human beings as rational if and only if their thought processes are programmed according to rational principles. At most, the recent empirical research highlights the difficulties we have in living up to our aspirations of rationality, difficulties that perhaps we traditionally did not sufficiently recognize. As we have seen, to infer in light of such shortcomings that human beings are not rational is in fact rather paradoxical, since the empirical research on which such a conclusion is based presupposes the very same traditional conception of humans as rational animals. It assumes that human beings are normatively required to be responsive to norms of reasoning since otherwise the fact that we do not seem to follow such norms would be as interesting as the fact that baseball players do not follow the rules of soccer. Baseball players, however, have no reason to follow the rules of soccer. Moreover, in defense of the claim that the conjunction rule is indeed the appropriate norm by which to judge a subject's inferential behavior in the context of probabilistic reasoning, it is also often pointed out that not following the rule would have very undesirable—irrational—consequences. We would for example accept a set of bets as fair, even though we would necessarily lose money. "Betting money when there is no chance of winning—which is what people who violate the conjunction principle are committing themselves to doing—" we are told "is irrational behavior" (Stein 1996, 97) because it seems to be behavior that everybody recognizes as being inconsistent with what one really desires. But such a defense of the conjunction principle supposes that we are indeed rational animals who are able to recognize that such an inconsistency has to count as a reason for not taking such bets and for regarding the conjunction principle as an appropriate standard for the evaluation of our inferential behavior. We therefore have to conclude that empirical research in psychology cannot be used to disprove the traditional assumption of human beings as rational animals that we have shown to be central to an engaged conception of folk psychology. Properly understood, the traditional conception of a rational animal requires only that agents conceive of their beliefs and desires and so on as reasons for acting and as being evaluable according to norms of reasoning.

2 Charity and Rational Contextualism

The previous chapter has shown that the current debate about whether we are justified to consider human beings as rational animals is riddled with terminological confusion on both sides. For that very reason, one might get the impression that the rationality debate is merely verbal, that both sides talk past each other. Even if the concept of rational agency in the traditional sense has not in fact been jeopardized, proponents of the non-rationality conception could insist that psychological research has shown that our mind is not programmed according to the proper norms of reasoning. Prima facie they are also right in claiming that the attribution of any specific belief or desire to another agent is not constrained by rational norms, if we conceive of them according to the standard conception of rationality. Proponents of the nonrationality view could therefore concede that agents have to be understood as acting for reasons, while insisting that psychological experiments have shown that they tend to act for rather bad reasons. If you still wants to call such an animal rational, go ahead, they might say with a grin; unfortunately, such "rational" animals do not act very rationally.

Even though this is a possible philosophical response, it faces some conceptual hurdles. To suggest that we are able to describe others in folk-psychological terms and that we are able to evaluate them according to standards of rationality even though their reasoning or behavior does not conform to such norms, seems to be equivalent to claiming that a person can be regarded as a chess player and appropriately evaluated according to the rules of chess even though his behavior does not conform to any rules of chess. In such a case why should we regard him as a chess player to begin with? More importantly, if a person's wanting to play chess does not commit him to the rules of chess or his playing chess does not require conformity to the rules of chess, how could it be legitimate to evaluate his action according to the rules of chess? Wouldn't such evaluation of his behavior be an arbitrary normative imposition from an external point of view that has nothing to do with how the agent conceives of himself as an agent? A normative evaluation of an action is normally understood as an evaluation that is directed at the agent himself, as an evaluation that could in principle be accepted as appropriate from his perspective. This is, as I have suggested in the first chapter, a central aspect of what it means to view agents as acting for a reason within the folk-psychological context. By pointing out that an action is not rational in an objective sense, we seem at least to imply that the agent would accept this critique if he were able to recognize that some of his assumptions about the world turned out to be false. Otherwise, the act of criticizing an action as objectively irrational seems pointless; that is, it cannot be understood as addressing the agent. It would be merely a critique from the detached perspective aimed at another external observer of the action. In this manner the nonrationality position fails to account for the fact that a critical evaluation of each other's actions is an integral aspect of our folk-psychological practices, because we view each other as acting for reasons.

2.1 In Defense of Global Charity

Still, pointing out the difficulties of another position does not explain in what sense norms of rationality constrain our folk-psychological interpretation of other agents, if we are at times able to interpret them when their behavior does not conform to such norms. I will try to address this question in the following by arguing for the principle of charity understood in a *global sense* as a constitutive principle of folk-psychological interpretation. As I understand it, charity advises the interpreter to optimize agreement between him and the interpretee. As such it advises the interpreter to attribute a certain amount of what he regards to be true beliefs that are in some sense "rationally" organized. Furthermore, if the principle of charity is properly understood in a global sense then it is in no way contradicted by the above mentioned revelation of irrationality in human inference strategies. Global charity allows for the attribution of irrationality in localized circumstances if such interpretation best fits the available empirical evidence.

The discussion of the argument of the principle of charity, and in particular Davidson's argument for it, has been rather intense and widespread in the last thirty years. Nevertheless, a brief reminder of its main steps is necessary here. As the above debate about folk psychology has shown, it remains contested territory, and there is considerable uncertainty about how exactly one should understand charity as an interpretive constraint. Even though I regard my position as Davidsonian, I do not intend my reconstruction of the argument for charity to be an exegesis of Davidson (see, however, Stueber 1993 in this respect).[1] I follow Davidson in conceiving of an analysis of radical interpretation as the appropriate starting point for articulating the implicit assumptions of our interpretive practice. As is well known, radical interpretation is thought of as a situation in which an interpreter tries to understand the linguistic and nonlinguistic actions of an agent of an unknown culture without presupposing any knowledge about the agent's propositional attitudes and without any comprehension of the semantic or syntactic structure of the agent's language.

In understanding the analysis of radical interpretation in this manner, we are not implying that actual field linguists or anthropologists proceed on such an evidentiary slim basis. They are certainly allowed to use any interpretive shortcuts sanctioned by standard scientific practice and to "approach the study of a particular language on the basis of assumptions drawn from the study of other languages" (Chomsky 2000, 53). We are also not implying that in the domestic case we normally have to justify our linguistic comprehension of another speaker of the same language along the lines of radical interpretation.[2] Rather, the analysis of the thought experiment of radical interpretation is best understood in analogy to the well-known skeptical scenario like Descartes's evil demon hypothesis, or the brain-in-a-vat hypothesis. In our everyday practice of justifying knowledge claims, we are asked to defend our claims not against such radical skeptical doubts but only against more local and restricted doubts. Normally such doubts are calmed in light of other knowledge that is accepted by all parties in the dispute. Still, raising skeptical doubts seems to be prima facie a radicalization and generalization of the doubts about specific knowledge claims within our epistemic practices, which depends on the realization that all our empirical knowledge is derived from or is based on our senses (see Stueber 2001). Thus, reflecting on the exact nature of the epistemic challenge of radical skepticism has to be seen as a useful philosophical exercise that forces us to articulate more precisely our central epistemic notions and our epistemic situation. Similarly, the analysis of the thought experiment of radical interpretation is best understood as a radicalization of the demand to justify particular interpretations of another speaker in a situation in which the default assumption that the speaker means with his words the same thing as I mean with mine is frustrated. The thought experiment of radical interpretation is therefore best seen as derived from the recognition that folk-psychological interpretation is an intersubjectively accessible epistemic practice. Its philosophical use is to press in more general terms our ordinary requirement that meaning and belief or desire attributions can be justified in terms of publicly accessible evidence. That is, they can in principle be justified in light of the publicly observable behavior of the agent in his environment (see Bilgrami 1992 and Stueber 1997a). For that very reason, the analysis of radical interpretation can also be understood as revealing the criteria that implicitly govern our interpretive practices and that have to be seen as constituting the central principles of the folk-psychological domain.[3]

In his analysis of radical interpretation, Davidson tends to focus on the interpretation of linguistic agency and the attribution of beliefs in light of the interpretation of assertive utterances of the speaker, presupposing that in sincerely uttering a sentence p the speaker also intends to express the belief that p. For Davidson, this interpretive task can in large part be accomplished by constructing an empirically adequate and interpretive theory of truth for the language of the particular speaker. We can abstract from all of the logical subtleties that are involved in adopting such a proposal. Moreover, in viewing the analysis of radical interpretation as revealing something important about our ordinary conception of folk-psychological notions, we need not agree with Davidson's view that the capacity for language is a precondition for the ability to have thoughts (for a critical discussion, see Ludwig 2004). To accept an analysis of radical interpretation as being philosophically relevant in this context, one only has to realize that as a matter of fact folk psychology primarily deals with linguistic agents and bases its attribution of mental states to a large extent on the interpretation of the agent's linguistic utterances.

Focusing for the moment mainly on the notion of belief, the folk-psychological purpose of attributing beliefs to an agent consists in explicating his perspective on the world in a manner that allows us to understand his reasons for acting. The characterization of his perspective on the world requires us to attribute beliefs in the *de dicto* mode, characterizing the content of his beliefs in a manner that corresponds to his conceptual repertoire and conceptual sophistication. Otherwise, we would not be able to understand his beliefs as being part of the reasons that motivated him to act, and which he could view as his reasons for acting. Characterizing his beliefs merely in a *de re* mode, for example, in characterizing him as *believing of* the most famous student of Plato that he is a great author, will not allow us to make justified predictions about his behavior in a bookstore if he sees a sign advertising the distribution of free copies of books by the most famous student of Plato. Making such a prediction would also require us to know how whether he also *believes that* the most famous student of Plato is a great author. Similarly, in interpreting linguistic assertions, we have to interpret them in a manner that is sufficiently fine grained, as we normally assume that a speaker intends to express his *de dicto* beliefs in his assertion (see also Stueber 2000). The question of whether language is a precondition for thought is thus irrelevant for our purposes, since the problem of how to characterize the meaning of linguistic utterances and the *de dicto* content of beliefs is structurally similar. In the end, folk-psychological interpretation and the attribution of mental states to other agents based on his behavior and the observed interaction between the person and his environment—whether or not these at the same time involve the interpretation of linguistic utterances—situate the person in his environment in a manner so that his beliefs and desires can be conceived of as reasons for his actions.

The radical interpreter makes the central folk-psychological assumption that the agent interacts with the world because of his beliefs and desires, that they are his reasons for the observed action, and that for this very reason we can attribute beliefs and desires to him—that is, based on the observation of his behavior in a certain environment. Since such situated behavior constitutes our only interpretive evidence, interpretation of linguistic meaning and the attribution of beliefs have to proceed externalistically. Without situating the interpretee within a complex of causal relations to the external world, we would have no justified indication of what his thoughts could be about.[4] Particularly in the beginning of radical interpretation, in interpreting a linguistic utterance, for example, we have to assume that one reason the speaker makes certain utterances is that he believes them to be true, and also that they are true by the interpreter's beliefs to a person if none of those beliefs can be seen as consistent with the attribution of other beliefs. Under the assumption, for instance, that a speaker might have a system of beliefs in which every two beliefs contradict each other, no interpretive hypothesis could be justified. In such a case, his future behavior would always falsify our chosen interpretive hypothesis for a particular utterance or attribution of belief. Yet the consistency assumption is not merely limited to the agent's system of belief. In collecting evidence for the interpretation of one utterance, we assume, for example, that a person's past speech behavior tends to be consistent with his present and future behavior. If he would start referring to cows as "gavagai," we would have reason to revise our original interpretation of "gavagai" as referring to rabbits. Note that without the assumption of consistency we are not justified in taking his repeated use of "gavagai" in the vicinity of rabbits as further evidence for our original interpretation. Similarly, if somebody seems to have strongly and sincerely asserted his desire to eat ice cream right now, but refuses to eat the ice cream in front of him, I have reason to suspect that I have misunderstood him. Accordingly, we have to presuppose that the agent has some basic cognitive capacities and inferential abilities to maintain the consistency in his mental system required to conceive of him as having intentional states within the folk-psychological system.[5]

Davidson is right to insist that "holism, externalism and the normative feature of the mental stand or fall together" (Davidson 2004, 122). All of these claims are part of what has come to be called the principle of charity. As the above discussion has shown, charity has to be conceived of as a constitutive principle of interpretation within the folk-psychological realm. It advises us to optimize agreement between interpreter and interpretee such that we see the interpretee as in some sense conforming to the fundamental virtue of consistency and as holding a minimal number of true beliefs. Yet we have to be very careful about how exactly we understand the principle of charity. First, we could understand it as an algorithmic procedure that provides specific advice to the interpreter in every interpretive decision. Such a *local conception* of charity would advise us to always prefer that interpretation which attributes quantitatively the highest number of true beliefs to the interpretee. It would recommend that we interpret him so that his belief system approximates as closely as possible an absolutely consistent belief system and that his behavior conforms to all of the normative principles of our best theory of rationality. A local conception of

charity would encourage the view that the standard conception of rationality is a constitutive assumption of interpretation within the folk-
psychological context, and it would encourage the view that to understand
another agent as rational is to interpret each and everyone of his actions as
if they are what "they rationally ought to be."

Second, one can understand charity as a principle that constrains the interpretive process in a more *global* manner, and not as an algorithmic procedure that advises the resolution of interpretive difficulties for every local
context. According to the second conception, it is constitutive of interpretation that it reveal an agent as having some true beliefs from the interpreter's perspective and that it reveal, loosely speaking, a certain amount of
consistency within his belief system and between his set of belief and
desires and subsequent actions. To be more precise, since from a logical
point of view consistency does not come in degrees, it is constitutive of
interpretation that it reveal the total belief system as being divisible into
consistent subsets of beliefs—each of them with sufficient complexity and
structure—even though the overall system need not be consistent. For the
global conception of charity, truth and rationality are a priori yet locally
defeasible default assumptions. They can be overridden in each specific
case in light of considerations regarding the overall fit between various interpretive hypotheses and the overall fit between these hypotheses and the
behavioral evidence on which such an interpretation is based.

Charity in the local sense is an easy target of philosophical ridicule. As a
matter of fact, interpreters have no difficulties attributing false beliefs to
agents, nor have they any problems, as Goldman quite correctly points out
(1995a, 77), attributing inconsistencies and irrationality to various agents if
the behavioral evidence requires them to do so.[6] As I have already pointed
out, to expect ideal consistency among the belief sets of human agents
would not be a psychologically realistic assumption given our limited cognitive resources. For that very reason, I regard it as futile to try to defend
the local conception of charity. From my perspective it is an equally Pyr-
rhic victory to defeat the local conception of charity in the above manner.
Although some of Davidson's earlier writings might have encouraged such
an understanding even in regard to the question of truth, it is clear that he
regards attribution of error quite correctly as perfectly legitimate. At times it
is required in order to view the behavior of the agents as intelligible.[7] If an
agent insists on walking on thin ice without having any detectable desire

for suicide, for example, it is indeed more appropriate to interpret him as having a false belief about the ice rather than as having a true belief. The attribution of a false belief here is justified in light of its fitting better with the empirically justified interpretation of his other beliefs and desires and his other verbal and nonverbal behavior. Charity, globally conceived, however, implies that such attribution is intelligible only if a certain amount of agreement between interpreter and interpretee has been established (Davidson 1984, 168–169).

The above global understanding of charity seems also to be Davidson's position all things considered insofar as the issue of rationality is concerned—or at least I take this to be his position, as he says that "the possibility of irrationality depends on a large degree of rationality" and that "inconsistency, or other forms of irrationality, can occur only within the space of reasons, inconsistencies are perturbations of rationality, not mere absence of rationality" (Davidson 2001, 99, 125). Nevertheless, it has to be admitted that in regard to the rationality assumption, the local conception of charity is much more plausible than it is in regard to truth.[8] To make some headway in the perplexing debate about rationality, it is important to understand why defenders of the principle of charity have been understood as committing themselves to a local conception of charity and to the standard conception of rationality. One reason certainly consists in the fact that even defenders of the rationality conception of interpretation distinguish insufficiently between the standard and the traditional conceptions of humans as rational animals. Within the context of viewing interpretation through the analysis of radical interpretation, there are two other systematic reasons why a local reading of charity in the debate about rationality has been encouraged and why merely pointing to isolated cases of interpretable irrationality has been seen as an argument against charity and the rationality assumption.

The first reason has to do with what I acknowledge to be a real tension within Davidson's position. Davidson declares, for reasons that have nothing to do with the analysis of radical interpretation, that an interpretation of an agent's speech and action has to have a certain form, favoring Jeffrey's decision theory and Tarski's truth definitions.[9] Besides regarding the notion of truth as intuitively central to our understanding of meaning, Davidson, for example, chooses the form of a Tarskian theory of truth as the appropriate form for a theory of meaning because he feels that only such a theory will allow us to conceive of the compositional structure of language in a logically conspicuous manner. It will enable us to understand the creative aspect of natural language and our comprehension of a potentially infinite number of sentences through a structural analysis that allows us to theoretically grasp how the semantic properties of complex linguistic expressions are based on the semantic properties of a finite number of linguistic elements (see Stueber 1993, chap. 2). Yet in making these theoretically motivated choices about the form of the end product of interpretation, Davidson suggests that the norms of logical reasoning and decision making that "give structure" to these theories are constitutive assumptions on part of the interpretive process itself. On the other hand, Davidson is more than willing to admit that these theories are "true only of the perfect logician" (2004, 126). As far as the "empirical application" of such theories—or their empirical adequacy—is concerned, Davidson states explicitly that there is no "list of 'basic principles of rationality'" and that "the kinds and degrees of deviation from the norms of rationality that we can understand or explain are not settled in advance" (2004, 196). Seen from this perspective, Davidson would advocate a process of interpretation that is very similar to Dennett's recommendation that "one starts with the ideal of perfect rationality and revises downward as circumstances dictate" (1987, 21).[10]

If we view the process of interpretation as necessarily involving a downward revision of our ideal or standard conception of rationality, then it is quite appropriate to ask, as critics of the rationality approach of interpretation have done, whether the notion of rationality has become so "flexible" and "slippery" (Dennett 1987, 94, 97) that it can no longer be regarded as a meaningful constraint on our empirical practice of interpretation. If folk-psychological interpretation allows the attribution of irrationality, why should we regard the norms of ideal rationality as constraints on interpretation in the first place? Davidson's contention that it is only in light of such a theory that we can articulate the compositional structure of language does not seem to be directly relevant in this context. It seems not to sufficiently distinguish between issues in theoretical linguistics regarding the structure of the best theory for theoretically representing our linguistic competence and questions of how we empirically justify the interpretation of linguistic agents with the help of folk-psychological terminology.

The second reason for regarding proponents of the rationality conception of interpretation as committed to the standard conception of rationality— at least in regard to the consistency of agents' systems of beliefs—has to do with a confusion about the exact nature of meaning holism and belief holism and the tendency to conceive holism in a very radical manner as suggested by Fodor and Lepore (1992). According to this understanding of holism, only "whole languages or whole theories or whole belief systems have meanings, so that the meanings of the smaller units ... are merely derivative."[11] Accordingly, a sentence has meaning and an intentional state has content if and only if other sentences and other beliefs do. Since the individuation of an intentional state depends on the individuation of its content, it follows that the identity of an intentional state can be determined only in relation to other intentional states. Thus far this conception of holism seems to correspond to the holism revealed in the context of radical interpretation. Yet Fodor and Lepore suggest that holism, in conjunction with the widespread rejection of the analytic–synthetic distinction in current analytic philosophy, is a rather radical doctrine. It implies that there is no principled way of distinguishing between those inferential relations among beliefs that should be regarded as content-determining ones and those relations that are irrelevant in this respect. If one rejects the analytic–synthetic distinction, all relations of a belief to other intentional states are constitutive of its content. Consequently, if there is any difference in the belief system between two persons they cannot share even one belief (for discussion, see Devitt 1996).

Fodor and Lepore are quite right to point out that if this would be implied by meaning holism then it would indeed be a "crazy doctrine" (Fodor 1987, 60). I do not want to dwell on the various disastrous consequences that Fodor and Lepore focus on if one accepts such a radical conception of meaning holism (see Stueber 1997a in this respect). I only want to suggest that such a conception of holism would also imply the implausible claim that ideal consistency is a requirement for interpretation of an agent's belief set. Any inconsistency between beliefs, however far apart they are from each other, would have to be understood as creating a equivalently severe crisis in our confidence regarding our interpretive hypotheses. Only in light of this radical version of holism can one understand Dennett's assertion, put so clearly in his earlier writing, "that intentional explanation and prediction cannot be accommodated to either breakdown or less than optimal design" (1981, 20), and that "in cases of even the mildest and most familiar cognitive pathology—where people seem to hold contradictory beliefs or to be deceiving themselves—the canons of interpretation of the intentional strategy fail to yield clear, stable verdicts about which beliefs and desires to attribute to the person" (1987, 28). Yet we ordinarily have no problems attributing beliefs and desires in cases of irrationality, certainly not in cases of "mild cognitive pathologies," as proponents of the nonrationality conception correctly point out. These cases are counterexamples only against a local conception of charity that is also implied by the above radical conception of holism. It is important to note that my conception of radical interpretation does not in any way commit me to such a view, because it does not imply the radical conception of holism. Based on the analysis of radical interpretation, meaning and content are holistically constituted because the attribution of even one belief can be empirically justified only in light of the attribution of other beliefs, and it is in this context that interpretive decisions are made about degrees of agreement between the interpreter's own belief system and the interpretee's. None of this implies that one cannot have a belief about the earth if one does not share all of the interpreter's beliefs about it or knows nothing about modern astronomy and physics. Radical interpretation implies only that to justifiably attribute a belief, an interpreter must be able to attribute *a sufficiently large enough belief system with a certain amount of structure and complexity*. More specifically, this implies that some sufficiently large enough subsets of beliefs can be understood as logically consistent from the interpreter's perspective. Only then is the interpreter justified in attributing false beliefs as well as beliefs that seem inconsistent with other beliefs.

It is therefore misleading to characterize the doctrine of meaning holism as maintaining that the meaning of smaller units is somehow strictly or in any formally precise manner determined by its more encompassing context. Holism as revealed by the analysis of radical interpretation minimally implies that sufficiently large enough islands of consistency and rationality have to be found within the belief system of a particular person. The cognitive deficiencies that have been discussed in the recent psychological literature can therefore not be used to argue against my interpretive position. The results of various psychological experiments merely imply that it is not to be expected that an agent's beliefs form a completely consistent set.

Nevertheless they do not prove that no subset of the belief system is consistent. Such a claim, I would maintain, cannot in principle be empirically justified since the interpretation of the relevant experiments presupposes the attribution of numerous other beliefs and desires to agents, some of which have to form a consistent set.

Even though overall consistency of the agent's belief set is not required according to the global conception of charity, the assumption of consistency and rationality has to be regarded as an a priori default yet defeasible standard for interpretation, even in cases of attribution of irrationality. Recognizing that the attribution of a particular belief is inconsistent with a subset of the agent's belief allows us to raise prima facie legitimate questions regarding the correctness of the interpretation of the agent so far.[12] Being able to legitimate a probing question about the correctness of an interpretation does not imply that attribution of irrationality can never be justified or that the question cannot be sufficiently answered in light of the available empirical evidence. One has to remember that in the end an interpretation is justified by how well it accommodates all of the empirical evidence available to an interpreter in light of his own knowledge of the world. Part of this knowledge is the recognition that human beings have limited cognitive capacities and are prone to error and inconsistencies. The rationality assumption can be overridden in localized circumstances by holistic considerations having to do with the likelihood of an attribution of irrationality, given the observed behavior of the agent and further psychological knowledge about him in particular and human beings in general. The rationality constraint can thus be overridden in localized circumstances in a manner similar to how the assumption of truth can be overridden in light of holistic considerations about the assumption of consistency and rationality of agency (see also Henderson 1993 and Thagard and Nisbett 1983 in this regard).[13] For example, knowing that a particular person is a highly regarded mathematician, I will feel less inclined to attribute a mathematical inconsistency that even I could recognize. On the other hand, knowledge that the person was depressed, tired, drunk, generally not paying attention, or was in a car accident that severely injured part of his brain and so on would increase my justification for an attribution of irrationality.

In this context, it is useful to compare my account of radical interpretation with the one that Stich advocated at one point (1983, 1990). For Stich, if rationality is a constraint on interpretation, it is so only in a derivative sense. Primarily, "in intentional description we characterize cognitive state via similarity to actual or possible states of our own" (1990, 50). Since we are as a matter of fact rational to a reasonable degree, creatures that are "intentionally describable" within the folk-psychological framework will be interpreted accordingly. An attribution of irrationality creates a problem that would undermine our ability to characterize another creature in intentional terms only when it involves "errors or incoherence that we cannot imagine falling into ourselves" (1994, 344). Stich bases his claims on a projectivist understanding of our concept of belief. Following Quine, he maintains that asserting that S believes that p has to be seen as being equivalent to saying that "S is in a belief state identical in content to the one which would play the central role if I were now to produce an utterance 'p' with a typical causal history" (1983, 81), or, more broadly, as saying that "S has a belief state similar to the one which would underlie my own assertion of 'p' were I (just now) to have uttered 'p' in the earnest" (1990, 49).

In the end, Stich's account of interpretation depends on the plausibility of his projectivist analysis of belief attribution. The central intuition behind such a projectivist account is the fact that one way of finding out about whether we have a particular belief that p is to find out whether we would assert p sincerely (see Evans 1982). I have no problem accepting this intuition as sound, but it does not imply a projectivist analysis of our concept of belief. Certainly we can find out what we believe by considering what we would assert sincerely, because we conceive of a sincere assertion as the expression of a belief. For that very reason, a belief can also be understood as a state that in connection with other mental states leads to an assertion. If interpretee and interpreter are in the same belief states, they are indeed in a state that in connection with other mental states leads to an assertion with the same content. This alone follows from a functionalist conception of the nature of belief. Yet all of this does not imply that in asserting "K. S. believes that p" I am asserting that K. S. has a belief state similar to one that would underlie my assertion of p. As Fodor and Lepore have pointed out, such analysis seems to have the unfortunate consequence that "what you can believe depends on what your interpreter can say" (1992, 140). More significantly, a projectivist explication of belief ascription cannot account for the fact that in the folk-psychological context, first-person and third-person ascriptions are taken to have the same content. According to the projectivist analysis, to say that K. S. believes that p is to say that he is in a state similar to the one that causes the interpreter to assert p. It is, however, absurd to suggest that in asserting that I believe that p, I assert anything about what possible interpreters would assert, especially in light of the fact that knowledge of my own mental states is supposedly not based on any inference. Also, even if one accepts a projectivist account of belief (which I have suggested one should not), it is not clear how such an account could be applied to the attribution of other mental states. Hence it is also not clear why similarity to ourselves should be a general constraint on the interpretation of other agents in the folk-psychological context.

My critique of Stich should not be misunderstood. In defending empathy as playing an epistemically central role in our folk-psychological practices, I am obviously not opposed to the view that in our folk-psychological interpretations we use ourselves as models for the other person's thought processes. But my conception of empathy's central role is tied to the crucial fact that within folk-psychological practices we view each other as rational agents who act for reasons. From my perspective, Stich's insistence that similarity rather than charity and rationality has to be seen as a primary constraint on interpretation is ultimately grounded in an insufficient distinction between the local and global understandings of charity. As a result, he distinguishes insufficiently between the topic of whether norms of rationality such as consistency have to be regarded as defeasible default assumptions that govern the interpretive process globally and the epistemic question of how we can justify a specific interpretation that construes a particular agent as deviating from such interpretive standards in localized circumstances. Obviously, if I do not recognize the inconsistencies in the belief system of the other agent—as is very likely given my own limited cognitive capacities—questions of interpretive adequacy in light of interpretive standards do not arise. If I am logically challenged, I will not think twice about attributing irrationality to agents that are logically challenged to the same degree. If psychologists are right, we can expect such interpretive behavior certainly as far as probabilistic reasoning is concerned.

But in order to recognize the validity of my argument for the global principle of charity, one only has to realize that the interpreter's epistemic situation changes dramatically once he recognizes an inconsistency from his own perspective. In that case he has to answer the question of why his interpretation is correct even though it seems to contradict his prior

of rationality, but they also have to be viewed as conforming to some of those norms of reasoning. Only if we view agents as satisfying the logical norms of consistency to a sufficient degree are we able to characterize them as creatures with intentional states. This also implies that agents have to be thought of as having the capacity to maintain the consistency of a suitably large and complex belief set. They will have to be thought of as being able to draw some of the logically appropriate inferences, since otherwise it would be mysterious how they could have acquired a consistent set of beliefs in the first place. Nonetheless, so far I have not directly addressed the issue of whether general and abstract logical rules of consistency should also be regarded as normatively binding from the perspective of the agent himself as the standard conception of rationality assumes. The fact that one organizes one's cognitive system according to such rules or that one can attribute beliefs to a person from the third-person perspective only if he conforms to such rules does not thereby give such standards any normatively binding force from the perspective of the agent himself. An organism that merely organizes its cognitive system according to our norms of rationality, yet for whom the question of the normative appropriateness of its action or belief never arises, is prima facie conceivable.[14] For the issue of normativity to arise, mere rational organization of one's belief system is not sufficient. The question of normativity becomes pertinent only in the context of organisms that have the capacity of second-order reflection, that is, organisms that not only have beliefs but also have the notion of a concept of a belief and beliefs about their beliefs and other first-order mental states.[15]

However, since we are such creatures, we also have to regard the principles that guide our attribution of mental states within the folk-psychological framework as normatively valid standards for the evaluation of our belief system, as standards we should try to conform to. These claims require more extensive considerations, but we can at least note that the normative force of rules of consistency seems to reside in the fact that each agent can reflect on the implications of conceiving of himself and others as believing something to be true. Each recognized contradiction within his belief system raises, from his own perspective, the question of what exactly he believes. Without resolution of such conflict, the agent undermines his own conception of agency from the first-person perspective. In the extreme he is unable to conceive of himself as acting for a reason, as he is unable to think of himself as believing anything in particular. It is for this reason that I suggest that the principles of logical consistency should be regarded as general norms of reasoning that should govern our considerations in any domain of investigation.

Yet in saying that rational agents should regard rules of logical inference such as modus ponens as normatively binding, I am not implying that those inferential rules should be understood as norms that tell agents what particular inferences they should draw. Rather, norms of logical inference should be understood as distinguishing for rational agents between inferences that are normatively permissible to draw and those that are not. They do not advise them that they have to believe q in case they believe that p and that p implies q. Rather, they tell them that it is impermissible to believe not-q in case they believe p and that p implies q. Stated more positively, they direct agents to draw only normatively permissible inferences if they have to draw any inference at all. Whether agents are expected to draw certain inferences is not decided solely by laws of logic. Rather, it is settled by further normative considerations relevant for a particular agent. According to the standards of their profession, mathematicians and philosophers, for example, might be expected to draw more of the logically permissible inferences than persons in other professions. In this regard, logical norms of inference should be understood as analogous to moral norms. Moral norms tell agents which actions are morally permissible and which are impermissible. They do not, for example, advise an agent to act in order to achieve the greatest number of moral actions. To understand moral norms in this fashion and to judge the moral worth of a person quantitatively in terms of number of moral actions performed is to confuse questions of morality or moral worth with "moral fetishism" (Smith 1994, 76). I do not deny that the contemporary rationality debate at times has committed the sin of logical fetishism by requiring that rational agents have deductively closed belief systems.[16] My interpretation of the normative status of the principle of logical consistency with its associated logical rules escapes this critique. For that very reason, I also see no need to reconsider the normative status of logical rules of inference in view of the psychology of actual reasoners and the fact that some inferences are psychologically "easier" to draw than others, as Cherniak (1986) seems to suggest in arguing for a position of "minimal rationality." The normative status of the standards of consistency and related principles of logical inference is derived from the fact that rational reasoners, in reflecting about themselves as believers or agents and in considering the question of consistency *in isolation from* other factors, recognize that they are committed to having a consistent rather than an inconsistent set of beliefs.

I would also like to address another possible misconception of my interpretation of consistency as a normatively binding principle for rational agents. I am not suggesting that a violation of such norms can never be normatively excused or that any violation of such a norm implies that the agent acted or reasoned irrationally. In deciding the rationality of a particular action, we have to consider a multitude of normative standards besides consistency, such as the standards for evaluating the empirical evidence for a particular belief, norms for conducting searches for evidence, norms for rational time management, and so on. Hence, the situations in which subjects of the above-mentioned psychological experiments find themselves are not representative of real-life situations in which we normally have to evaluate the rationality of their actions. In the artificial situation of the psychological experiment, the only decidable question was indeed whether or not subjects' inferential behavior violated one particular norm of reasoning. In those situations, one is inclined to judge the subjects' reasoning as irrational. Yet this does not imply that our judgments regarding the rationality of an action are normally decided by determining whether or not subjects violate logical norms taken in isolation. The only question that is decided in this isolated fashion is the question of whether we should regard particular principles as normative standards for the evaluation of an agent's action from the first- and third-person perspective. Judgments regarding the rationality of a particular action, on the other hand, are, as has been already suggested, contextualized judgments that evaluate the agent in light of various relevant normative standards, his goals and belief system, his resources and abilities to reach those goals in those specific circumstances. More specifically, in evaluating the rationality of an action we take into account aspects of the internal organization the human mind as well as the objective likelihood of an agent to satisfy his goals in a particular environment. It is for this reason that we evaluate the activity of an agent according to the dimensions of both objective and subjective rationality. The normative standards of rationality are best compared to the normative standards of morally and socially appropriate behavior. To be able to live up to those standards and in order for one's action to be judged as socially or rationally appropriate behavior is to be able to negotiate the various normative standards that are taken to be relevant for such judgment in particular circumstances. Except in a situation of artificial restriction as in the above psychological experiments, the question of the rationality of a specific action is rarely exhausted by considering whether a particular norm has been violated.

To explore the analogy between judgments of the rationality of an action and judgments about the social appropriateness of behavior in a bit more detail, I will consider the judgment about the normative correctness of an agent's social behavior according to the relevant standards or virtues such as honesty, generosity, bravery, and so on. All of these standards are relevant for the evaluation of an agent's behavior in a social context. In understanding honesty as such a normative standard, however, we do not regard honesty as a norm that should be relativized to our morally fallible nature; we do not suggest that all we can require from agents like us is that we should be a little bit honest, because it is almost impossible to be honest all the time. Rather, the norm of honesty is regarded as a general principle of behavior that has normative relevance in all possible situations of human action. Still, a violation of a particular norm can at times be excused and even normatively justified in terms of higher-order norms. In considering the virtue of an action we have to consider the norms that are relevant in a specific situation, and then we have to decide whether the agent properly negotiated these norms in this situation given his beliefs and desires, resources, and capacities. A violation of a single relevant norm does not by itself show that the agent was not virtuous, particularly in situations in which these rules come in conflict with each other. Consider the following: norms of honesty, truthfulness, and politeness are certainly all norms of good behavior. Yet the rules of politeness and honesty might come in conflict with each other in case a neighbor asks me whether I like the color that he used in repainting his house. Given that I desire to maintain good neighborly relations and given that this goal is normatively sanctioned by my community, the fact that I violate the rule of honesty in this case does not imply that I am not a virtuous person. Notice, however, that in "justifying" a deviation from the norm of honesty, I do not imply that honesty has no normative relevance in these circumstances. Rather I regard the situation as one where I have overriding normative reasons not to conform to this specific rule. At the same time, I acknowledge my commitment to the norm in regretting having to violate it. The general desirability of maintaining good neighborly relations, however, does not morally excuse every normative "violation." Giving up a Jewish friend, whom one is hiding, to a neighbor, who works for the Gestapo, would not be morally excusable in light of the fact that one wants to maintain good neighborly relations. In general an action is not regarded as socially or morally appropriate merely because it violates one norm of good behavior; rather, one judges an action as morally or socially inappropriate because the agent fails to properly negotiate the demands of a variety of norms relevant for consideration in this particular circumstance.

Whereas logical norms are certainly less ambiguous than social rules of honesty and politeness, I would suggest that their status for our judgments of rationality should be understood in an analogous manner. Consistency should be understood as a norm of rationality, but not as the only norm relevant for deciding questions of the rationality of an action in particular circumstances. Given our limited resources, it certainly cannot be expected—as Harman (1999) has pointed out—that we could successfully interact with the world while also maintaining the complete coherence of our belief system. We would spend all of our time merely checking our belief system for consistency instead of trying to reach other important goals. Trying to maintain absolute consistency is irrational not only because it conflicts with certain facts about our limited cognitive capacities but also because it clashes with normative considerations about time management and maximizing one's utility. All of this does not imply that considerations of consistency have no normative force for rational agents (Bermudez 2001). Given my above suggestions, conceiving of myself as having beliefs implies that I am committed to consistency among my beliefs; I have to at least acknowledge that inconsistency within my belief system is a potential problem requiring resolution. Yet, as considerations from post-Kuhnian philosophy of science have certainly made clear, how such inconsistency is resolved involves a whole set of other norms about evaluating the empirical evidence and criteria for choosing between different theories. It is not necessarily irrational to continue to hold onto a particular theory even if it does not fit smoothly into my overall belief system. Instead we have to ask in part whether another theoretical alternative is available to me that would allow me to interact with the world in an instrumentally successful manner as the old theory.

The foregoing considerations, however, do not allow us to deduce a priori anything about how the capacity to preserve some consistency among beliefs, which is presupposed in folk-psychological interpretations, are cognitively implemented in our biological hardware. Such questions about the underlying mechanisms of our reasoning abilities are important empirical questions. Gaining knowledge in this area also helps us gain a better understanding of the difficulties human beings have in living up to or even recognizing the appropriate norms of reasoning. Giving my contextualized analysis of judgments regarding the rationality of specific actions, knowledge of those limitations of the human mind is undoubtedly relevant for evaluating the rationality of an agent's action in particular circumstances. We excuse more easily a violation of a norm if we know that agents generally have great difficulties in recognizing that situation as falling under the relevant norm. In those situations, we are less inclined to call the action irrational.[17]

An evaluation of the by now rather extensive empirical literature on this topic is beyond the scope of this book. But it is important to discuss briefly whether and to what extent empirical research about the psychological mechanisms underlying our reasoning capacity has repercussions for how we should conceive of the norms in light of which we decide questions about the rationality of the actions and inferences of a particular agent. According to my position, questions about which standards are normatively relevant to answering such questions are decided independent of questions of our underlying cognitive organization. Questions of the underlying cognitive organization of the mind become relevant only in light of our contextualized judgments about the rationality of actions in view of a number of normative standards and the relevant facts of the situation, which include facts about the cognitive organization of the acting subject. Within the context of evolutionary psychology, on the other hand, Gerd Gigerenzer and his collaborators seem to suggest that even the normative questions can only be decided in terms of the actual cognitive organization of a creature's mind and in terms of how well its cognitive mechanisms are adapted to the structure of the environment. Researchers within this rather recent research program take the term "mind" to refer to a collection of more or less independent but interconnected mechanisms or modules. They regard these modules as biological adaptations and as mechanisms that have been selected for in order to solve specific cognitive problems that an organism faces in a particular environment.[18] The mind is no longer conceived of as a general-purpose tool to solve problems in various domains of investigation as envisioned by Descartes, Leibniz, and even today's cognitive scientists. To use Gigerenzer's apt metaphor, it is understood as an "adaptive toolbox," "a collection of specialized cognitive mechanisms that evolution has built into the human mind for specific domains of inference and reasoning" (Gigerenzer et al. 1999, 30). It is not surprising that within this research paradigm, particular attention is paid to our limited resources and the manner in which a creature with such limited resources can take advantage of the structure of the environment in order to further its goal of survival or proliferation of genes—depending on how one is inclined to describe the basic "goal" of natural selection. Interestingly, Gigerenzer uses the ecological perspective not only for the project of describing the underlying cognitive structure of our mind; in arguing for what he calls *bounded* and *ecological* rationality, he also challenges the standard picture of rationality presupposed in the previously discussed psychological research into the shortcomings of human inferential strategies. For Gigerenzer, a cognitive mechanism is "ecologically rational to the degree that it is adapted to the structure of an environment" (Gigerenzer et al. 1999, 13). He rejects the standard approach of defining rationality primarily in terms of "content-blind" and "context-independent" criteria that are concerned with the logical coherence among judgments or beliefs (ibid., 19). Instead he emphasizes correspondence criteria such as "accuracy, speed and frugality in real world environments" (ibid., 29). Yet the plea for a notion of bounded rationality should not be misunderstood as implying that traditional criteria of coherence never play any function for an ecologically rational animal or even for the evaluation of the rationality of such animal. Gigerenzer objects to the standard picture of rationality only because it conceives of norms of rationality in a formal and "content-independent" (2000, 216) manner. For this reason he rejects the standard picture's "a priori imposition" of these norms as "context-independent yardsticks of rationality" (2000, 202).

Gigerenzer's writing tends to be ambiguous about the exact scope of this claim, since it allows for a strong and a weak reading. Weakly read, his claim implies only that rules of formal logic and decision theory and "principles such as consistency and maximizing are insufficient for capturing rationality" (2000, 209). Understood in this manner, Gigerenzer does not wholeheartedly deny that the formal and "content-independent" rule of consistency plays *a* normative role in determining the rationality of an action. He only denies that formal rules of inference are sufficient for deciding whether an agent acted rationally in a particular situation. I take this weak reading of Gigerenzer to be compatible with my contextualized conception of judgments of rationality, even though it can be argued for independently of any evolutionary considerations. I am also critical of the standard conception of rationality as it insufficiently accounts for the contextualist nature of our practice of evaluating the rationality of specific actions.

More radically (and more often), Gigerenzer's texts support a stronger reading of his claim (see, e.g., Gigerenzer 2000, chaps. 4, 9, 10, 12). According to the strong reading, the rejection of content-independent norms of consistency implies that the normative relevance and validity of coherence criteria is merely derivative and cannot be supported by abstracting from the particular domain an organism is thinking about. They can be justified only by evaluating the adaptive success of a cognitive mechanism conforming to such abstract rules in a specific domain of operation. If a cognitive mechanism can fulfill its adaptive function independent of conforming to such logical standards, such standards would have to be regarded as completely irrelevant to judging the rationality of the organism's actions. A fortiori, human beings need not regard logical rules of consistency as normatively binding if they are able to successfully interact with the world and solve problems in a particular domain without paying any attention to such rules. As Peter Ayton, a sympathizer of the bounded rationality approach, has remarked while discussing the fact that honey bees seem to violate the transitivity axiom in choosing between flowers:

Bees have been successfully going about their business for millions of years. As they have managed to survive for as long as they have, whilst violating one of the basic axioms of rationality, one feels that it is the axiom that is limited in capturing what it means to be rational—not the bees. (Ayton 2000, 667)

Gigerenzer therefore pleads for a positive reevaluation of the use of mental heuristics that do not conform to formal models of decision making and belief acquisition. He objects to conceiving of them in a negative fashion as irrational biases of the mind, as they have tended to be in the recent psychological literature. Instead of interpreting them as deviations from proper norms of rational decision making, we should see the "fast and frugal heuristics" that allow organisms to arrive at adequate decisions in a reasonable amount of time as serving adaptive purposes, and as the "way that the human mind takes advantage of the structure of information in the environment" (Gigerenzer et al. 1999, 29). Given the obvious limitations of the human mind and time constraints within which human agents and other biological organisms have to make decisions, the traditional idea of rational behavior, according to which we "carefully have to look up every bit of information, weigh each bit in your hand, and combine them into a judgment" (ibid., 76), is psychologically and biologically implausible. Following simple rules of decision making (such as the rule of *recognition heuristic*: "if one of two objects is recognized and the other is not, then infer that the recognized object has the higher value") can lead to the reliable formation of true beliefs and successful interaction with the environment *in an environment in which recognition as a matter of fact is correlated with the value in question.* Such rules not only allow rats to avoid poisonous food (ibid., 40). They also enable humans to correctly answer questions about the comparative sizes of cities in an unfamiliar country. If American students unfamiliar with Germany are asked which of two cities, Hamburg or Flensburg, has the larger population, they should choose the city they have heard of, since in the environment we live in one tends to hear more about cities with large populations. Even in cases in which both objects are recognized (and the recognition heuristic does not apply), a complete weighing of all possible criteria for deciding which object has the higher value tends to be unnecessary if the environment is structured such that "each cue is more important than any combination of less valid ones" (ibid., 121). Basing one's decision on just one criterion—the best, or the first one that comes to mind, which is known to have some cue validity regarding the value in question and which is a criterion according to which the two objects in question differ—does quite well if compared to more traditional and standard models of decision making that require a complicated weighing of all possible cues.

Ecological rationality also concerns the "adaptation of mental processes to the representation of information" (Gigerenzer 2000, 58) in the "environment in which our ancestors evolved," or what Tooby and Cosmides (1992) call the EEA, the "environment of evolutionary adaptiveness" (59). It is particularly in this context that Gigerenzer challenges the standard conception of rationality and its reliance on abstract, content-independent rules presupposed by the standard interpretation of the inferential short-comings of the human mind. As Gigerenzer points out, whereas it is quite true that humans tend to fail Wason's original selection task, they are rather successful at a structurally very similar task if the content of the conditional is changed. In particular, Gigerenzer, following Cosmides and Tooby, is partial to the thesis that our mental modules dealing with such conditional reasoning originally developed for the specific purpose of allowing social cooperation among nonrelatives. For such cooperation to be an "evolutionary stable strategy" that does not succumb to the free-rider problem, creatures dependent on social cooperation require the cognitive ability to recognize cheaters. As it turns out, humans perform quite well in conditional reasoning tasks similar to the Wason selection task if they are primarily concerned with the detection of cheaters in the context of maintaining social contracts.

Yet, as Gigerenzer and others have shown, it is not merely the content that activates this module in an appropriate manner. It is also required that the perspective of a cheater detector is taken in this situation. Depending on the perspective they were asked to adopt, subjects differed significantly in performance when confronted with the task of determining the truth of the conditional "If someone stays in the cabin, then that person must bring along a bundle of wood from the valley." When asked to take the perspective of a guard, who checks whether people comply with the rule of the Swiss Alpine Club, they performed rather well. Their performance deteriorated significantly, however, when they were asked to take the role of an impartial observer deciding whether the behavior of hikers conformed to the rule (Gigerenzer 2000, chap. 10). No wonder, then, that in the context of the original Wason selection task subjects tend to give the logically inappropriate answer; they are not asked to detect cheaters, which, according to this interpretation, is the proper function of the involved cognitive module.[19] Similarly, in the context of probabilistic reasoning, Gigerenzer suggests that those of our reasoning mechanisms involved in processing probabilistic information were designed to manipulate information not in terms of percentages but in the "format of natural frequencies, acquired by natural sampling" (2000, 62). According to Gigerenzer, representing probabilistic information in terms of percentages is a relatively recent intellectual heritage. Biologically speaking, we are designed to store and report information about the environment in absolute numbers relative to specific samples of objects encountered in the environment. From an evolutionary perspective, it is more "natural" to say that out of 100 deer which one has seen, 15 were ill, than it is to say that 15 percent of the encountered deer were ill. This evolutionary suggestion seems to be supported by the fact that subjects are not as prone to the common mistakes in probabilistic reasoning such as the conjunction fallacy if the information is presented in a frequency format rather than the probability format, a fact already noted by Tversky and Kahneman (1983).

Gigerenzer also observes that to conceive of the observed shortcomings in probabilistic reasoning as fallacies and violations of normative standards is largely to ignore what researchers in statistics departments regard as "conceptual and technical distinctions *fundamental* to probability and statistics" (2000, 244). Psychologists ignore what Gigerenzer sees as the "dominant school of probability theory," which interprets probability in terms of frequency and regards judgments about the probability of a single event as meaningless (ibid., 246). Judgments about the probability of Linda's being a bank teller or Linda's being a feminist bank teller cannot be regarded as violations of probability theory because, according to the frequentist interpretation, such judgments do not fall within the scope of its theory. Deciding the correct interpretation of the normative theory of probability is certainly beyond the scope and interest of this book.[20] More importantly, questions about how to conceive of probability theory are independent from Gigerenzer's general arguments for bounded rationality, which motivates his general rejection of the normative status of content-independent norms and leads him to view frugal heuristics in a more positive light. Even if we acknowledge a frequentist interpretation of probability theory, we should not thereby concede that content-independent rules of logic cannot be conceived of as standards for the evaluation of the rationality of agents.

It is this claim, however, which is implied by the strong reading of Gigerenzer's position, that is philosophically more interesting and far reaching. For Gigerenzer (2000, 216), the fundamental mistake of the standard psychological research consists in overlooking the fact that our reasoning capacities are primarily concerned with particular content and the manipulation of specific forms of representation. Judging our cognitive systems by formal and content-independent rules, as directed by the standard picture, is like judging a thermostat as making a mistake because it is unable to regulate the different cycles of a washing machine or a dishwasher. The mistake is here clearly in the person who makes the judgment since he does not recognize the objective function for which the thermostat was designed. Conceiving of rationality in a bounded and ecological manner implies that formally "defective" reasoning cannot be judged to be irrational if it is reasoning that is outside the boundaries of the domain for which our reasoning modules were originally selected.

Gigerenzer's conception of bounded and ecological rationality can certainly be challenged from a variety of venues. One might, for example, contest the claim that the frequentist mode is the most "natural" form for the presentation of probabilistic information. In this context, one could point out that the frequentist assumption presupposes an implausibly "unbounded" memory capacity. Given our limited memory capacity, it has been suggested that humans are able to process the probabilistic information with the help of a general reasoning mechanism organized according to "content-independent logic" (Over 2002). Such empirical considerations will not concern us here. Instead we will focus only on the question of whether Gigerenzer's negative conclusion about the normative status of content-independent logic follows even if he is right about the modular organization of our brain. In this context, it must first be emphasized that Gigerenzer's reasoning does not constitute a form of the naturalistic fallacy, where "ought" is merely derived from "is," as some authors have claimed (Stein 1996, 233; Stanovich and West 2000, 651). As already noted, even within our ordinary conception of rationality, questions about the objective probability of achieving one's goal via a chosen means is just one aspect to consider when evaluating the overall rationality of that action. Gigerenzer's plea for the notion of bounded and ecological rationality is better seen as playing one dimension of our normative conception of rationality—objective rationality—against the other—the subjective rationality of the internal organization of our mental states.

Gigerenzer's evolutionary perspective is certainly a welcome corrective to the assumption—predominant in cognitive science and the study of animal behavior—that our normative theories of logic and decision making also provide us with a suitable model for the underlying mechanisms of human and animal behavior (Gigerenzer et al. 1999, chap. 15). It demonstrates that to look primarily to content-independent rules of logic is not necessarily the most productive route in answering the question of how to build a system with limited cognitive resources that can also survive in the real world. To answer this question, it seems indeed wiser to look primarily at the correspondence of internal cognitive mechanisms and the environment. In this manner one would be able to exploit the stable structure of the environment and adapt the limited resources of a specific information-processing system to its surroundings. Gigerenzer and his collaborators are right in insisting that our formal theories of logic and decision theory should not guide the descriptive project of specifying the underlying cognitive organization of biological organisms with an evolutionary history. In that endeavor we should be led by the criteria that evolution uses for "evaluating" decisions—that is, success—since "evaluation" in terms of these criteria "are the processes that led to the decision making mechanisms we use." Hence, "we must adopt the same success-oriented perspective if we want to uncover and understand what is going on in our head when we make choices" (Todd and Gigerenzer 2000, 776).

Nonetheless, the question of whether rules of logic are normatively valid for humans as they are conceived within the realm of folk psychology cannot be reduced to the question of whether our reasoning competence is organized in a domain-specific and modular fashion, or whether it is instead endowed with a general reasoning competence programmed according to the rules of the standard conception of rationality. Here Gigerenzer seems to be as mistaken about the exact implications of the traditional conception of humans as rational animals as the psychological research that he criticizes. As far as folk psychology conceives of agents who act not only according to reason but also for the sake of reason—that is, as having a conception of their reasons for acting—the dimension of subjective rationality has to be admitted as an independent domain for the evaluation of rationality. Logical and formal rules of reasoning are normatively relevant because a recognized violation of the consistency requirement would make it difficult for the agent and his interpreter to conceive of the content of his thoughts, and more specifically, to conceive of his thoughts as his reasons, regardless of what specific topic the agent is thinking about. From the folk-psychological perspective, Gigerenzer's evolutionary perspective encounters two hurdles in particular. First, even if we focus on the notion of objective rationality, within the folk-psychological realm we decide questions of an action's rationality by focusing on the actual situation each individual agent finds himself in, and by considering the goals, intentions, and resources this specific individual has in a particular situation.

Success is thus not evaluated primarily in terms of reproductive success; even dying an honorable death can count as a goal of an agent. Folk-psychological evaluations of an action's rationality are primarily made at the personal level and not the subpersonal level. They do not require taking into account successful interaction with the original "environment of evolutionary adaptiveness" (EEA), but rather with the agent's actual social and cultural environment. Even if a simple rule like "What one does not know one should not eat" (which, according to a north German folk saying, characterizes the behavior of a farmer—"*Wat de Buer net kennt, dat fret he net*") has been successful from a evolutionary perspective, it would hardly be rational to adopt it in the environment of a global economy. It would certainly put German or American businesspersons at a serious disadvantage if they want to sign a business deal in Japan.

If an agent's actual environment is the primary evaluative context for judging the rationality of her action, then Gigerenzer's evolutionary assumptions are no longer pertinent for questions regarding the normative status of specific principles of inference. The evolutionary perspective would only be helpful for finding out why we have the cognitive mechanisms we have and in explaining why we might have cognitive difficulties in certain contexts. If we want to continue to support the normative claim for bounded rationality in the folk-psychological context, we would have to reconceive the specific evolutionary perspective in more general terms on analogy with an externalist and reliabilist conception of justification in the context of philosophical epistemology. (See also Samuels, Stich, and Bishop 2002 in this respect.) Broadly described, epistemic reliabilism and externalism take a belief to be epistemically justified if and only if it has been produced in a particular environment by a mechanism that tends to produce true beliefs in those types of circumstances. For a belief to be justified the agent does not have to know or have any epistemic access to the fact that his belief-producing mechanism is reliable in this sense. Analogously, one could think of a reason for action as a set of mental states that has been produced by mechanisms that tend to lead to successful interactions with the environment, without requiring that the agent knows about this fact. Hence, Gigerenzer's strategy to raise doubts about content-independent norms of reasoning depends on being able to defend a general reliabilist and externalist conception of reasons. (For a discussion of epistemic externalism and reliabilism, see Goldman 1986; Alston 1989; and Grundmann 2003.)

I am quite favorably inclined to accept some form of epistemic externalism, but only within limits. Within our epistemic practices, I regard as context dependent the answer to the question of whether or not the agent's access to the justificatory facts of a belief are required for the belief to be epistemically justified. If questions of the reliability of my belief-producing mechanisms are raised compellingly—for example, by a trustworthy friend telling me that I just drank a hallucination-inducing drug—it seems to be epistemically irresponsible and subjectively irrational to continue to regard my perceptual beliefs to be justified, even if, unbeknownst to me, my friend lied to me. Even if one insists on regarding my perceptual beliefs to be epistemically justified in such situations, the example raises serious doubt about the viability of conceiving acting for a reason in a purely externalist fashion. From my cognitive perspective, at least, I do not have any reason to continue trusting my perceptual beliefs. Continuing to do so would be as irresponsible as the behavior of someone getting into a car and driving off even though a trustworthy mechanic just had told him that the brakes of his car are not working properly. In this situation, the question of the actual reliability of the belief-producing mechanism or of the brakes is irrelevant, since the agent has prima facie persuasive evidence against their reliability. The agent himself cannot understand his perceptual beliefs as being sufficiently justified to constitute a reason for his action or for the adoption of further beliefs.

I am inclined to agree with Gigerenzer that following the recognition heuristic is in certain circumstances indeed a rational strategy, even if I do not have sufficient reason for regarding the criterion as being a reliable indicator, or if I have not read Gigerenzer's study about the recognition heuristic. I agree with Gigerenzer, as far as the rationality of the behavior of nonreflective animals is concerned, that an externalist conception of reason is the only game in town. Questions of the internal inconsistency of belief sets are indeed normatively irrelevant because such animals do not conceive of themselves as acting for a reason. A radical externalist conception of reason and rationality becomes inappropriate, however, if we are dealing with agents who conceive of themselves as acting for reasons. For such agents, I am not so sure anymore whether I would regard their behavior of, say, guessing the size of cities using the recognition heuristic as rational if such a guessing strategy involves betting large sums of money. From the perspective of the agent, such behavior is certainly not more rational than playing the lottery, even if it is, as a matter of fact, guaranteed to be more successful. He may be lucky, but a lucky fool nonetheless. More significantly, the agent's epistemic situation changes dramatically if he starts having serious counterevidence against the reliability of the criterion used for guessing the size of a city. He might, for example, be told that even though newspapers—the source of his normal acquaintance with foreign cities—normally tend to mention larger cities more often, this is not true for country B. Rather, in B, smaller cities are more often mentioned because it is in those cities that newsworthy activities occur such as the training of terrorists. In this situation agents would no longer be able to follow the normal recognition heuristic as a reason for their action. From the perspective of the agent, such counterevidence—regardless of whether it is in fact true—undermines the confidence with which "something can be said" for the action from his perspective.[21]

If I am right, it is exactly on this level of reflective agency that questions about the normative status of content-independent logical rules arise. Agents who on reflection recognize a contradiction within their belief set, which is relevant to planning their actions, are thereby challenged in their attempt to conceive of themselves as acting for a reason. Even if, each time the agent recognizes an inconsistency in his belief set, a subpersonal mechanism forces the agent to act on the belief that is objectively true, it would not change the fact that from his perspective nothing could be said for the action. His action would be rational only from an external observer's point of view. From his own perspective, he would be seriously alienated from his action. For these reasons, Gigerenzer's critique of content-independent norms of reasoning as suggested by the strong reading of his position ultimately fails. The problem is similar to that for the detached conception of folk psychology: he does not sufficiently take into account that within the folk-psychological context mental states are viewed not merely as internal events that cause an outward motion, but as states that agents can be reflectively aware of as reasons for their actions. A merely external and evolutionary conception of rationality is thus inappropriate. Moreover, nothing that Gigerenzer says shows that the folk-psychological conception of agency in the folk-psychological realm is inappropriate or false. Indeed he himself in his argument for the ecological rationality adheres self-reflectively to norms of proper reasoning and argumentation.

To summarize the results of my exploration of the status of rational agency within the folk-psychological context so far: *pace* the influential and detached conception of folk psychology dominant in current philosophy of mind, I have argued for an engaged conception of folk psychology. According to this conception, the notion of rational agents who act for a reason and who have to be understood as responsive to normative standards is at the center of the explanatory and interpretive concerns of folk psychology. In defending the principle of global charity, I have also argued that within the folk-psychological context we can interpret other agents only if we conceive of them as conforming to the rules of logical consistency to a sufficient degree. In addition I have shown that psychological research documenting the inferential shortcomings of human subjects does not contradict the above assumption of folk psychology or the traditional assumption of humans as rational animals, since viewing humans as rational animals does not commit us to the view that they are programmed according to the principles of the standard model of rationality. It also does not conflict with viewing charity in a global sense as a constitutive principle of folk-psychological interpretation. Finally, I have resisted the widespread temptation to "downsize" our norms of reasoning as conceived by the standard model of rationality in light of our finite cognitive capacities. I agree with the standard model of rationality that the rules of logic, probability theory, and decision theory have to be understood as normatively relevant to the evaluation of the rationality of a specific action. Yet I criticize the standard model of rationality for not having recognized the contextualized nature of such judgments. Having clarified my understanding of the central features of folk psychology and my conception of rational agency, it is time to address the central epistemic question of this book, namely, whether or not the egocentric method of empathy is epistemically central to our folk-psychological practices. In the following chapters, I will argue for this claim by critically evaluating the interdisciplinary debate between theory theorists and simulation theorists and by addressing the pertinent objections against empathy from the traditional philosophy of social science.

Naturalized" in his 1969 (for a survey, see Kornblith 1994). Epistemological naturalism follows the Quinean dictum that philosophy cannot provide the various sciences with epistemic foundations from the perspective of cosmic exile. Naturalists conceive of epistemology as a project that is part of the scientific exploration of the causal structure of the world, specifically the exploration of the causal mechanisms underlying our acquisition of knowledge in particular domains.[2] It is only in light of knowledge of such underlying mechanisms that we can sensibly address questions regarding the scope and limitation of our specific strategies for knowledge acquisition.

While I agree with the epistemic naturalists that philosophy cannot be conceived of as speaking from an inaccessible cosmic exile perspective, it is a mistake to think that traditional armchair philosophizing is committed to a perspective of cosmic exile and that one can completely discount it in empirical investigations of the world. Rather, as the previous chapters discussing rational agency have shown, conceptual considerations become centrally important for assessing the validity of interpretive conclusions drawn from such evidence. Such a priori considerations are also significant for answering the question of how best to conceptually frame the empirical investigation of our folk-psychological capacities. In our context, they will be important for deciding whether such important research should be understood as trying to, and being able to, decisively demonstrate the correctness of either of the main paradigms that is put forward this context, that is, the theory theory or the simulation theory. In light of the centrality of the notion of rational agency to our folk-psychological practices, I will argue that framing the empirical debate in this manner might indeed be misleading. Empirical considerations about underlying mechanisms alone—especially neurobiological mechanisms—as important as they are for our understanding of our folk-psychological abilities, can never decide the issue for either simulation theorists or theory theorists. For that purpose, the empirical research has to be further buttressed by more traditional a priori or conceptual considerations. In particular, a defense of empathy and simulation theory is ultimately successful only if it is able to address the conceptual concerns that made the detached conception of folk psychology so attractive to philosophers of mind. First, simulation theorists and defenders of the empathy proposal will have to say something about how they understand the nature of mental concepts and how they conceive of the epistemic status of folk-psychological explanations. Second, and of even greater consequence, a priori considerations focusing on the notion of rational agency make it appear highly implausible that a theory-theory account adequately describes the inferential processes underlying our folk-psychological abilities. Yet in order to substantiate this claim it is necessary to provide a better sense of the parameters of the empirical investigation of our folk-psychological mindreading abilities and a bit of the flavor of the empirical facts that have driven the debate so far.

Psychologists also refer to research into our folk-psychological mindreading abilities as "theory of mind" research, since the recent surge of interest in this topic has been triggered by Premack and Woodruff's 1978 publication "Does the Chimpanzee Have a Theory of Mind?" In this article Premack and Woodruff construe having a theory of mind as the ability to impute mental states to oneself and others. They thus define having a theory of mind not primarily in terms of specific underlying causal mechanisms but in terms of engaging in a conceptual and interpretive practice. At times psychologists refer to our folk-psychological abilities as theory-of-mind abilities without implying a specific thesis regarding the underlying psychological mechanism on which such abilities supervene. At other times, they use this term for a more detailed proposal about how we should conceive of the underlying mechanism of our folk-psychological abilities.[3] To avoid such unfortunate ambiguity, we will use the theory of mind terminology only when it refers to a specific proposal accounting for what I will otherwise call folk-psychological or mindreading abilities.

The developmental facts that have been central to this debate include the enormous cognitive advances that children seem to make between the ages of three and four in their folk-psychological understanding of other agents. Within this period of time children come to understand that other persons can have false beliefs and that they act because they subjectively misrepresent objective states of affairs. Child psychologists have regarded it as particularly noteworthy that only children older than four are able to pass the false-belief task. In its classic conception by Heinz Wimmer and Josef Perner (1983), children were shown a puppet "Maxi" who observed his mother putting a piece of chocolate in a cupboard. Afterward Maxi is seen leaving the room and during his absence his mother uses part of the chocolate and puts the rest at another location. Children are now asked where Maxi will look when he comes back and wants to eat the chocolate. The correct answer is—needless to say—that he will look where he thinks the chocolate is, not where the chocolate actually is. Yet children under the age of four tend to say that Maxi will look in the cupboard where the chocolate actually is. This inability to predict Maxi's behavior was often taken to indicate that children under four years of age are unable to conceive of a belief as a subjective representation of an objective state of affairs that could be objectively false (Wellman 1990).

Further research has shown, however, that such a conclusion based only on the results from false-belief tasks has been premature. Children's folk-psychological abilities, and specifically the ability to attribute false beliefs and explain behavior in light of false beliefs, do not develop overnight. Rather it seems to be a gradual three-stage process. First, from around 1 1/2 to 2 years of age, children start using desire terminology such as "want" and "wish" to talk about their own desires and the desires of other people. Desire talk precedes belief talk and its equivalent for about a year. Children start using terms like "think" and "believe" to refer to genuine mental states at around 3 years old, even before they pass the standard belief task. Between 3 and 4 years, they are able to attribute a false belief to another person in the context of being asked to explain their behavior (Bartsch and Wellman 1995). Moreover, even if children are not able to solve the standard false-belief task, they tend to look at the location where Maxi saw the mother put the chocolate. This has been interpreted as indicating that children have a tacit understanding of the logical possibility that agents can possess false beliefs (Clements and Perner 1994). Other experimental results suggest that children "find it significantly easier to track a false belief in the context of a word-learning task than in a standard test of false belief" (Happe and Loth 2002, 30). Children within the age group of 3 to 5 years old, for example, are more successful in recognizing the intended reference of a person's naming ceremony even if the person has a false belief about which object he is actually pointing to. If a person, for example, points to a closed container and uses a novel word to name $object_1$ that he thinks is in the container—as the children observed, he put it there a short while ago—children are able to figure out that he refers to that object rather than $object_2$, which has been substituted for $object_1$ unbeknownst to the experimenter. Further research has also shown that children of around 3 years old in general have less trouble attributing a false belief in contexts where they have to make sense of the intentional and goal-directed behavior of other agents. Children, for example, did not have trouble understanding that a person who tried to pour milk on cereal from a carton full of dirt falsely thought that there was milk in the carton (Moses 2001, 76).

The second set of centrally relevant phenomena in this debate is that of the observed deficiencies and abnormalities in social behavior and cognitive development resulting from certain psychopathologies, particularly autism, ever since such psychopathologies have been diagnosed as specific deficiencies in mindreading abilities (Baron-Cohen 1995; for a useful summary of research on autism, see Frith 2003). Autistic children, who show a variety of deficiencies in their ability to relate socially to other people and in their linguistic and communicative competence, do not pass the false-belief task at the normal age, in contrast to normal children and even in contrast to children with Down syndrome. In contrast to normal children, autistic children also do not engage in spontaneous pretend play, such as pretending that a banana is a telephone, or more cooperative role play, such as playing Mommy and Daddy. According to Leslie (1987) both deficits are closely related, since for him the same conceptual resources and mechanisms that underlie our ability to engage in pretend play or to recognize pretense in others also enable us to attribute false beliefs to other people. For that very reason, providing a theory of pretense has been crucial within the context of current theory of mind research (Harris 2000; Nichols and Stich 2003). Whatever one thinks about Leslie's controversial proposal, being able to explicate certain deficiencies in psychopathologies as a breakdown of normal mindreading mechanisms would certainly strengthen one's claim of providing a psychologically realistic account of our normal mindreading abilities (Scholl and Leslie 1999). Any competing theory would have to find another way of accounting for the deficiencies of an autistic person within its particular explanation of our mindreading abilities or would have to point to other general cognitive mechanisms that could also explain the observed deficiencies.[4]

In attempting to describe the underlying mechanisms of our mindreading abilities, the research for a long time has tended to stay on what one could call the functional or conceptual level of investigation—what one could call with Dennett (1987) the design stance. Researchers focusing more on the developmental data were interested in describing the conceptual sophistication or cognitive abilities that on the whole characterize the

child's understanding of the mind at its different stages of development (Wellman 1990; Perner 1991; Gopnik and Meltzoff 1997). Other
researchers with a slightly different theoretical outlook, more focused on
psychopathology, were interested in characterizing the various subsystems
of our cognitive system that contribute to our mindreading abilities (Leslie
1987; Baron-Cohen 1995). Baron-Cohen (1995) has proposed that our
mindreading abilities rest on the interaction of four subsystems: the intentionality detector (ID), the eye-direction detector (EED), the shared attention mechanism (SAM), and what he calls the theory of mind module
(TOMM). ID and EDD are quasi-perceptual systems that respectively process information about bodily movements in terms of primitive intentional
agency—for instance, "agent wants ball"—and important information
about the direction of another's gaze, such as "agent sees ball." Both feed
the information into SAM, which determines the exact relationship between the observed agent and self. It then decides whether the observed
person sees what I am doing or whether we are looking at the same object.
Afterward this information is fed into the TOMM and interpreted in
terms of a full range of mental concepts characterizing our ordinary folk-
psychological practices. Baron-Cohen diagnoses autism as due to a shortcoming in SAM and TOMM, since children with autism have difficulty
passing the false-belief task and deficiencies in "joint-attention behavior"
(1995, 66).

Each of these systems is characterized functionally in terms of its infor-
mational interaction with other cognitive systems and in relation to certain
perceptual inputs. The justification for the postulation of each individual
subsystem rests on its perceived unique contribution to explaining our
normal and abnormal mindreading abilities.[5] EDD and SAM, for example,
have to be regarded as separate subsystems because individuals can be
impaired in joint attention without being impaired in recognizing the direction of the gaze of another person. Nevertheless, since these subsystems
have been proposed mostly independent of neurobiological insights it is
to be expected that our understanding of the various subsystems might
change dramatically in light of new findings of how the brain implements
specific mindreading functions. Researchers have only very recently begun
to integrate new information from the neurosciences in the context of our
mindreading abilities. One can anticipate that various proposals about the
explication of our mindreading abilities will have to be adjusted in order to

accommodate recalcitrant and new experimental evidence in these various domains of investigation. (For a recent survey see R. Saxe et al. 2004.)

Nevertheless, even though research in mindreading abilities should be seen as an ongoing empirical research agenda, the investigation so far has provided two general explanatory paradigms for our mindreading abilities, which have framed the debate for the last two decades about the nature of our folk-psychological abilities: the theory-theory and the simulation theory. To put it abstractly, theory-theorists conceive of our folk-psychological abilities as constituting a detached theoretical strategy that utilizes "knowledge-rich" mechanisms. Simulation theorists, as proponents of empathy, conceive of mindreading as an ego-centric, "knowledge-poor" strategy (Goldman 1995b, 191).

3.1   The Theory-Theory Paradigm

Before providing a more detailed description of these two paradigms, a word of caution is necessary. The terms "theory theory" and "simulation theory" are best understood as labels that subsume under their headings a group of distinct positions that are controversially discussed on both conceptual and empirical grounds within and between these two camps. It should be noted that whereas early in the debate simulation theorists and theory theorists tended to take diametrically opposed positions, one can nowadays observe a certain rapprochement between these two views. More and more authors seem to argue for a hybrid position and acknowledge that, depending on the exact subject matter and context, normal human beings use both knowledge-poor and knowledge-rich strategies (Perner 1996; Stich and Nichols 1997; Nichols and Stich 2003). Yet, although I regard such rapprochement between these two camps as an intellectual advance, merely admitting that simulation or empathy does play a role in our folk-psychological abilities and that our mindreading abilities are a hodgepodge of various theoretical and egocentric strategies does not sufficiently recognize and delineate the centrality of empathy for understanding other agents in the folk-psychological context.

For our purposes a brief characterization of the theory-theory position will suffice, since the differences between positions traditionally regarded as falling within this paradigm primarily concern questions of how exactly knowledge-rich strategies are psychologically organized. It does not concern topics that are directly relevant to the main question of this book of whether or not in understanding other minds we essentially use an ego-centric method. The theory-theory paradigm has been what one can call the "dominant explanatory paradigm" within the psychological community (Stich and Nichols 1995). The allure of the theory-theory paradigm has to do both with the philosophical attractiveness of the detached conception of folk psychology, which I discussed earlier, and the explanatory paradigm provided by Chomskian linguistics, according to which our linguistic abilities are seen to rest on some tacit knowledge of grammar. Similarly, psychologists within the theory-theory camp conceive of our folk-psychological abilities as based on causal mechanisms that represent or make use of some tacit knowledge of folk psychology and general psychological principles. In contrast to the case of linguistic competence, psychologists tend to view the conceptual structure that underlies our folk-psychological abilities to be identical or very close to the conceptual structure of ordinary folk-psychological talk. Furthermore, and equally important, the theory-theory paradigm is attractive because it provides a paradigm that allows us to see a child's cognitive development and increasing conceptual sophistication in various domains of investigation in a unified manner. It allows us to conceive of our maturation in understanding the physical, biological, and psychological aspects of the world as due to the acquisition of increasingly more complex knowledge structures about these various areas of human interest (Carey 1985; Keil 1989; Gopnik and Meltzoff 1997).

Theory theorists differ in regard to how seriously to take the analogy between knowledge of folk psychology and knowledge that is represented by a scientific theory. For some of them (Wellman 1990; Gopnik and Wellman 1995; Gopnik and Meltzoff 1997), thinking about folk psychology on analogy with scientific theory and thinking of the child on analogy with a scientist is appealing because folk psychology, like a scientific theory, does not merely store information in an unconnected manner but seems to enable us to provide an explanatory account of observed macrophenomena in terms of underlying regularities that are postulated to hold between unobservable theoretical entities. More importantly, scientific theories undergo changes in light of recalcitrant experience. They have to be modified or are replaced by very different conceptual frameworks. Within this model a child's cognitive development can be conceived of as a data-driven process in which less complex theories about others are replaced by increasingly complex theories.[6] To account for the observed development during the ages of 2 through 5, proponents of this version of the theory theory postulate, for example, a transition between three stages of theoretical sophistication: a "desire psychology," an "intermediate desire-belief psychology," and a "belief-desire psychology" (Bartsch and Wellman 1995, 144). Only in the last phase is the child able to attribute false beliefs and to use such attributions consistently in the explanation of observed behavior. In the second phase the child already has some understanding of the concept of belief but it is not yet fully developed; compared to the concept of desire the concept of belief still plays a marginal role. Particularly, the attribution of false beliefs to another person, though possible, does not seem to be widely used at this stage for accounting for or predicting another person's behavior.[7]

On the above theory-theory model of accounting for the observed developmental stages in a child's understanding of others, the driving force behind theory change is a general learning mechanism. As the child acquires a better understanding of the world around it, it develops a more appropriate conceptual and theoretical framework to make sense of the experiences it has in encountering the natural world and other people. Proponents of the modularity conception of the theory-theory paradigm (Leslie 1987; Leslie and German 1995; Baron-Cohen 1995) disagree with other theory theorists in this respect. For them, our increased conceptual sophistication cannot be understood as theory building due to general learning mechanisms. They point out that there is a standard sequence of stages according to which children acquire their folk-psychological sophistication. All children go through the same sequence and by around four years of age are able to pass the false-belief task. Even if this sequence shows some individual variability in that some children are able to pass the false-belief task a bit earlier than others, these variations are not sensitive to IQ differences as one might expect if general learning mechanisms were involved (Leslie 2000). Modularists prefer to view our folk-psychological abilities as based on the interaction of various cognitive modules or—to use Gigerenzer's metaphor again—as specialized and domain-specific tools for recognizing other people as minded creatures. The different stages of cognitive development are thus seen not as due to a conceptual revision of a particular theory but rather as activations of various relevant modules comprising our folk-psychological abilities. According to Baron-Cohen, our concepts of volitional states are associated with ID and SAM. The function of the theory of mind module consists in providing the child with the concepts of epistemic states such as belief and to integrate these various concepts into a theory as proposed by Wellman (1990) and others. For Leslie, on the other hand, the function of the TOMM consists primarily in providing us with a reservoir of mental state concepts that allow our cognitive system to form what he a bit misleadingly calls a metarepresentation or "an agent-centered description of a situation," such as mother PRETENDS (of) the banana (that) "it is a telephone" (Leslie and German 1995, 126). For Leslie, it is the implementation of such a module that also accounts for the child's ability to engage in pretend play without such play interfering with the forming of an adequate representation of the real world. Representing its mother's pretense in this manner enables the child to cognitively quarantine what mother says about the banana-telephone from his other knowledge of bananas. Even though Leslie is identified with the theory-theory label, in his more recent publications (2000) it seems clear that he regards the function of the TOMM as providing a reservoir of mental state concepts but not necessarily a full-blown psychological theory. He distinguishes explicitly between concepts and our conceptions involving those concepts. Rejecting a theory-theory or descriptivist account of psychological concepts, he also proposes a strictly causal-referential account of concept possession, according to which one possesses a concept if one has a mechanism that "locks" a concept to the corresponding property in the world.

In light of the considerations about meaning and belief-content holism reviewed in the last chapter, I am doubtful of Leslie's atomistic conception of psychological concepts. Additionally, it can be asked whether in conceiving of psychological concepts in this manner Leslie can still be regarded as a genuine proponent of the theory-theory proposal, or whether his position could be better accommodated within the simulation paradigm. The answer to that question would depend on the role Leslie grants to general psychological knowledge that we associate with our mental state concepts of our ordinary folk-psychological abilities. I will leave both questions in this context undecided.[8]

For our purposes, it is also not important to decide whether it is more plausible to regard our knowledge of folk psychology as stored within a specialized theory of mind module or whether it should be regarded as a theory acquired because of a general learning mechanism that is stored like any other theoretical knowledge in our general belief system. In the context of our discussion, I regard any position as falling within the theory-theory paradigm if it conceives of our folk-psychological ability to predict, explain, and interpret other agents to centrally involve and to be causally dependent on mechanisms that represent general knowledge about the psychology of other agents. At its core, our folk-psychological ability to interpret, predict, and explain the actions of other people has to be understood as a type of theoretical inference that utilizes knowledge about psychological generalizations.

To be more concrete, passing the false-belief task and being able to predict that Maxi will look where he thinks the chocolate is would involve something like the following inferences:[9]

I Determining Maxi's belief about the location of the chocolate

i. Maxi observes that the chocolate in cupboard$_1$ (because he saw his mother put it there).

ii. *Principle of the formation of a perceptual belief*: If somebody observes that *p*, then he normally forms a belief that *p*.

iii. Maxi believes that the chocolate is in cupboard$_1$.

II Recognizing that Maxi did not change his belief

i. Maxi did not observe during the time he played outside (nor did he get any information in this regard from other trustworthy sources) that his mother put the chocolate in cupboard$_2$.

ii. *Principle for changing a perceptual belief*: Somebody normally changes a belief that *p* based on his perception that *p* if and only if he observes at a later time that not-*p* or he receives information that not-*p* from other trustworthy sources.

iii. After coming in from playing outside, Maxi still believes that the chocolate is in cupboard$_1$.

III Predicting where Maxi will look for the chocolate

i. Maxi wants to eat the chocolate, and he believes that the chocolate is in cupboard$_1$, and he believes that looking for the chocolate in cupboard$_1$ is a means of satisfying one's desire of eating it.

ii. *Central action principle*: If somebody desires x and believes that A-ing is a means of achieving x, then, ceteris paribus, he will do A.

iii. Maxi will look for the chocolate in cupboard$_1$.

Before turning to a critical discussion of the simulation alternative I want to emphasize a point about the relationship between the theory-theory view and what I have called the difference between the detached and the engaged conceptions of folk psychology. As a matter of fact proponents of the theory-theory position in psychology tend to conceive of their position as detached and do not seem to regard the notion of rational agency to be at the center of our folk-psychological practices. Yet in this context it has to be stressed that recognizing rationality as a central notion to our folk-psychological practices and to understanding agency does not logically entail an argument for empathy or simulation. Declaring that in understanding agency we not only have to grasp the inner causes of a person's actions but also have to comprehend them as his reasons for his action does not imply that in explaining and predicting another person's action we do not also have to implicitly appeal to a theory of rational agency that outlines how rational agents should act and how they normally would act (see, e.g., Botterill 1996). For that reason, I find Collingwood's (1946) and Dray's (1957) argument for empathy—which is to merely assert that it is necessary for understanding rational agency—a bit underdeveloped, even if it points in the right direction (Stueber 2002a). Certainly a theory of rational agency would differ from a merely "causal-psychological" theory in that it also would contain some general normative principles. Yet the different epistemic status of these general principles, lawlike generality versus normative universality, alone does not suffice to show that our understanding of other minds essentially involves the first-person perspective. In both cases we could account for an action in light of certain general knowledge of the world, knowledge of what normally happens and knowledge of how humans are normatively supposed to act in certain situations. Thus, even if one admits that rationality is a central notion to our folk-psychological practices, as I have urged, a theory theorist could easily accommodate his position to that fact. If there is indeed a connection between the central notion of rational agency and the epistemic centrality of empathy to understanding other minds and other agents, this claim has to be argued for in greater detail.

3.2   The Simulation Paradigm

Simulation theory is best understood as denying the centrality of theory involvement in the above sense to our folk-psychological abilities. Simulation theorists do not merely assert the existence of some knowledge-poor strategies but also challenge the claim that theory-rich mechanisms are at the center of our folk-psychological practices. It is this specific contention that simulation theorists have challenged in various publications, after Gordon (1995a), who first used the term "simulation" in this context, and Heal (1995a) articulated their doubts about the dominant framework's account of our folk-psychological abilities (see also Ripstein 1987; Goldman 1995a; Harris 1989, 1995). Simulation theorists, as the proponents of empathy before them, claim that in contrast to other domains of investigation our folk-psychological understanding of other persons cannot be comprehended as predominantly based on an implicit psychological theory. In contrast to theory theorists, simulation theorists—regardless of important differences between them—emphasize that our folk-psychological abilities to understand other agents rest primarily on "the use of one's own motivational and emotional resources and one's own capacity of practical reasoning" (Gordon 1996, 11) as we "put ourselves in his shoes," imagine the world "as it appears from his point of view," and "then deliberate, reason and see what decision emerges" (Heal 1995a, 47).

At the heart of the simulation proposal is the claim that our cognitive relation to other persons is radically different from our cognitive grasp of other domains of investigation because nature has provided all human beings with a mind that is structured and that functions psychologically in a similar manner. Moreover, it has endowed us with a mind that has the power of imagination, in that it can use essentially the same cognitive machinery—to use common cognitive science terminology—to think about actual or possible worlds, to process beliefs or mere "make-beliefs" (Heal 1995, 49), and to react emotionally to such imaginary worlds as our common experience with literature and movies suggests and has also been experimentally demonstrated (Harris 2000). We use the same cognitive or reasoning processes whether we are actually looking at a particular configuration of chess pieces and trying to find the solution of how white can checkmate in two moves or whether we merely imagine in our mind the same configuration. In these cases our reasoning begins with very different inputs—perceptual stimulation versus mere images—and it might be more difficult to imagine such a configuration in the head. Yet we do not seem to reason any differently in trying to find a solution to a chess problem when we are trying to solve it in our imagination.

Using my cognitive resources for such imaginative purposes requires the ability to quarantine some of my beliefs and desires and use my cognitive system for reasoning about facts that I do not believe exist. As simulation theorists correctly point out, we ordinarily use this ability of quarantining some of our beliefs not merely for imaginative projects but also in rather mundane tasks of ordinary decision making. In deliberating about what to do next we regularly entertain thoughts about hypothetical state of affairs and consider what would follow if such hypothetical scenarios would turn out to be true. In deciding which car to buy, we might raise questions like "what if the gasoline prizes should rise another fifty cents?" and we might consider the various consequences and effects that such a possible state of affairs would have on my budget or my driving habits. It is for this reason and in light of the fact that we all seem to be cognitively structured in a similar manner that I can use myself as a model for finding out about how another person might think about a chess problem by either looking at the same configuration on a chess board or by imagining it. Imagining myself to be a bat, to use Nagel's famous example, would not tell us much about bats, however, since the cognitive and perceptual mechanisms of bats and humans are very different (Nagel 1979). Imagining myself to be a bat seems only to tell us, as Nagel correctly pointed out, about how I would feel and think as a bat, but not necessarily how the bat feels and thinks. Without a heavy dose of theory about bats and human psychology, my cognitive processes in imagining to be a bat cannot provide me with any information about bat psychology. Only if our minds are organized in a psychologically similar manner can my cognitive processes provide information about another's mind, particularly if I pay sufficient attention to differences between me and the other person and adjust my own cognitive system in light of "relevant differences" in doxastic and conative states between us. What simulation theorists call simulation is essentially a procedure of using one's own cognitive processes in an imitative fashion in order to gain information about other minds and in order to predict or explain the actions of another person. In simulating another person I try to understand his reactions by asking myself how I would react to his situation either by thinking through his problem "in reality"—as in the case of setting up a problem on a chess board—or "in imagination,"[10] by imagining myself to be in a similar situation. In using my own cognitive devices in this manner, I might make use of further theoretical knowledge about the world—knowledge that I assume I share with the other person. In order to predict your reasoning about a particular issue in astronomical theory I certainly will have to utilize my knowledge of astronomy and astronomical theory. Such use of theory (Currie and Ravenscroft 2002; Goldman 2001) provides no support for a theory-theory position since the theory in question is not a theory about the cognitive processes of other human beings or a specific theory about the cognitive processes of the astronomer. Rather, I gain information about your cognitive processes by using my own cognitive processes and by thinking about a particular subject matter. At no time in this process do I consult a theory whose subject matter includes the cognitive processes of human beings. Using one's own cognitive system in this manner is, in Goldman's terminology, a "process-driven" and not a "theory-driven procedure" since it depends on my using my own cognitive devices instead of appealing to a general *psychological theory* of the use of such processes (Goldman 1995a).[11]

Empirically, simulation theorists argue for simulation as an important and central mechanism underlying our mindreading ability by suggesting that:

(i) simulation theory is compatible with all of the developmental and psychopathological facts even though most of the research has been done within the theory-theory paradigm (Harris 1995);

(ii) it is implausible and uneconomical to postulate implicit and rich knowledge about the functioning of our cognitive mechanisms (Goldman 1995; Heal 1995a,b; Harris 2000);

(iii) simulation theory can more easily explain why we at times do display an emotional reaction in conceiving of the situation another person (Gordon 1996; Harris 1989, 2000; Ravenscroft 1998); and

(iv) there exists direct evidence for simulation on the neurobiological level (Gallese and Goldman 1998; Goldman 2001; Goldman and Sripada 2004).

The first and second argumentative strategies of simulation theorists are best illustrated by the manner in which they account for pretend play, an ability regarded as a central phenomenon within current theory of mind research. If simulation can be shown to be relevant in the context of pretense, then simulation theorists would indeed have strong evidence for the fact that simulation is central to our folk-psychological abilities because simulation would be established as a developmentally early phenomenon. Researchers within the simulation paradigm emphasize the cognitive flexibility that children show early on in creatively engaging in pretense and in cooperative role play.

Pretend play cannot be conceived of as being due only to an increase in conceptual sophistication, as Leslie (1987) has suggested. It has also to be understood in terms of the child's increased ability to identify with the role of another person and to respond creatively and flexibly to a sequence of events as they unfold in the imagined pretend play situation. In playing out a particular role, like pretending to be an astronaut or Mommy, it seems implausible that the child has a general theory about what astronauts, Mommy, or people in general would do in each situation. Such assumption would require a rather uneconomical duplication of information in the mind of the child. On the one hand, the child would have to represent Mommy's knowledge about the world, and independently of that, he also would have to represent facts about the world as he knows it (Harris 2000, 35–36; Heal 1995a,b). More importantly, the child has probably never seen Mommy or an astronaut responding to a type of situation that he encounters in pretend play, for example, that a neighbor's dog has injured its leg. It is more likely that the child decides that he has to bring the dog to the veterinarian based on his knowledge of the world— specifically, knowledge that veterinarians treat injured pets—rather than his psychological knowledge that Mommy or an astronaut would bring injured dogs to veterinarians. Similarly, to predict how another chess player might respond to a particular situation, it is more plausible that we put ourselves in her position and use our own knowledge about the rules of chess in predicting what next move she might likely come up with, rather than assuming that in addition to our ability to play chess we also rely on a general theory about how chess players will act in a certain situation.

Simulation theorists therefore understand the developmental sequence in a child's folk-psychological ability not as a change in theory. Instead they interpret it as an increase in the child's power to imagine the perspective of the other person and to quarantine pretend-beliefs from its own cognitive grasp of the world (Harris 1995; Gordon 1995a). Passing the false-belief task does not imply the use of an inference involving general psychological principles or greater conceptual sophistication but rather is understood as an increase in imaginative sophistication, which allows the child to look at the world from Maxi's position. It implies that the child is able to recognize that in Maxi's position it would have looked at the location where it thought the chocolate was, since all the information one would have in Maxi's situation would be that the mother put the chocolate in cupboard$_1$. As Harris points out, the simulation account of the developmental sequence in the child's mindreading abilities is further supported by evidence that links individual differences in children's abilities to solve the false-belief task to their prior opportunity to have engaged in cooperative role play with other children. It seems that children from larger families who have more opportunity to engage in cooperative role play are also able to solve the false-belief tasks earlier (Harris 2000).[12]

Recently, simulation theorists have pointed to fascinating neurobiological findings that prima facie seem to support the case for simulation theory understood as a thesis about underlying causal processes. Simulation theory understood in this manner postulates that processes of "inner imitation" underlie our mindreading abilities. Simulation theorists assert that in recognizing the mental processes of another person, humans utilize the same causal mechanisms that underlie the production of mental phenomena in their own case, whereas theory theorists would deny this thesis. To put it in simplifying terms: simulation theory is committed to the *one-and-the-same-mechanism thesis*, whereas theory theory is at least committed to the *two-and-different-mechanism thesis* (Currie and Ravensroft 2002, 67ff.; Goldman 2001; Goldman and Sripada 2005). More carefully understood, simulation theory postulates a significant overlap between the mechanisms that underlie our understanding of others and those that underlie our own mental processes and states. It is for this reason, for example, that various authors point to neurobiological research in visual imagery—imagining being in my favorite pub of my childhood town—or motor imagery—imagining walking through the rooms of my house or moving my hand—that suggests there is a significant overlap between the mechanisms of visual imagery and of real perception and of real motor behavior and of motor imagery. In pointing to this evidence, simulation theorists assume that if such forms of imagination utilize the same underlying neurobiological mechanisms as their corresponding nonimaginary psychological processes, then it is also plausible to assume that other forms of imaginative uses of our mind work in a similar fashion.

Evidence more directly supporting the simulation claim comes from findings regarding the existence of so-called mirror neuron systems in humans and other primates. It has been found that there is significant overlap between the neural areas of excitation that underlie our observation of another person's action and the recognition of his emotion based on his facial expressions and the neural areas that are stimulated when we ourselves feel the same emotion or execute the same action. More precisely, it has been demonstrated—originally in single-cell studies on macaque monkeys by the Italian neuroscientists Rizzolatti, Gallese, and their colleagues—that particular neurons in the premotor cortex discharge both during the execution of an action and during the observation of the same action, such as the grasping of a particular piece of food. It could be shown that the mirror neurons in monkeys do not merely code the physical movements of the hand but that they discharge during a particular movement of the hand if and only if it is directed toward a particular object such as grasping a nut or grasping a cup. These mirror neurons do not respond when the other monkey moves its hand but not toward an object, or when the monkey only observes the object without making the corresponding movement with its hand. Similarly, mirror neurons underlie not just the visual observation of actions; they also respond when we hear a particular noisy action such as the opening of a peanut or the tearing of a sheet of paper. More importantly for the simulation thesis, the existence of such mirror systems for a variety of observed biological movements and actions in humans has been confirmed through a variety of brain-imaging studies and studies of motor-evoked potentials in arm and leg muscles during the execution and observation of action and of hand and arm movements. In humans, furthermore, such mirror systems are not merely utilized in the coding of transitive or goal- and object-directed actions, but are also involved in the observation of intransitive movements. (For a survey, see Fogassi and Gallese 2002; Rizzolatti, Craighero, and Fadiga 2002; Gallese 2003a,b.)

Moreover, such physical resonance phenomena do not only underlie the observation of actions and bodily movements. In the last few years research has identified mirror neurons in a number of areas. It has been suggested that mirror neurons underlie our speech perception in that hearing certain phonological sequences automatically excites the specific tongue muscles responsible for the production of those heard sounds (Fadiga et al. 2002; Fadiga and Craighero 2003). For our purposes, even more significant is the realization that neuroiological resonance phenomena play an important causal role in human recognition of the particular mental states of other. Observing pain in others and experiencing pain, for example, seem to activate some of the very same areas of the brain (Holden 2004). Likewise, our recognition of basic emotions such as fear, disgust, and anger based on facial expression activates similar areas of the brain as experiencing these emotions ourselves. Seeing fear in your face, for example, activates the same neural areas (particularly in the amygdala) as my experience of fear. Furthermore, the inability of experiencing fear due to damage in this area also leads to a sharp decline in the ability to recognize fear in the facial expression of others (for a survey, see Goldman and Sripada 2005).

For now the above review of the kind of evidence appealed to in support of various positions in the empirical debate about our mindreading abilities has to suffice. It should be abundantly clear that the empirical evidence has been accumulated from a bewildering array of very different levels of psychological description. It includes observations of personal-level abilities, such as the development of linguistic competence with mental terminology; the results from various psychological experiments on the normal developmental sequence of various capacities for understanding other agents; and investigations about our the ability to engage in pretend play and to understand characters in fictional narratives. The evidence is also concerned with trying to understand the cause of various psychopathologies, particularly autism, and it is receptive to neurobiological studies probing the underlying neuronal structures that are regarded to be associated with our abilities to understand others. In my opinion, the evidence regarding children's creative flexibility in pretend play and the recent findings about mirror neurons speak strongly in favor of the thesis that mechanisms of simulation or inner imitation, as Lipps has already suggested, play at least some role in our folk-psychological abilities,[13] a fact that has been partly acknowledged by some theory theorists (Perner 1996; Botterill and Carruthers 1999; Stich and Nichols 1998). Yet it must be noted that the evidence does not provide conclusive support for either theoretical paradigm. So far no one has been able to synthesize and integrate all the levels of evidence; nor has anyone comprehensively justified either paradigm in this debate as providing an adequate theoretical explication of the central mechanisms of our mindreading abilities. A committed theory theorist, it seems, can always respond to evidence favoring simulation by suggesting that theoretical inferences and theoretical knowledge are central to mindreading while at the same time admitting a marginal role for nontheoretical skills necessary for acquiring information to run or develop the knowledge-rich machinery underlying folk psychology.

In just this manner, Meltzoff has been able to recognize the importance of nontheoretical abilities for our interpersonal understanding without forgoing the interpretive framework of a theory theory. Meltzoff, a prominent theory theorist, has been influential in investigating imitation in young infants and has been important for our recognition that our ability as children to imitate other people is a foundation for the development of our mindreading abilities (see Nadel and Butterworth 1999; Meltzoff and Prinz 2002). Meltzoff and his collaborators have shown that very young infants (under two months old) are able to intentionally imitate observed tongue protrusions and mouth openings of other people. Eighteen-month-old infants seem to be able to recognize the underlying intentions of bodily movements. If they are shown an adult unsuccessfully trying to achieve a certain goal, such as pulling a toy apart, they will imitate the intended target act and not merely the bodily movement of the failed attempt (for a summary, see Meltzoff and Moore 2001). Yet Meltzoff sees such imitative abilities not as evidence for the simulation paradigm but as mechanisms for "developing and elaborating" a theoretical framework (Meltzoff and Gopnik 1993, 337). These innate imitation mechanisms allow children "to map some of their internal states on to the behavior of others" (360) and provide children with data for their "theoretical investigations" in the realm of folk psychology. More importantly, within his theoretical framework mirror neuron systems can be interpreted as cross-modal matching mechanisms required to provide an innate basis for these imitation phenomena. Since both observation and execution of bodily actions involve the same neuronal systems, mirror neurons allow us to explain how it is possible that my observation of another person's bodily actions enables me to imitate the very same bodily movements (Rizzolatti et al. 2002; Rizzolatti and Craighero 2004; Blakemore and Decety 2001; Decety 2002).

I would argue that this fluent state of affairs in the current theory of mind debate is particularly due to the fact that simulation theorists have been unable to dislodge the philosophical background motivation for the detached conception of folk psychology and that they have not been able to account persuasively for ordinary folks' conceptual sophistication in the use of mental terminology. For the final evaluation of the simulation position and for my argument for empathy it is thus important to evaluate how these conceptual issues have influenced various contemporary theorists in their conception of the simulation proposal.

3.2.1 Different Conceptions of Simulation Theory

So far I have mainly characterized simulation theory as a paradigm that opposes the theory-theory paradigm. Yet, even though simulation theorists are unified in their opposition to theory theory, they tend to be divided about the appropriate level of formulating and supporting the simulation alternative, a fact that can be partly explained in light of their different opinions regarding the centrality of rational agency to our folk-psychological practices. Whereas in the psychological discussion the conceptual motivations for adopting a theory conception of folk psychology have faded into the background, some simulation theorists, such as Jane Heal, prefer supporting the simulation proposal for conceptual and a priori reasons. As philosophers of social science before her, Heal emphasizes that the nature of thought itself entails that simulation is essential for understanding other minds. To distinguish herself from other versions of simulation theory, Heal also speaks of co-cognition instead of simulation. Accordingly, simulation theorists often differ in their understanding of the metaphor of putting oneself into the shoes of another. Simulation theorists who understand their proposal mainly as an empirical thesis conceive of it as a hypothesis about underlying subpersonal and internal mechanisms of our folk-psychological abilities, whereas others understand it as a thesis about personal-level activities that mainly describes what the person does and not what is going on in his brain. In conceiving of understanding other agents as a personal activity, one views it as an activity that is analogous to activities such as writing a check, visiting a city or a friend, traveling by airplane, and so on. All such activities certainly require that some brain activity is going on; but for purely conceptual reasons it is not to be expected that we can decide how to characterize the personal activity only by looking at neurological evidence.[14] I will first describe the two ways of characterizing the simulation proposal. Afterward I will address the question of whether and in what respect conceptual topics traditionally reserved for a priori consideration are significant for deciding the debate between the proponents of theory theory and simulation theory.

Within the philosophical community, Alvin Goldman has been the main champion of understanding the simulation proposal in a strictly empirical manner and as making claims about internal causal mechanisms. Such understanding also seems to be suggested by Gordon's claims that simulation rests on our ability to feed our cognitive system with pretend inputs and run it "off-line," that is, without leading to a decision that determines our own action (Gordon 1995a, 70). According to Goldman, in using simulation to read another mind I proceed in the following manner: I first refashion myself as a model for another person's cognitive processes by "matching" or "recreating" in my mind his initial cognitive states, feeding into my cognitive systems certain pretend inputs (pretend "beliefs" and "desires"). I then observe how those mental states are processed within my cognitive system, and afterward I infer in an analogical fashion what the other person would do in a particular situation, what inference he would draw, or how he would feel and react emotionally.

Schematically, we can think of the simulation theorist as proposing that our folk-psychological understanding of other minds consists of a causal process separated into three distinct phases:

(i) The matching phase The simulator matches the initial state of the target by introducing the relevant "pretend-beliefs" and "pretend-desires," as necessary.

(ii) The simulation phase The cognitive system of the simulator processes these states in a fashion that mirrors the internal processing of the target, and the simulator simultaneously observes such processing.

(iii) The attribution phase In light of knowledge introspectively gained in the second phase, the simulator attributes to the other person states of mind, actions, or plans. This attribution is based on an analogical inference from the simulator to the target.[15]

Notice that simulation theorists are able to admit the relevance of some kind of propositional knowledge in the first and third phases as long as such knowledge does not render the central simulation phase superfluous. Consequently, simulation theorists can grant that the matching phase of the simulation process has to utilize propositional knowledge about differences between me and the other person in order to properly construct the initial phase (Goldman 2000, 184). Such knowledge might concern, for example, doxastic and conative differences between me and you, such as that I know that you in contrast to myself do not like potatoes. At times, however, I might even have to utilize knowledge of a more general kind, such as that all Christians believe in the existence of God, that all Azande believe in the existence of witches, or even more explicitly psychological knowledge such as that Peter the Great probably did not share any of my beliefs about airplanes since he was not perceptually acquainted with airplanes as I am. Admitting the use of such knowledge in getting the simulation started, however, does not invalidate the claim that during the simulation phase such theoretical knowledge about mental states of other people is not causally involved in the processing of the relevant pretend states, and that we, as a matter of empirical fact, are creatures that use their own cognitive system for the understanding of other agents in this manner.

Goldman is also willing to acknowledge that the attribution phase depends on the tacit assumption that "my psychology works the same as the target's psychology" (2002, 16, n. 10). This acknowledgment raises important normative questions of justification that I will address later on. In this context, where I primarily address the debate about underlying causal processes, it is sufficient to point out that admitting the involvement of such a principle in the third phase does make the central simulation phase causally superfluous. Using such a principle would not enable us to derive anything specific about another person's behavior (Davies and Stone 2001). It is important to stress that simulation theorists are able to recognize the involvement of psychological knowledge in propositional form in our mindreading activities as long as the propositional knowledge in question does not *infect* the simulation phase or make it causally unnecessary for reading other minds. If that would be the case then simulation could no longer be understood as a knowledge-poor strategy, and it certainly could no longer be understood as a strategy that is centrally important to our mindreading abilities. In the same vein, a simulation theorist who advocates the simulation proposal mainly as an empirical thesis can admit that mindreading at times does not proceed in a simulating fashion but rather makes use of theoretical knowledge. As long as such strategies can be empirically regarded as mere shortcuts that are derived from the more basic simulation strategy (Goldman 1995) or understood to be less important or less frequently used for providing the causal underpinning of our mindreading abilities than simulation, the simulation proposal remains a clear empirical alternative to the generic theory-theory paradigm stressing "knowledge-rich" mechanisms.

Goldman himself calls his view the "introspection-simulation view" (2000, 183). This is certainly an appropriate label for his conception. I would prefer to call it the detached conception of simulation since Goldman views his simulation proposal explicitly in contrast to a rationality conception of folk psychology for reasons that are very similar to the ones we have discussed in the above chapters. Mental states are conceived of as mere internal states that happen inside me, that are causally processed by my cognitive system, and whose causal processing I can introspectively observe. Goldman's simulation proposal is best seen as a proposal in which I take an observer perspective toward my own cognitive processes for the purpose of gaining information about others' cognitive processes. Thoughts are not primarily understood as my reasons for my actions; instead, they are conceived of as causal events that happen inside me which I can observe in a detached manner. From the perspective of the engaged conception of folk psychology, for which I have argued in this book, Goldman is mischaracterizing what one might call the directionality of attention involved in having thoughts and in attributing a thought to another agent. In conceiving of thoughts, beliefs, and desires in the folk-psychological context as potential reasons for agents, we are not conceiving of mental states as mere internal events happening inside the person, even if it is the case that we can only attribute thoughts to agents that have a normally functioning brain. Thoughts, beliefs, and desires are not mere objects that agents have in their mind analogous to the manner in which their organs are in their body.[16] In thinking, believing, or desiring that p an agent is primarily oriented toward the world. In grasping that one has certain thoughts, one is grasping one's own subjective attitude toward that world, a recognition that also subsequently allows for a critical evaluation of this attitude. Thoughts characterize the agent's perspective on the world in terms of which they themselves can make sense of their actions in the world. In thinking of thoughts as internal objects, however, it would remain a complete mystery why the internal perception of an object should reveal for the agent his orientation toward the world. Objects are normally not transparent in this respect, at least not without the help of a lot of theory. For reasons similar to these, Gordon

(1995b,c; 2000a) and Heal (2003b) suggest that thinking is best understood as a personal-level phenomenon, attributable to the whole person and not to any specific part of his body. Thoughts (including beliefs and desires) characterize a person's "outlook" toward the world and not primarily the functioning of a mechanism under his skin.[17] If thoughts have to be understood as personal-level properties, however, then simulating another person's thoughts and mental states would a fortiori have to be understood as a personal-level phenomenon. In simulating another person I situate myself toward the world in such a way that I start thinking about it very similarly to the person whose mind I am trying to read. Simulation understood in this manner still has to be conceived of as a mirror phenomenon, but as mirror phenomenon on a different level. It primarily characterizes the change of perspective involved in thinking about the world from another's point of view. Yet it does not necessarily desribe an internal process that happens inside of me while I am taking the other's perspective.

Following Gordon, we could characterize personal-level simulation as involving (if necessary) a shifting of my "reasons for action" and "a personal transformation" through a "recentering of my egocentric map" in which I make "adjustment for relevant differences" (Gordon 1995a, 63; 1995c, 56).[18] Gordon also likes to compare this imaginary transformation of my perspective into another's perspective as a process that is akin to the manner in which an actor identifies with his role by fully immersing himself in the adopted character. In the context of such immersion, the first-person pronoun "I" seems to lose its ordinary reference and refers to the simulated character (Gordon 1995c, 1996). When an actor playing Wellington, for example, says "I wish it were night and Blücher was here," the "I" indeed seems to refer to the enacted character Wellington instead of the persona of the actor. Similarly, Gordon suggests that when I am simulating another in my imagination, my "I" refers to the other person and not myself. While I do not doubt that such whole-hearted identification is at times possible, I do not think that it is necessary for a successful simulation of another's perspective. Specifically, if we are concerned with simulating someone's thinking only on a particular issue, taking that person's perspective on a certain issue is in that respect not very different from entertaining thoughts about a different scenario in hypothetical reasoning. Yet it seems to be taking it too far to suggest that in such hypothetical reasoning the "I" refers not to my normal self but to my hypothetical twin. All that seems to be necessary for simulating another's perspective is that I recognize myself as simulating a different perspective and as not considering those of my beliefs that I know the other does not share. Indeed, it seems to be for this very reason that we can also critically engage with the thoughts of another person and recognize their shortcomings or their superiority to our own line of reasoning. This seems to be possible, however, only if we recognize them as thoughts that the other thinks and are able to reflect critically on their status as appropriate reasons for the other's actions by comparing them to our own beliefs.[19]

Moreover, Gordon introduces the idea of the shift of reference for the first-person pronoun in order to suggest that contrary to Goldman's model, simulation does not have to be conceived of as an "inference from me to you," from a simulator to a target. Yet regardless of whether one thinks that a wholehearted identification is possible or even necessary for simulating the thought processes of another person, even a personal-level conception of simulation has to recognize that in the folk-psychological context we ascribe mental states from our perspective on the world. In saying that another person believes that p, I describe him or her from my perspective, while being myself and not pretending to be somebody else. For the simulation proposal to be plausible as an account of our folk-psychological practice, simulation would need to involve not only the identification with another person but also a "de-identification" (Perner 1996, 97–98). According to the simulation proposal, this later attribution depends on the knowledge of what I did or thought of while "being" the simulated person and not on knowledge of a psychological theory.

Hence, despite the differences in formulating the simulation proposal, simulation articulated as a personal-level phenomenon would still have to be thought of as involving three distinct phases, albeit characterized slightly differently as consisting of:

(i) *The matching phase* I entertain different beliefs and adopt a different conative relation to the world in order to recreate the other's perspective on the world.

(ii) *The simulation phase* Having adopted the other's perspective, I start thinking about the world from that perspective and entertain reasons for possible actions and thoughts.

(iii) The attribution phase   After having completed the simulation phase, I cease to entertain the other's perspective and base my folk-psychological interpretation of the other's action on my knowledge of what happened during the simulation phase.

For this very reason, similar considerations regarding the use of propositional knowledge in the first and third phase apply to models that conceive of simulation as a primarily personal-level phenomenon in which I think of thoughts as reasons for actions. Simulation theorists, whether they prefer formulating simulation as a personal-level phenomenon or in terms of internal mechanisms, can accept the use of propositional knowledge as long as it does not infect the simulation phase or make it superfluous.

It has to be stressed that the considerations so far do not entail that the debate between simulation theory and theory theory should not be seen as an empirical debate for which the investigation of subpersonal and neurobiological mechanisms becomes relevant. Indeed, even though Gordon and Heal both agree on conceiving of simulation as a personal-level phenomenon in the above manner, they disagree about the status of the debate between simulation theory and theory theory in this very respect. Heal suggests that the simulation alternative can be defended on purely a priori grounds and that it can be shown in this manner that theory theory is "unacceptable as an account of our personal-level abilities" (2003b, 91–92). Investigations into subpersonal mechanisms cannot be understood as providing further empirical evidence for or against simulation theory, since at this stage "strong theory theory is nowhere in the running as an option in the imagined investigation" (ibid., 111). Instead such explorations can only provide additional illumination about the "exact boundaries" of simulation's role and the exact manner in which simulation as a personal-level ability is "realized or embodied" on the subpersonal level.

Gordon, on the other hand, aligns himself with an empirical understanding of this debate, suggesting that evidence about subpersonal mechanisms, especially neurobiological ones, might prove "an empirical tie-breaker that vindicates simulation theory" (Gordon 2001, 191, n. 1). Even if simulation has to be formulated primarily as a personal-level phenomenon, Gordon conceives of such phenomenological considerations as a "poor guide to how it's really done" (quoted in Davies and Stone 2001, 139). As the following will reveal, I tend to agree with Heal, particularly insofar as the centrality of what I will call reenactive empathy to understanding rational agency is concerned. At the same time, I think that we have to be cautious in articulating this insight. Moreover, Heal seriously underestimates the philosophical relevance of neurobiological findings in the context of conceptual considerations for our explication of the basis of interpersonal understanding.

Prima facie, Gordon's stance reflects our general understanding about the relation between our commonsense classification of natural kinds and a more scientific classification of such kinds in terms of their underlying microphysical structure. At first, we classified elements as being gold or water not according to their microphysical properties but using their observable macroproperties. Nonetheless, we did and do understand our commonsense classification to be responsive to future investigations about the underlying microphysical structure. In light of the results of such investigation, we recognize that we need to further refine our classification of the world. It might also make us realize that we made certain mistakes, say, in classifying two objects as belonging to the same kind. New insights about the microphysical structure of gold have forced us, for example, to distinguish between real gold and fool's gold. Similarly, biological and medical research about the underlying causal mechanisms that maintain our bodily functions has led to a radical reconceptualization of the classificatory scheme of diseases that has moved the medical sciences from an understanding of diseases as based largely on an imbalance of bodily fluids to a more complex understanding of diseases as based on various forms of infections, nutritional deficits, and genetic abnormalities. More recently, insight into the causal mechanisms responsible for peptic ulcers, for example, has made us realize that ulcers should be seen not as a psychosomatic condition but as a disease due to bacterial infection (Thagard 1999). To a large extent, scientific advance can thus be understood as a refinement of and readjustment to our classificatory schemes of the world in light of our increased knowledge of nature's underlying causal mechanisms. Given that we ordinarily accept such reclassification as justified, we might speak of our commonsense scheme of classification as having an implicit *dimension of microphysical depth* that allows it to be responsive to such advances in our microphysical knowledge.

Given that our knowledge about the neurobiological basis of our cognitive mechanisms has been minimal until very recently, it is not surprising that our classifications of various psychological phenomena have been primarily personal-level characterizations. But admitting that personal-level criteria have up to now been central to our commonsense classification of psychological phenomena does not entail that psychological categories should lack the dimension of microphysical depth that we ordinarily grant our classificatory concepts of nonpsychological aspects of the world. Our ordinary understanding of personal-level psychological phenomena has already benefited greatly from advances in the neurosciences, and it is to be expected that our personal-level classifications will be refined further in light of future neuroscientific knowledge. One need only point to our increasingly sophisticated understanding of the neurobiological mechanisms that make up our perceptual systems. Without doubt, our understanding of the neurobiological basis of perception has provided us with a more sophisticated understanding of the nature of perception, which we originally characterized as a personal-level phenomenon. It also is to be expected that our ordinary classification of psychological phenomena will take notice of new findings on the neurobiological level. For example, realizing the function of systems of mirror neurons and recognizing that the perception of action and the planning and execution of action in contrast to perception of other objective features of the world use the same neuronal mechanisms might force us to speak in a more fine-grained manner about perception. It might force us to distinguish between action-perception and object-perception, or between perception of bodily movements and perception of other events as two very different types of perception (Tversky, Morrison, and Zacks 2002). It certainly requires us to rethink and gain a more complex understanding of the relation between our perceptual abilities and our volitional abilities to initiate action. Traditionally these abilities were regarded to be separate, one having to do with the processing of externally and passively received stimuli, the other having to do with initiating voluntary action based on the decision of a deliberating mind. However, given that our perception of action appears also to prepare us for action in using mechanisms of action planning, perception can no longer be conceived of as a phenomenon of passive reception (Clark 2001, chap. 5).

Without difficulty we could multiply these examples, particularly from the area of our understanding of psychopathologies that are mainly diagnosed according to personal-level criteria of the DSM.[20] For our purposes the above considerations should suffice to motivate Gordon's and

Goldman's view that even the debate about our mindreading abilities has to be conceived primarily as an empirical debate in which further neurobiological research could turn out to be decisive. Hence Heal's claim about the a priori nature of the argument for simulation theory is at first glance very implausible. Simulation theorists and theory theorists might both describe personal-level phenomena, but in order to decide who is right about the nature of such phenomena, neuroscientific evidence certainly could turn out to be relevant. Moreover, if we follow a suggestion by Goldman (2001), Currie and Ravenscroft (2002), the debate between simulation and theory-theory has a clear dimension of microphysical depth. Only simulation theorists postulate a significant overlap in the mechanisms that underlie our mindreading abilities and the making of one's own decisions, being in a particular mental state, attributing mental states to oneself, and so on.

Yet in this context it is important to distinguish between two claims. One has to differentiate between

(i) The claim that neuroscientific and other psychological research investigating the underlying neural correlates of our mindreading abilities is intrinsically a worthwhile pursuit because it provides us with important information about how our mindreading abilities are biologically implemented, and

(ii) the claim that such empirical research is best framed in terms of the theory-theory and simulation paradigms, because empirical research is decisive for adjudicating between the respective accounts of those underlying causal processes.

Nobody should be understood as denying the first claim. Certainly I do not want to be understood as denying this claim. Yet (i) does not logically imply (ii). Before one commits oneself to claim (ii) it should be remembered that our folk-psychological practice of interpreting other agents is primarily a practice that uses a conceptual repertoire and for which the notion of rational agency as explicated above is central. It is exactly at this stage that traditional a priori considerations become important. As I have shown, simulation theorists conceive of the simulation procedure implicitly as consisting of three distinct phases. While the simulation theorists can admit the influence of some propositional knowledge during the first and third phase, it is crucial for them to maintain that the simulation phase itself is not dominated by such knowledge. However, if we describe the other person in the attribution phase in terms of mental predicates such as belief and desire and such a description is derived from the results of simulating that person, then we need to be able to categorize our observations of what happens in the simulation phase in exactly those same terms.

Hence, if a theory-theory account of psychological concepts is to be regarded as the most persuasive account, then it would appear also to be plausible to suppose that the simulation phase has to involve some form of theoretical knowledge. No evidence regarding an overlap of underlying neurobiological mechanisms would help in countering this argument, since it would no longer appear plausible to interpret such mechanisms as knowledge poor. Goldman and Gordon are not willing make this concession to the theory theorist, and they try to develop alternatives to the theory-theory conception of psychological concepts. But in their concern with such conceptual investigations, they implicitly acknowledge that thinking about folk psychology also involves some level of traditional "armchair" philosophizing.

4 Basic Empathy and Reenactive Empathy

Thinking through the nature of our grasp of our folk-psychological concepts will show that neither of the accounts of folk-psychological concepts associated with either simulation theory or theory theory—despite the prima facie plausibility of each—is without significant blind spots. For that very reason neurobiological research on mirror neurons should not be understood as decisive evidence for simulation theory and against theory theory. Instead, it should enable us to reconceive of the debate between the two approaches on a new level that recognizes basic empathy as the primary perceptual mechanism for interpreting other agents. As I will argue, the centrality of empathy or simulation to our understanding of other agents on this new level is not decided merely by appealing to empirical arguments about underlying causal mechanisms. Rather it requires an appeal to a priori considerations that reveal empathy to be epistemically essential for our understanding of rational agency—a concept that, as argued in the previous chapters, is central to our conception of other persons in the folk-psychological realm.

Before I address various attempts by simulation theorists to provide an account of folk-psychological concepts, it is important to remind ourselves of the central and at times conflicting constraints on any philosophically plausible account of folk-psychological concepts. First, it has to meet what I would like to call the *constraint of first-person authority*; that is, any explication of folk-psychological concepts has to be compatible with the fact that within folk psychology we grant a special even if limited authority to first-person reports and take first-person knowledge in contrast to third-person knowledge to be somehow direct and noninferential. Second, it has to meet the *univocality constraint*: within the folk-psychological perspective we assume that the same mental concepts are used in first-person reports and third-person ascriptions. If I explain my behavior by pointing to a particular belief and desire that I have, I provide the same explanation for my behavior that Peter would give were he to cite the same beliefs and desires. Both of our explanations have the same content and have to have the same truth value; they are either true or false. The theory-theory account of psychological concepts has been regarded as philosophically attractive because of its prima facie ability to meet the univocality constraint and its capacity to say something interesting—and not obviously wrong—about the first-person authority constraint. Third, though this is not specifically a constraint on the explication of folk-theoretical concepts, any philosophical explication of any conceptual domain has to attempt to be *comprehensive*, that is, has to provide a general explication applicable to all members of the relevant set of concepts.

4.1   Mindreading, Folk-Psychological Concepts, and Mirror Neurons

It is particularly in this last respect, as has also been pointed out by Goldman (2000), that Gordon's attempt to link our comprehension of psychological concepts directly with our ability to simulate runs into trouble. Gordon denies that the possession of psychological concepts or a conceptual sophistication in the psychological realm is a necessary prerequisite for simulation. Rather, it is the other way round; we gradually acquire psychological concepts through becoming more sophisticated in our simulative abilities. As the basis of his account of our concept of belief Gordon relies on the recognition that whenever I assert that p I commit myself to the assertion of "I believe that p." To find out whether or not I have a certain belief I use what Gordon calls the "semantic ascent routine." I answer the question about my mental state by answering a factual question about the world, that is, by answering an "'object-level' question" (1996a, 15). Similarly, to apply the concept of belief to another person, I rely on the same ascent routine by asking within the context of the O-simulation whether p is the case. To say that another person O believes that p is equivalent to asserting "that p within the context of a simulation of O."[1]

Children can be thought of as acquiring a basic understanding of the concept of belief by first recognizing the centrality of the ascent routine and then applying it within the context of simulation. For Gordon such a grasp of the concept of belief would not constitute a full mastery of the concept of belief. But it would enable the child at least to grasp one primary aspect of our notion of belief, that is, the idea that a fact can have a "mental location," "that it can be a fact to a particular individual."[2]

Gordon does not say much about what more is required to confer a full comprehension of the concept of belief. In this context I will not worry about Gordon's explication of our concept of belief, since this has been discussed in the literature. I am inclined to think that Gordon's account of the concept of belief has trouble meeting the univocality constraint, a problem similar to the one faced by Stich's projectivist account of belief. According to Gordon's account, my saying that I believe that p and your saying that K. S. believes that p seem to follow very different procedures. Gordon (2000b, 112–113) suggests that he does not have to consider the univocality constraint because in both first-person and third-person ascriptions we make use of the ascent routine and our attention is in both cases directed toward the world. But this response is insufficient. In making a third-person ascription, there is the question of the epistemic adequacy of my simulation procedure: I have to go through the matching phase and adopt the perspective of the other person based on the available evidence for doing that. Hence first-person and third-person ascriptions do involve very different sets of criteria.

More importantly, it is not obvious how Gordon's simulationist account of psychological concepts can meet the comprehensiveness constraint, as it is doubtful that our comprehension of other psychological concepts can be explicated analogously to the above analysis of the concept of belief. How, for example, would one apply the simulationist approach to concepts like pretense, intention, decision, fear, anxiety, and so on? I do not share Gordon's conviction that it is possible in the case of other concepts to coordinate "one type of verbal behavior, self-reports of a mental state episode, with another, the outward looking 'expression' of the state or episode" (2000b, 112–113) in a manner that would allow us to analyze the content of the psychological concept without vicious circularity. As an example of such coordination between these types of expressions, Gordon mentions utterances such as "I am pleased" and "This is delightful." Gordon is certainly right that one normally can assert the first sentence if and only if one is prepared to assert the second. Yet in contrast to the case of belief it is less plausible to maintain that one's assertion about the world's being delightful is independent of one's understanding that such a judgment does not express an objective state of affairs but rather is uttered from a particular subjective perspective expressing the emotional effect the world has on a particular person.

Moreover, if the simulationist approach to psychological concepts is sustainable, it would also have to account for the claim that mental concepts are holistically constituted. According to such a holistic position, we can grasp the content of mental concepts only in light of other mental concepts. Such a holistic position in regard to psychological concepts is certainly compatible with the Davidsonian considerations given in chapter 2. In order to be granted a comprehension of the concept of belief, one must have some beliefs about beliefs. Intuitively, it is at least be required that one has some understanding of how a belief, for example, differs from a desire and from other mental states. It was exactly for this reason that the proposal of logical behaviorism to analyze mental concepts in terms of certain subjunctive conditionals failed. In order to count as a plausible analysis of a specific mental concept, it seems the conditional must mention other mental concepts either in its antecedent or consequent. To meet the comprehensiveness constraint, Gordon would have to reject such a holistic doctrine in favor of a purely atomistic or at least hierarchical account of mental concepts, in which higher-order concepts are determined by atomistically constituted lower-order concepts, which are defined purely in terms of our ability to simulate and to perform the ascent routine. That such a comprehensive account could be forthcoming on Gordon's model is, after all that has been said, rather doubtful.

In this respect, Goldman's proposal is prima facie more promising. In contrast to Gordon, Goldman decouples his explication of psychological concepts from his account of simulation. For him each mental state concept is primarily defined in light of some "inner features"—either phenomenal properties or some other internal properties—that are accessible primarily from the internal first-person perspective (Goldman 2002, 1993). In defining mental state concepts in this manner, Goldman seems to circumvent the holism problem and avoid conceding to theory theorists that the simulation phase itself requires any involvement of theory.[3] Yet Goldman's account of psychological concepts can meet the comprehensiveness constraint only if it is indeed plausible to assume that each concept for a mental state type has a phenomenal feature or some other introspectively detectable internal feature associated with it. Alternatively, it at least has to be plausible that there is a basic set of mental state concepts for which this assumption is true and in terms of which higher-order mental states could be defined. Such an assumption is intuitively plausible for phenomenal states. It is less apparent that all types of intentional states including beliefs and intentions could be identified on the basis of phenomenal or other internal features. But even if Goldman was right in this respect, a purely first-personal account of mental state concepts is in principle unable to provide an account of folk-psychological concepts that can meet the other two constraints.

In associating his simulation proposal with a Cartesian conception of mental concepts, Goldman has to conceive of the attribution phase as implicitly based on analogical inference from me to you, from the simulator to target. He thus opens his position up to the well-known objections against analogical reasoning and Cartesianism. Analogical reasoning, as Goldman himself admits, requires at a minimum the assumption that the other person's psychological organization is very similar to mine. It requires that I can at least conceive of the other person as having similar mental states as I do and that I can conceive of the other person in terms of the same mental terms that I apply to myself. Wittgenstein objected to analogical reasoning because within the Cartesian framework I cannot even think of somebody else being in the same mental state as I am, given that my conception of what it means to be in such a mental state is defined in a purely first-personal manner. If my grasp of a mental concept is constituted by my experiencing something in a certain way, then it is impossible for me to conceive of how somebody can be in the same mental state, for that would require that I can conceive of my mental state as something that I do not experience or is not essentially accessible to me from the first-person perspective.

Wittgenstein's critique of analogical reasoning is well known. What is less well known is that Theodor Lipps, the main champion of empathy at the beginning of the twentieth century, made essentially the same point much earlier. As he expresses it, what I find in my own case "is my sadness or my anger, in short it is me, not another person, or just sadness or anger or an ego itself" (Lipps 1907, 708, my translation). Analogical reasoning, however, requires that I infer from the existence of my anger or sadness in certain circumstances the existence of something characteristically different, even if somehow related to my anger and sadness. Analogical reasoning requires the contradictory undertaking of inferring another person's anger and sadness on the basis of my sadness and anger, while thinking of that sadness and anger as something "absolutely different" from my anger and sadness. More generally, analogical inference requires the contradictory undertaking of "entertaining a completely new thought about an I that however is not me, but something absolutely different" (ibid.).

Even though they saw the problem of analogical reasoning in similar terms, Wittgenstein and Lipps parted ways when it came to a proposed solution for overcoming the problem of other minds. Wittgenstein claimed that the fundamental mistake of Cartesianism consists in conceiving of mental concepts in a purely first-personal manner, whereas Lipps (1907, 713) retained a first-personal conception of mental concepts. Instead, Lipps suggested that what is wrong with our thinking about other minds within the Cartesian framework is the manner according to which we traditionally think of our epistemic relation to other minds. Instead of understanding our grasp of another person's mental states—particularly the recognition of another person's emotions based on his facial expressions—as the result of an inference, we should think of it as a form of knowledge *sui generis* (a form of instinctive knowledge) and as based on mechanisms of empathy, as I have explained earlier.

Knowledge of the functioning of the brain was limited in his time, and Lipps's account of empathy lacked sufficient empirical grounding. The recent work on mirror neurons that I have described above, however, provides strong evidence for the existence of phenomena of "inner imitation" that Lipps postulated rather speculatively. All of this seems to indicate that Lipps's suggestions about the mechanisms of inner imitation were indeed on the right track. Yet, despite Lipps's adamant insistence that empathy is not an inference from analogy but a very special form of knowledge, it is not clear how this can be interpreted as more than mere hand-waving, a philosophically ad hoc maneuver. In particular it is not clear how Lipps can avoid the analogical inference "from me to you" that Goldman explicitly postulates, since he agrees with Goldman that the meaning of psychological terms is defined only in regard to our own inner experiences (Lipps 1907, 713). Even if my observation of another person's actions and facial expressions causes the stimulation of the very same neurons that are stimulated when I act in a certain manner or when my face shows certain expressions, the question that needs answering is how we should understand the mechanism that allows me to project my mental state onto the other. More significantly, we need to explain why such mechanisms allow me to apply concepts that are defined solely in terms of my experiences to another person whose experience I do not directly share.

In implicitly extending on Lipps's theory, Goldman (2002) appeals to mirror neurons not only as evidence for simulation theory as a thesis about underlying psychological mechanisms but also as evidence about how mental state concepts, which are defined primarily in first-person terms, can become associated with behavioral characteristics that we ordinarily also associate with somebody's being in pain, being angry, wanting to grasp the cup, and so on. It is those criteria that we seem to rely on in our third-person attributions of mental states. Mirror neurons allow us to match the perceived behavioral characteristics with the inner features of our concepts because the perception of these behavioral characteristics activates the appropriate mirror neurons. Yet, as has been correctly pointed out (Child 2002), all that such resonance phenomena can establish is a relation between observed behavioral characteristics (primarily in others) and my experience or my private concept. It thus would allow me to understand how my mental state concepts and my inner experiences might be become related to observations of the other person's behavior. It is difficult, however, to see how it would enable us to recognize that the other's observed behavior can be understood as indicating that he is in the same mental state as I am. It seems to remain a mystery how the existence of mirror neurons should enable me to think of my mental concepts, defined in terms of my internal features or experiences, as applicable to another person, especially in light of the fact that I ordinarily know nothing about the existence of mirror neurons and that they play no role in the explication of psychological concepts in the folk-psychological realm. Thus, Goldman's line of reasoning still cannot account for the existence of psychological concepts that allow us to conceive of another as being in the same mental state as I am. What we get is a bifurcation of psychological concepts, a public concept based on behavioral criteria and private concepts that each person defines in terms of his internal or phenomenal features. Hence, the problem of Cartesianism cannot be overcome merely by appealing to certain neurobiological mechanisms of inner imitation or by appealing to empathy, if one retains an essentially first-person conception of mental concepts.

In his anti-Cartesian reflections, Wittgenstein concentrated on the nature of psychological concepts of our public language and the criteria according to which they are used. In particular he claimed that it was a fundamental mistake to conceive of mental concepts as being defined purely in terms of an act of inner ostension supposedly referring to an inner mental state that is privately accessible only from the first-person perspective. According to him, mental concepts should be conceived of as intrinsically related to behavioral evidence accessible from the third-person perspective. As he famously declared, "the inner process stands in need of outward criteria" (1958, 508).[4] The functionalist or theory-theory conception of mental concepts can certainly be seen as satisfying this Wittgensteinian constraint. It thinks of folk psychology not as a conceptual framework in which each term can be defined in isolation but as a theoretical framework that as a whole meets its confirming or disconfirming evidentiary basis, in this case the observed behavior of the other agent. Yet Wittgenstein would have been very uncomfortable with Sellars's explication of the detached conception of folk psychology.[5] First, as is well known, Wittgenstein and Wittgensteinians like Peter Winch (1958) did not consider folk-psychological descriptions to be the basis for causal explanatory accounts of another person's behavior. Second, even though Wittgenstein stayed on the level of a conceptual or grammatical investigation and, in contrast to Lipps, was not interested in exploring and investigating the biological mechanisms that allow us to relate to each other as minded creatures, he did think of our folk-psychological language game as resting on and extending our primitive—that is, prelinguistic—and natural forms of engaging with each other. Wittgenstein's objection toward the detached conception of folk psychology in this respect is expressed in the following remarks.

But can't I imagine that the people around me are automata, lack consciousness, even though they behave in the same way as usual?—If I can imagine it now—alone in my room—I see people with fixed looks (as in a trance) going about their business—the idea is perhaps a little uncanny. But just try to keep hold of this idea in the midst of your ordinary intercourse with others, in the street, say! Say to yourself for example: "The children over there are mere automata; all their liveliness is mere automatism." And you will either find these words becoming quite meaningless; or you will produce in yourself some kind of uncanny feeling, or something of the sort. (1958, 420)[6]

Recognizing another person as being minded is for Wittgenstein not merely the acquisition of a theoretical belief but a manner of interacting with him: "My attitude towards him is the attitude towards a soul. I am not of the *opinion* that he has a soul" (1958, 178). Accordingly, recognizing that another person is in pain or is afraid or happy is a fact directly accessible from—can be "read off from"—the facial expression or behavior of the other person. Such an ability to directly recognize certain mental states of the other person has to be understood as part of our primitive, noninferential, prelinguistic relation toward each other (1980 I, 927; 1980 II, 170, 570).

Although Wittgenstein's remarks point to an alternative way of thinking about our relation to other people within the folk-psychological framework, a way that is different from both a Cartesian and a theory-theory account, they have proven to be insufficient for derailing the dominant theory-theory paradigm. As Davidson (1963) has shown, Wittgensteinian arguments against the causal explanatory character of folk-psychological notions are riddled with logical confusion. Moreover, in staying for the most part on a conceptual level and rejecting any attempt to provide explanatory accounts of our prelinguistic relation toward others as incompatible with the project of philosophical clarification (1958, 109, 654, 655),[7] Wittgenstein lacks an argumentative basis to counter a purely theory-theory account as proposed within the detached conception of folk psychology. The detached conception can always respond to the above Wittgensteinian phenomenological observations about the apparently direct perceptual apprehension of the mental states of another person by reinterpreting those observations. The detached conception of folk psychology understands the phenomenology of direct perception as a feature of an originally purely theoretical practice that has become embedded in our practical dealings with each other and the world. A theoretical physicist, for example, is able to directly observe the movement of a subatomic particle by looking at the graphic representation of the results of a particular experiment without consciously going through any inferential derivations. By conceding that overcoming Cartesianism requires us to think of mental concepts as internally linked to behavioral features, Wittgenstein is left without the resources to explain how his account of folk-psychological concepts ultimately differs from the theory-theory account, even though his expressed intentions point in a different direction. It is no wonder then that the theory-theory account was seen as the most plausible alternative given Wittgenstein's scathing and influential critique of analogical inference.[8]

Still, it would be a mistake to think that the theory-theory account is without significant blind spots and that it is able to meet the constraints for the explication of folk-psychological concepts. More specifically, theory theory fails to explicate the role of first-person reporting in mental concepts that do not seem to be directly based on any behavioral evidence—at least, it fails to explicate it in a manner that honors the univocality constraint. Within this framework, the standard approach to the problem of a first-person-reporting function of mental concepts defined primarily in a third-person manner consists in claiming that we acquired the capacity of first-person avowals in a process of linguistic conditioning (Sellars 1963). Somehow our first-person usage started to inexplicably correspond to the usage of the same terms from the third-person perspective. Privileged access is no longer conceived of as introspective acquaintance with mental states but is viewed merely as a feature of our language game (Rorty 1970). Wittgenstein tries to make the process of conditioning a bit more plausible by suggesting that our first-person usage of mental concepts be seen as replacing the natural expression of mental states; for example, "I am in pain" gradually replaces the cry that is part of the definitional criteria of our concept of pain (Wittgenstein 1958, 244). Finally, it has been suggested that we think of the first-person and direct application of mental terms to other people analogously to the use of theoretical concepts by an expert who has become very familiar with the usage of those theoretical terms (Gopnik 1993; Churchland 1989). The direct application of a term either in the third-person or the first-person case should not count against its being identified as a theoretical term that is defined in terms of its role in a theoretical context.

In the end, however, such reasoning cannot explain how we acquire first-personal competence with a wide range of our mental state concepts. To see this, consider emotional terms that we seem to apply effortlessly to other people—at least as far as the basic emotions are concerned—based merely on a perception of their facial expressions.[9] The analogy to how theoretical terms can be used as observational terms is appealing as an explication of first-person reports only at first glance. Using a theoretical term in an observational manner normally means that the person who is familiar with a certain theory is able to apply that term directly without going through all the inferences and conscious shifting of evidence that a novice painstakingly has to go through. This model might indeed explain how I will be able to realize directly that you are angry instead of having to go through all the inferences that a novice would have to go through. I see directly that the other person is angry. I see it in his facial expressions, whereas a novice would have to infer that the other person is angry based on the evidence from his facial expression. The observational use of a theoretical term is possible normally only in situations in which the evidence for its application would still be available to the novice. For this reason, it is difficult to see how this account can illuminate my own recognition that I am angry. I recognize the emotions of other people because I see their facial expressions; yet in my own case such evidence is typically not available to me. Whereas I know how your face looks like when you are angry, I normally do not have a visual representation of my own facial expression available when I am angry. All that I have to go on is a kinaesthetic–proprioceptive representation of the tension in my facial muscle. Wittgenstein's claim that the utterance "I am in pain" replaces my natural expression of pain is a plausible suggestion for how a term that is defined in terms of evidence accessible to the third person could be applied in the first person without being directly based on such evidence precisely because my crying and your crying are both represented in the same sensory modality and can therefore be compared. It is credible to suggest that in both first-person and third-person attribution we use the term with the same meaning. In such cases the analogy to the observation of an expert is also somewhat plausible. But the example is specific to this particular expression of pain and does not generalize to other emotional terms.

As a final option we could consider the possibility that we are simply trained to express our emotions in language even without having a visual representation of our own facial expressions.[10] One could imagine that we are trained to do so when our facial expressions are observed by a third person; whenever we show a certain facial expression others approve of our use of an emotional term, otherwise they correct us. For such a tale to be plausible it seems that we need to have some criteria to distinguish between the many emotional terms that we are able to use. The only option that seems available is to rely on a kinaesthetic representation of the simulation theory nor the standard theory-theory account is tenable in the end. The lesson we should draw is that neither working from the inside out (as suggested by Cartesianism) nor working from the outside in as suggested by theory theory will enable us to construe the use of mental concepts in the folk-psychological realm in a way that honors the univocality constraint. I do think that the research on mirror neurons and imitation provides a secure middle way that avoids the Scylla of pure introspectionism and the Charybdis of pure theory theory. Indeed I regard this as a position that is able to incorporate Wittgenstein's suggestion that our folk-psychological practice be seen as an extension of our natural and prelinguistic interactions with each other. Yet since Wittgenstein stayed on the conceptual level and refused to explore the underlying mechanisms for such natural engagement, he was unable to insulate his position from the problems that plague the detached theory-theory position. I regard it as the philosophical implication of the research on mirror neurons that it will allow us to overcome these specific shortcomings. In various articles, Meltzoff has suggested that cross-modal mechanisms underlying our imitative capacities allow us to encode other agents as being "like me" and allow the infant to divide the world of objects "into those that perform human acts (people) and those that do not (things)" (Meltzoff and Brooks 2001, 174). It has also been suggested that imitation and the relevant underlying mechanisms of physical resonance might be nature's way of solving the other minds problem (Meltzoff and Gopnik 1993; Gopnik and Meltzoff 1997). To a certain extent I agree with all of the above characterizations. Still, I regard the "like me" terminology as placing the emphasis merely on one side of the equation, thereby indicating the powerful intellectual influence of the Cartesian tradition of conceiving of ourselves as having to work our way from the inside out. Imitation and its underlying mechanisms should be understood not only as allowing me to recognize others to be "like me" but also as allowing me to recognize myself as being "like you." More pointedly and in more traditional terminology, one could say that within nature I understand my subjectivity as a moment of interpersonal intersubjectivity. Nature, one might say, *does not solve* the problem of other minds. In fact, this is a problem had only by philosophers within certain intellectual traditions. Nature *does not have* the problem of other minds. In endowing us with resonance mechanisms like the discussed systems of mirror neurons nature has endowed us with intersubjectively valid perceptual "objects" it encounters or interacts with in the world. It is also in this manner that we can develop a conceptual framework for which the univocality constraint holds, since at no time in the child's development should we conceive of its mind in a Cartesian manner. The infant does not first encounter a fully developed mind in the privacy of its own mental den. It does not first define its mental state concepts through an act of inner ostension, as Goldman seems to suggest, and then worry about how to apply such concepts to other persons or how to translate mental concepts of a public language into terms of its private language.[11] Rather, the above remarks suggest a very different picture of the psychological basis for the acquisition of mental concepts of the public language of folk psychology. It suggests that I understand mental state concepts as used by another person in light of perceptual similarity spaces due to the mirror neuron systems *as being applicable to both myself and other persons*, particularly those that are closely tied to certain behavioral manifestations such as is the case with certain emotions. I grasp implicitly that, when my mother says about another person that he is angry, she is using a predicate that also has conditions of application in my own case. Infants do not have to solve the problem of other minds in the manner in which philosophers have traditionally conceived of the problem. However, infants do have to develop a deeper understanding and a more complex conceptual grasp of various domains of interests that are innately circumscribed by various perceptual similarity spaces based on a variety of neurobiological mechanisms.

How then does the existence of mirror neurons and other resonance phenomena affect the debate between simulation theory and theory theory? Prima facie, the existence of such neurobiological mechanisms cohere more with the simulation alternative. First, such mechanisms seem to be knowledge poor. Second, as predicted by simulation theory, our understanding of another person's behavior and emotions involves similar mechanisms that are also involved in the production of our own actions and emotions. For that reason, I am inclined to refer to such mechanisms, in light of Lipps's understanding of empathy, as mechanisms of *basic empathy*. Basic empathy should be conceived of as the fundamental level of interpersonal relations. I would like to suggest, however, that we regard the investigation of such neurobiological phenomena as the investigation of certain perceptual phenomena. What such phenomena certainly show is that Sellars's myth of our Rylean ancestors is a myth that should no longer inclined to do, as a quasi-perceptual mechanism that allows us to directly recognize what another person is doing or feeling. Such an ability is a necessary precondition for a wide range of cognitive development. Without it we can hardly comprehend how language learning should be possible, as such learning requires some grasp of the referential intentions of the other speaker (Bloom 2000). Accepting basic empathy as the foundation for all interpersonal relations does not prove simulation theory right. Rather, it implies that the debate between simulation theorists and theory theorists—if it is taken to be an empirical debate—should be conceived of on a new level, without being limited by traditional concerns of behaviorism and Cartesianism that even today unduly constrain the debate in philosophy of mind. Accepting that in encountering the other person we do not primarily encounter him or her merely in physical terms, as both behaviorists and Cartesians assumed, still leaves room for the question of whether in predicting and explaining the other's behavior in terms of folk psychology we rely on knowledge-rich or knowledge-poor procedures. Basic empathy allows us to recognize the other intuitively as being same minded in that it allows us to directly recognize, for example, *that* he is angry or *that* he is intentionally grasping a cup. Yet we also have to be able to further explain and predict a person's behavior in complex social situations vastly exceeding the mental state attributions due to the mechanisms of basic empathy. We need to understand why that person is angry, why he is grasping the cup, or why he responded to a particular situation in a special manner; that is, we need to understand the reasons for his actions. Here we need to use the full realm of folk-psychological concepts, particularly belief and desire. And a theory theorist will claim that this involves a heavy dose of theory.

Moreover, the above considerations about the nature of our grasp of psychological concepts do speak partly in favor of attributing some theoretical knowledge to the competent folk psychologist. In this context I would like to emphasize that my considerations about mirror neurons should not be taken as implying that basic empathy allows the infant a full grasp of all mental concepts that we attribute to the typical adult. I also do not take myself as having provided a sufficiently rich account of the various stages of how children gain conceptual competence in this area. My considerations are intended as showing only that the traditional philosophical paradigms of introspectionism and behaviorism are unfounded from a naturalist perspective. I understand basic empathy as a mechanism that allows us to recognize the other as being same-minded in a direct perceptual manner. Basic empathy is the basis for the development of a conceptual framework for which the univocality constraint holds.

Given my interpretation of mirror neurons, however, I regard some of our mental concepts—even those of the fully developed mental scheme of the typical adult—as more directly linked to a perceptual basis than others. The traditional theory theorist is wrong in claiming that we can understand all of our psychological concepts only in respect to their embeddedness in a theoretical context or that all of our mental concepts are theoretically embedded to the same degree. As far as our recognition of basic emotions such as anger, fear, and disgust, or even the recognition of the goal-directedness or what one might call a primitive intentionality of actions are concerned, this claim is certainly misguided. In this respect there is a difference between concepts of basic emotions and concepts like belief and concepts of more complex emotions such as shame, guilt, or anxiety that do not seem to have a specific and unique behavioral expression. This is a fact that has generally been overlooked in the discussion about the holism of the mental. Given my Davidsonian explication of meaning holism, I am inclined to favor the thesis that possession of the latter concepts entails the having of some beliefs about the corresponding mental states.[13] Or to say it differently, having such concepts requires having some conceptions associated with those concepts. In particular, one has to have some knowledge of how those states interact with other mental states. It has been pointed out (Malle and Knobe 2001), for example, that our adult concept of an intention implies some grasp of how intentions differ from mere desires and how they are formed in light of an agent's beliefs and desires. Similarly, in order to be granted possession of the concept of the emotion of guilt, it seems necessary that one has some understanding of how guilt differs from other emotional states in that it involves the belief that one has done something morally wrong. It is therefore less clear that one could attribute a concept of guilt to someone unless the person also has some understanding of how guilt interacts with other mental states such as beliefs and desires, how it can be caused, and how it might express itself in behavior.

Yet these holistic intuitions lose some of their grip in case of the concepts of basic emotions. Intuitively I would have no trouble crediting somebody with having *a* concept of fear if all he can do is attribute fear to another person based on his facial expressions without knowing much more about how fear interacts with other mental states. Even though such a concept might be regarded as different from the normal adult concept of fear since adults tend to have considerably more knowledge about the nature of fear, it seems to be sufficiently similar in that it has the same perceptual basis for attributing fear to others. I would also suggest that such concepts linked to mechanisms of basic empathy form the foundation of children's conceptual development in this area. My considerations are confirmed by recent discussions among psychologists about children's concept of intention. Children under the age of three certainly do not have the adult concept since they do not even have a concept of belief. Yet children are able to recognize in observing the behavior of another person that agents act in a goal-directed manner. For this reason, psychologists attribute a perceptually based and primitive concept of *intention-desire* or *conation* to children of that age (Astington 2001; Moses 2001; Wellman and Phillips 2001). How exactly we acquire the conceptual competence of adult folk psychology on this basis—what role linguistic conversation (Garfield, Peterson, and Perry 2001), role play (Harris 2000), or scientific curiosity (Gopnik and Meltzoff 1997) have in this context—is certainly a topic that requires further empirical research.

The issues relating to the nature of concepts are controversial within contemporary philosophy. I have to admit that I do not think that it is possible to provide strict necessary and sufficient conditions for the possession of each mental concept, since I tend to follow Quine and Davidson in rejecting a strict analytic–synthetic distinction. For the sake of argument I am willing to grant that competence in the full range of folk-psychological concepts that we normally attribute to adult human beings requires some minimal theoretical grasp of the nature of mental states and how they might interact. In my opinion such a concession does not imply that having folk-psychological concepts requires the possession of a very rich theory that involves knowledge of detailed theoretical principles about the interaction of various mental states. A theory theorist thus cannot argue against a simulation theory solely basing his argument on considerations about psychological concepts, since only knowledge of such detailed principles would make it prima facie plausible that the simulation phase is superfluous for our interpretation of other agents.

Yet even independent of the question of whether such knowledge of a general framework theory is required in order to be credited with a grasp of folk-psychological concepts, it appears to be a plausible thesis that, as a matter of fact, our grasp of folk-psychological concepts is associated with knowledge of some such theoretical principles. It should not be forgotten that in contrast to simulation theorists, theory theorists focus in their research on children's cognitive development, not merely on our folk-psychological abilities. According to the theory theorist, children become cognitively more competent in various domains of investigation such as folk psychology, folk physics, and folk biology by acquiring a theoretical understanding in these areas. The theory-theory position provides a comprehensive account of children's cognitive development. For these reasons I am indeed inclined to give theoretical considerations their due: it would be puzzling if children would construct various theories about different subject matters except in the mental realm, a realm that after all seems to be of primary importance for their well-being.

Nevertheless, despite these concessions, the above considerations are certainly not sufficient to vindicate a theory-theory position that conceives of our folk-psychological abilities as implicit theoretical inferences that use knowledge of psychological generalizations in the manner that I have described. First, the theory theorist would have to argue specifically that we possess each and every principle that he assumes in his account. Second, a simulation theorist could always insist that the debate between simulation theorists and theory theorists is not primarily about whether or not ordinary folk possess theoretical knowledge about matters of psychology. They certainly do possess some theoretical knowledge. Rather the main question that needs to be answered is whether using such general knowledge of a framework theory in the manner envisioned by the theory theorist should be seen as necessary and sufficient for our folk-psychological abilities to read other minds. Admitting that the grasp of folk-psychological concepts is linked to the possession of some folk-psychological knowledge does not imply that in reading other minds we use the folk-psychological knowledge in the manner suggested by the theory theorist.

Thus, acknowledging that some minimal theoretical knowledge is involved in folk-psychological competence does not fully settle the issue in favor of theory theory. Once possession of such knowledge has been granted, however, it is quite plausible to assume that it does play a role in our folk-psychological interpretation of other agents. Furthermore, granting the possession of psychological knowledge also leads to the suspicion that such psychological knowledge seriously infects the simulation phase and that simulation at most can be seen to play a marginal role in the understanding of an agent's complex social behavior. In order to demonstrate the epistemically central role of empathy or simulation, the simulation theorist therefore needs additional arguments proving that such knowledge is not actually used in or that it alone cannot be viewed as necessary or sufficient for our mindreading abilities.

Given these considerations, it might appear that the debate between simulation theorists and theory theorists on this level is a straightforward empirical debate to be settled by evidence about knowledge of specific theoretical principles and their use in folk-psychological tasks. My arguments in the following will suggest that this appearance is misleading and that a priori considerations in favor of simulation on this level or what I will call *reenactive empathy* are of central importance. We should agree with Heal that considerations that speak in favor of simulation theory are not straightforward empirical arguments buttressed by the results of specific psychological experiments. Rather they are derived from a priori philosophizing that focuses on the central assumption of our folk-psychological practice, defended in the first chapters of this book, according to which agents are rational creatures who act for reasons. If we conceive of agents in this manner and articulate simulation primarily as a personal-level phenomenon, then it is increasingly implausible that a theory-theory conception of folk psychology could be justified through further empirical research and neurobiological findings. But in contrast to Heal I do not consider the following considerations to be conceptual knockdown arguments. It is always possible for a committed theory theorist to dig in his or her heels and insist that while the argument shows that simulation should be allowed a role, it does not prove that simulation plays a central role in our mindreading abilities. Theory theory could accommodate the a priori defense of simulation in a manner analogous to its interpretation of mirror neurons. For a theory theorist such mechanisms have to be seen merely as mechanisms that provide some basic psychological knowledge necessary for running a theoretical apparatus.

Nevertheless, I will suggest that this defensive move on part of the theory theorist has to be regarded as a rather implausible ad hoc strategy. It is therefore best to conceive of ongoing empirical theory of mind research as being outside the theory-theory and simulation-theory framework. Empirical research provides us with a sophisticated understanding of the developmental stages, the conceptual sophistication associated at each level, and the biological mechanisms implementing our folk-psychological abilities. It should not be conceived of as deciding the debate between theory theorists and simulation theorists. Insofar as we try to account for rational agency in the folk-psychological context, our mindreading abilities have to be seen for more a priori reasons as essentially involving reenactive empathy.

There are two principal arguments central for the a priori considerations in favor of simulation or reenactive empathy, both of which are suggested in a rudimentary fashion by Collingwood (1946): the *argument from the essential contextuality* and the *argument from the essential indexicality of thoughts as reasons*. It is also because of this Collingwoodian legacy that I refer to our folk-psychological ability to understand the behavior of other agents in more complex terms as *reenactive empathy*.

4.2   The Essential Contextuality and Indexicality of Thoughts as Reasons

Within contemporary philosophy of mind, Jane Heal (1996) has been the original proponent of the argument from the contextuality of thoughts as reasons and has given it its most precise articulation. Before I proceed with a discussion of the argument and highlight what I think is basically correct in this line of reasoning, it is important to understand a bit more precisely in what sense such reasoning constitutes an a priori argument. In talking about the a priori, I take Heal to have learned Quine's lesson that it is impossible to distinguish on a principled basis between a realm of purely conceptual truths and a realm of purely empirical truths. Her use of the notion of an "a priori" should be understood in a "low-grade" manner (Henderson and Horgan 2000a) and as conceiving of it in a contextual fashion. A priori truths are truths that are accepted because they "are deeply embedded in our world view" (Heal 2003b, 94). They are a priori because they cannot be directly verified or falsified in terms of results of any particular experimental setup. Hence, a priori arguments are "armchair" considerations that have been traditionally taken to constitute the domain of philosophy because they do not require us to run to the laboratory or read articles revealing any specific laboratory results. A priori arguments, however, are not completely independent of centrally held beliefs of our accepted explanatory paradigms in the sciences. Indeed, as I will suggest, the argument for reenactive empathy from the essential contextuality of rational thought depends on insights gained from the empirical study of the mind and the realization within this context that certain aspects of our cognitive lives are almost impossible to model within the cognitive paradigm of "good old-fashioned artificial intelligence" (GOFAI).

In Heal's writings, we can detect two strategies of arguing for the claim that to think about another person's thoughts requires first-order thinking about the same "state of affairs which are the subject matter of those thoughts" (2003b, 99) and not a general theory of thought. First, Heal stresses the fact that in thinking that Peter thinks that p we have to able to think that p ourselves. Otherwise we would not be able to know what Peter is really thinking about. Identifying the content of a particular thought is only possible, or so it seems, in light of the content of a first-order thought that we ourselves can entertain.[14] Notice, however, that this claim is true only if we implicitly assume that when we characterize another person's thought we identify it comprehendingly. We are undoubtedly able to refer to the thought of another person in a noncomprehending manner without being able to think about the same subject matter. Even if we do not know any German, for example, we can recognize that Peter has the same thought as Karl since both of them utter the sentence "Der Schnee ist weiß." In order to do this we need only know that both of them speak German and that in making an assertion we normally express a belief we hold. We could also assert that Peter thinks the thought that German speakers normally express by saying "Der Schnee ist weiß." I do not think it is necessary to belabor this point in this context.[15] Such noncomprehending identification should without doubt be regarded merely as a second-best manner of identifying the thoughts of other agents. Without knowing in the sense of comprehending what the other person is thinking about, we hardly can claim that we understand how thoughts can be reasons for a person's action that provide the agent with a perspective on and orientation toward his environment. The idea that folk-psychological interpretation is based primarily on a comprehending identification of the thoughts of other people seems to be implicit in our conception of agency as it has developed earlier on.

Still, admitting that thinking about another person's thought implies a comprehending identification of his thoughts does not in itself constitute a decisive argument against theory theory. The question of how we understand complex social behavior concerns primarily the relations between various thoughts and the relations between thoughts and behavior. It has mainly to do not with the problem of how we comprehendingly identify single thoughts of other persons but with how we, based on our knowledge of a set of such thoughts, can grasp—explain and predict—another person's subsequent behavior. A theory theorist is free to maintain that we are able to do this exactly by appealing to various principles such as the central action principle of folk psychology and other principles such as "if a person believes that p and q he tends to believe that p."

Considerations that have proven to be quite popular in this context, and which have even persuaded some formerly die-hard card-carrying theory theorists like Stich and Nichols to make some concessions to simulation theory regarding our ability to predict the inferential behavior of others, are empirical considerations about cognitive economy. From the perspective of the design stance, it seems to be a waste of cognitive resources if Nature endowed us with an additional theory about the nature of thought processes to be used for the prediction of others' behavior. Why waste limited cognitive space for the use of a theory of mind for that purpose if we could use our own mental mechanisms in a manner suggested by simulation theorists? Yet one should contain one's enthusiasm for arguments from cognitive economy. First, the process of evolution cannot be compared to a process in which we start a design from scratch. *Pace* creationism, we should not forget that we did develop from the animal kingdom. Besides, Nature designs organisms—if I am allowed for a moment this anthropocentric formulation—"wishing for" and "trying" to guarantee their survival. Yet Nature does not have to justify its design choices to a penny-pinching accountant. Second, as I have pointed out, theory theory provides us with a unified account of cognitive development in respect to various domains of investigations that are of human interest. Developing a theory of mind or activating a theory of mind module is from this perspective not uneconomical but an expression of a generally theoretical stance that we implicitly have to take for survival's sake. Given our natural curiosity in this respect, it seems that Nature would have to provide us with additional inhibitory mechanisms for not developing a theory of mind and for using merely our own cognitive resources for that purpose.

Thus, empirical arguments from economy, even though they are broadly appealed to by simulation theorists and by Heal (2003b, 101) herself, have to be taken with a grain of salt. Fortunately there is a more powerful argument also appealed to by Heal that claims that our understanding of rational thought processes cannot be based on a theory, namely, the argument from the essential contextuality of thoughts as reasons. The basic assumption of this argument is not merely that we have to comprehendingly identify another person's thoughts but also that we have to understand them, in some minimal sense, as being "rationally or intelligibly linked." It is not always clear how Heal understands this requirement, but I take it as implying that the initial sets of thoughts have be conceived of as reasons for the derived thoughts, in the sense I outlined earlier. Thought processes have to be viewed not merely as causal sequences but as processes that, even though they might not conform to the standards of our best theories of rationality, are nevertheless evaluable in light of such theories. More importantly, it has to be noted that the theories philosophers and psychologists most often appeal to in this context like theories of logical inference tend to characterize the normatively sanctioned forms of reasoning in a formalized and syntactic manner through rules such as modus ponens, modus tollens, conjunction elimination, and so on. Given any arbitrary set of beliefs or class of sentences, such rules allow us to distinguish between logically permissible and impermissible inferences. They allow us to characterize believing that p and believing that q as reasons for believing that p & q. If we for a moment counterfactually assume that we conform in our reasoning habits to the inferences that are sanctioned by such theories, one might argue that knowledge of such theories would be sufficient for predicting and explaining the rational thought processes of another person. If this were to be taken as the appropriate account of rationality then it would be impossible to argue in an a priori manner that a theory theory account is insufficient for understanding the thought processes of another person.

In light of my argument for rational contextualism it has to be emphasized that such merely formal and syntactic theories of logical inference can never be sufficient for characterizing rational thought and decision processes. Formal theories of inference presuppose that it does not matter for the evaluation of the rationality of a person's thought processes how the subset of beliefs on which they operate is fixed. Such an assumption is completely off the mark insofar as human rationality is concerned. Humans are rational and are judged to be so only if they draw the inferences appropriate to a particular context, the inferences that lead to appropriate decisions and actions. Formal theories of inferences tell us which inferences are logically permissible to draw, but not which inferences are rational to draw within a particular context. At most they enable us to characterize necessary conditions for a thought's being a reason for a person whose action is judged to be rational in a certain situation. If I am sitting on the beach marveling at the sunny weather, blue sky, and rough sea, while at the same time hearing a boy in the water crying for help, I am certainly permitted according to our formal theories of inference to form the complex belief that it is a sunny day with a blue sky and a boy is crying for help in the water. Formally speaking, there is nothing wrong with drawing such an inference. One could even say that looked at it in isolation from the situation I find myself in these thoughts are my reasons for forming such a belief. Yet in this situation they are not sufficient for being the reasons of a person who would act appropriately and rationally in this particular context. If I remain seated—assuming that I also believe that one should help people that are in danger—something has gone seriously wrong. My action or rather nonaction cannot be seen as rational, since I have failed to recognize that a cry for help in this situation indicates that the boy is in danger—as I know quite well—and that this requires me to get him some help. My fundamental mistake consists in considering the boy's cry for help in the context of the wrong set of beliefs because I seem to be unable to recognize which of my beliefs are relevant for consideration in this particular situation.

Individual thoughts function as reasons for rational agency only relative to a specific framework of an agent's thoughts that are relevant for consideration in a specific situation. As the above example illustrates, not all of a person's thoughts are relevant in a specific context. Thoughts as reasons are sensitive to relevant background information that is accessible to a particular agent. On its own, President Clinton's relationship with an intern or more precisely my knowledge thereof would not count as a reason for anything. Furthermore it could not count as a reason for my deciding to vote against him or thinking any less of him as a president if I am of the opinion that one should allow politicians a private sphere of behavior and that behavior in the private sphere should not be taken into account for the evaluation of his public and political persona. On the other hand, if I am strongly committed to the idea that the private is political and that the distinction between the two spheres of behavior cannot be neatly drawn, my knowledge of his behavior has to influence my deliberations regarding for whom to vote and how to evaluate his presidency. Thoughts are constituted as reasons as long as they "match" in the appropriate manner with other relevant thoughts of an agent. Since we possess a huge amount of information about the world of which only a fraction is relevant for consideration in a specific context, understanding a thought as a reason requires us to be able to distinguish between the relevant and irrelevant parts of our belief system in each new context. As a matter of fact we are able to make these distinctions on a daily basis.

In predicting the rational thoughts of another person we have to figure out in a similar manner which thoughts the other person finds relevant in order to understand his thoughts as his reasons. Understanding thoughts as reasons of rational agents requires us to solve what has become known as the frame problem. Within the context of the classical computational paradigm, one tries to model human cognitive capacities in terms of operational rules that are defined precisely over discrete and context-free elements of a particular situation (see Henderson and Horgan 2000b). More precisely, within the computational paradigm such rules are defined syntactically, that is, in terms of properties of mental representations that remain invariant even if the context changes in which the mental representations occur. As Jerry Fodor puts it, the frame problem arises because in "classical machines the basic architectural as well as the basic computational processes are local," but "there appear to be mental processes that . . . respond to (irreducibly) non-local properties of belief systems" (Fodor 2000, 45). To modify an example of Dreyfus, we normally understand the sentence "The parachute is in the pen" as asserting that the parachute is in a child's playpen, given our knowledge of the relative sizes of playpens and parachutes. Yet in the context of a James Bond movie we effortlessly understand it as asserting that the parachute is in a writing utensil ingeniously devised by the British Secret Service, because this interpretation coheres better with what we know about the world and James Bond movies (Dreyfus 1972,

127ff.).[16] A machine can certainly "recognize" that the word "pen" has more than one meaning, as different meanings can be linked to a local property such as the syntactical shape of the word "pen." In defining a program for disambiguating the meaning of the word "pen" in a specific context, we would have to use a rule that refers to the global properties of our cognitive system, for example, "choose the interpretation that coheres best with the relevant knowledge of the world." To program a machine accordingly, we would have to computationally define a precise theory of relevance so that the machine could determine the relevant aspects of a specific situation. It is empirically highly unlikely that such a definition is possible within the paradigm of good old-fashioned AI. Any attempt to implement a general theory of relevance presupposes a precise understanding of how one decides what part of a "global theory of relevance" is relevant for a local context. And such understanding would again depend on our ability to recognize global features of our belief system and not merely specific local properties in terms of which we are able to articulate a programmable rule for a computer.

For these reasons it is indeed implausible that thinking about the rational thought processes of others could be solely dependent on a theory. Since we solve such frame problems in our mind daily even though we seem to lack any folk-psychological theory of relevance, it is more plausible that thinking about other people's thought requires that we ourselves think about the subject matter of their thoughts. We do not have a theory about how people who think about a particular subject matter *s* process their thoughts; rather we have to use our own thinking about *s* in order to find out about the other person's thought processes. Collingwood calls this egocentric method of grasping the thought processes of another person *reenactment*, whereas Heal, emphasizing that she conceives of it as a personal-level phenomenon, refers to it as *co-cognition*. Given that this egocentric manner of understanding the other agent has traditionally been referred to as a method of empathy I prefer to call it the method of *reenactive empathy*. Taking the theory-theory stance in this regard would imply that we attribute a theory to each person without having the faintest idea about its structure. Attributing a theory "we know not what"—to use Locke's characterization of our notion of substance—seems, however, to run against standard scientific practice. From a philosophy of mind perspective it seems equivalent to Descartes's sin of postulating of a mental substance without having a clue about how it might interact with the physical world. Notice, however, that even though the above considerations about the plausibility of the theory-theory position are "armchair" reflections, they are not completely independent of empirical research about the structure of the human mind. In fact they depend essentially on (by now generally recognized) shortcomings and principal limitations of the cognitive model of the mind within the approach of good old-fashioned AI, a framework that is committed to the empirical study of the mind. Thirty years ago, such considerations (as the generally hostile reception of Dreyfus's book *What Computers Can't Do* has shown) would not have been regarded as having much argumentative force, since good old-fashioned AI was the only game in town.

It is, however, too narrow an interpretation of the argument from the essential contextuality of rational thought to limit its scope to the predictions of the cognitive inferences another person will draw based on knowledge of his initial thoughts, as Heal and Collingwood are inclined to do.[17] This constitutes another reason to prefer the label of reenactive empathy over reenactment or co-cognition. It is important to realize that the above considerations are applicable to a whole range of psychological phenomena that can plausibly be seen as evaluable according to some norms of rationality and in which the response of an agent can be evaluated as rationally compelling or as rationally uncalled for. That is, the above considerations apply to the whole realm of normatively structured agency in which agents have to be understood as being responsive to and as implicitly acknowledging the validity of a variety of general normative standards for their behavior. If I am right, the rationality of an action has to be seen as the negotiation of various norms of behavior in light of the specific situation an agent with limited capacities finds himself in. As both Aristotle and Wittgenstein emphasize, however, even if we assume counterfactually that there are norms that govern our behavior in each situation, such norms could only be conceived of as formulated on a very general level and are therefore to a certain extent open ended. For each situation, as we have emphasized, a variety of normative considerations are applicable and need to be weighed against each other. Each rational decision requires that one is able to recognize which normative considerations are relevant in a particular situation, how a general norm is to be applied to the particular aspects of that situation, and how to weigh and negotiate among these various rules in that situation. Hence Aristotle views our ability to react rationally and appropriately in specific situations as resting on a practical capacity that is theoretically not further explicable. He also emphasizes the limitations of abstract philosophical considerations about ethical principles since in a specific situation only the ethical person will be able to judge in light of his practical ability how to act ethically. Understanding other agents seems to require that I am able to recognize particular aspects of their situation as relevant to their actions. And in order to do that I have to put myself in their shoes and practically evaluate what aspects of the situation have to be regarded as relevant using my own rational capacity for making such judgments.

One should therefore also regard the realm of emotions as falling within the scope of the above considerations, since in contrast to the moral psychologies of Kant and Hume, emotions belong within the normative realm of reason and are not merely part of the irrational passions. First, practical rationality, including ethical rationality, involves the ability to find among a myriad of features of a situation the ones that are relevant given one's interests and values. As Aristotle correctly and repeatedly pointed out, the ability to respond in a specific situation in such a manner presupposes that one is emotionally attuned to the world in the right manner. Various recent authors have suggested that emotions or the ability to respond emotionally to the world be regarded as Nature's way of solving the frame problem (DeSousa 1987; Damasio 1994; Goldie 2000). By wiring us to respond to certain aspects of the world in a particular manner, Nature has enabled us to automatically recognize those aspects of a situation that are relevant to our survival. And through moral education society fine tunes our emotional responses further according to criteria that are regarded as essential for its proper functioning. In this manner each individual is ideally provided with the emotional maturity to make rational decisions. As the saying goes, a coward dies a hundred deaths because he is unable to distinguish real threats from imagined ones. Without such emotional attunement toward the world acquired through natural selection and social education, any aspect of a situation could be regarded as relevant and worthy of consideration. In such a situation, making a decision as simple as what day to meet next would be an almost impossible task, since we would have to process and deliberate about every possible aspect that might be affected by such a decision (see Damasio 1994 for a description of such a

clinical case). It is for this reason that we ordinarily judge an emotional response to be appropriate or inappropriate; we recognize, as Aristotle put it,
that it is appropriate to feel angry at the right time, the right place, and toward the right person. We indeed take it to be a good reason for you to be
angry if somebody intentionally steps on your foot to hurt you. But we
would not find this reaction appropriate in the case where somebody steps
on your foot by accident.

In light of these reflections one also should reanalyze the example that
Goldman (1995a, 83) uses to argue for simulation theory independent of
the rationality assumption. Goldman presents us with the case of somebody who just missed a train (it left one minute before he reached the plat-
form) compared with somebody who misses a train by two hours. We
intuitively understand that the person who just missed the train is more
annoyed. Goldman suggests that we figure this out not by appealing to
any particular psychological theory but just by imaginatively putting ourselves in such a situation and seeing how we would feel. I agree with Goldman that we probably do not appeal to theory in this case. Yet I think
Goldman is not sufficiently analyzing what happens when we imaginatively put ourselves in such a situation. What we do understand—using
the method of simulation—I would like to suggest, are the aspects of the
situation that constitute our reasons for responding emotionally in a certain way or, to express it in a more neutral manner, the aspects of the situation that would allow such a response to be appropriate. We grasp that the
person who just missed the train has more reason to be annoyed than the
person whose train left over an hour ago, because if the latter, say, would
have avoided wasting time talking to the cab driver, or would have run or
driven a little bit faster, he probably would have made it in time.

There is another a priori argument for the claim that reenactive empathy
is of central importance to our ability to understand other agents and their
minds. This argument also derives from a reflection on the central aspects
of conceiving of other persons as authors of their actions who act for reasons
and not merely because of internal events inside them—mental or otherwise. I call this argument for the central importance of reenactive empathy
the *argument from the essential indexicality of thoughts as reasons*. It is inspired
by Collingwood's suggestion that our recognition of a thought—and here
we should add our recognition of a thought as a reason—cannot be conceived of as similar to the perception of an external object (Collingwood

1946, 291–292). Understanding our recognition of a thought as a reason on the model of object perception does not allow us to grasp it as something other than a mere internal event. Understanding how a thought can be a reason for someone minimally requires that we can understand how a thought can be a thought that somebody recognizes as his or her own. This is possible, or so Collingwood seems to claim, only if we are able to integrate them as thoughts into our own cognitive perspective by imaginatively identifying them as our own thoughts that could be reasons for our own action. The argument from the essential indexicality of thoughts as reasons consists of two steps. First, it claims that from the first-person perspective we can grasp a thought as a reason only if we identify it as our own. For me to conceive of the belief that President Clinton had an affair as a reason for my action, or at least as a reason for adjusting the rest of my belief set, I minimally have to conceive of it as my thought. Recognizing that Linda has such a thought could not constitute a reason for my actions. Second, the argument claims that in order to understand how Linda's belief could be a reason for her action we have to imaginatively entertain the belief ourselves—taking care of all the relevant differences—and imaginatively identify the thought as our own.

These suggestions are best understood in light of considerations about the essential and irreducible role of first-person concepts in our cognitive system, which has been recognized by thinkers as diverse as Descartes, Kant, Perry, and most recently, by Burge.[18] As Kant maintained against Hume, in order for thoughts to be recognized as constituting a conception about the world, they cannot be understood merely as temporally succeeding events in an ever-changing stream of consciousness. Such a conception of thought would not even allow us to understand the stream of consciousness as a singular stream of consciousness; it would be better described as a flickering of radically separated conscious events. For Kant, the fundamental mistake of empiricist epistemology was that it could not account for the possibility of the unity of consciousness, which it presupposed in taking sensory experience as the basis of all knowledge. Empiricists tend to overlook what Kant calls the transcendental unity of apperception, that is, the ability to recognize one's thought as one's own or, as Kant says, that[11] it must be possible for the 'I think' to accompany all of my representation" (Kant, *Critique of Pure Reason*, B131). I would argue that one can accept these insights without also accepting Kant's postulation of a noumenal world and his attempt to derive synthetic a priori principles from such considerations. Kant is right in insisting that thoughts can be understood to be about the world only if they are part of a subjective perspective on the world. Without constituting a worldview or a perspective on a common world, thoughts also cannot be understood to rationally compel an agent to act in the world, especially if we conceive of actions as the result of active deliberation. Without the unity of consciousness, provided by the ability to recognize thoughts in my mind as my own, I would lack the ability to rationally organize my own thoughts. I would lack the ability even to recognize that two thoughts might contradict each other and that this would constitute a reason for revising my belief system. Recognizing that two thoughts contradict each other does not compel me to revise any of my own beliefs, unless such a contradiction is recognized as arising between *my* thoughts.

It is important to understand that the unity of consciousness necessary for understanding thoughts as reasons is essentially a first-person phenomenon that is displayed in the psychologically unanalyzable and irreducible use of the first-person pronoun. John Perry (1993) talks in this context of an essential use of the first-person pronoun, or, as philosophers and linguistics like to call it, the essential use of the first-person *indexical*, because our knowledge of what the expression "I" and other indexical expressions like "here", "now," "today," and so on refer to depends on our knowledge of certain features of the context in which the utterance containing the expression was made. "I" always refers to the speaker of the utterance. For that reason, we have no difficulty recognizing that the sentence "I am not a crook" uttered by President Nixon has the same semantic content as the sentence "Mr. Nixon is not a crook." Nevertheless, the I-concept or first-person indexical plays a special psychological role that cannot be captured by semantically equivalent thoughts.

To use one of Perry's well-known examples, only if I recognize that it is me that is unintentionally making a mess will I have a reason to stop engaging in the behavior that is causing the mess. No uniquely identifying description of me, such as "The only person in aisle 5 in Shaw's supermarket in Sturbridge, Massachusetts on June 15, 2001, at 4:45 PM is making a mess," can replace the first-person indexical in its psychological efficacy. In order to have a reason for changing my behavior based on this description, I would also have to recognize that it is I who is being described in this manner. Similar remarks apply to attempts to replace the "I" with "the person who is making this utterance," "the person who is having this thought," or even a reference to the person by his or her proper name. Even thoughts that I recognize as belonging to Karsten Stueber could not be reasons for me unless I also recognize that I am Karsten Stueber and that these thoughts are my thoughts. Burge is thus right when he maintains that only in light of our use of the I-concept can we fully understand ourselves as being critical reasoners, as "reasoners who are moved by reasons":

Recognition that a thought is one's own—taking up the subjectivity and proprietary ownership in the first person concept—is the only basis for conceptually expressing having a rationally immediate and necessary reason to tend a point of view, to make the reasons effective on the attitude they evaluate. (Burge 1998, 258)

Much earlier, Kant seemed to have already recognized that these considerations about the essential status of the I-concept for our conception of ourselves as rational agents implies that reenactive empathy is epistemically central to our understanding of others as rational agents:

It is obvious that, if I wish to represent to myself a thinking being, I must put myself in his place, and thus substitute, as it were, my own subject for the object I am seeking to consider (which does not occur in any other investigation), and that we demand the absolute unity of the subject of a thought, only because we otherwise could not say, "I think" (the manifold in one representation). For although the whole of the thought could be divided and distributed among many subjects, the subjective "I" can never be thus divided and distributed, and it is this "I" that we presuppose in all thinking.[19] (Kant, *Critique of Pure Reason*, A353–354)

To understand how another person's thoughts are her reasons for her actions or deliberations, such as understanding why Linda decides to revise her beliefs about President Clinton in light of revelations about his private behavior, we have to understand how those thoughts can be thoughts that require the attention of the other person as a "critical reasoner." We need to understand others' thoughts as events that are not mere occurrences in their minds or bodies but that are their reasons for their behavior. This presupposes that we have to understand them as thoughts that they can recognize as their own thoughts. Being told that Karsten Stueber thinks that President Clinton had an affair does not immediately constitute a reason for me to do anything unless I also recognize that it is my thought. In the same manner, I do not just have to grasp that Linda thinks that President Clinton has had an affair; I also have to see that Linda thinks "I think that President Clinton has had an affair." We have to understand how another person can relate to his or her thoughts in an essentially first-personal manner. Given the above considerations about the essential use of the first-person pronoun, this is possible only if we conceive of her use of the I-concept on the model of my use. Only insofar as I treat her thoughts as thoughts that could be my own—and as thoughts that would move me to draw certain conclusions if I were to integrate them in my own cognitive system were I also to entertain Linda's other beliefs—can I grasp them as her thoughts and as thoughts that constitute her reasons for her action. If I am unable to do so I would have to treat them not as thoughts of a person, but as thoughts that happen to occur in a person. Such an alienated stream of thoughts might be the mark of a particular mental patient, but they are not thoughts characteristic of rational agency. Moreover, it is not even clear in what sense such "thoughts" can be regarded as genuine thoughts in the first place.

These two arguments suggest that reenactive empathy is central to our understanding of others as rational agents because we have to be able to understand that we would have acted or drawn certain inferences for the same reasons if we were in their situation. Only in this manner are we able to predict and explain behavior in the folk-psychological realm. A pure theory-theory account of our folk-psychological abilities therefore cannot be adequate. Moreover, the foregoing conclusion seems to be insulated from a critique based on, for example, empirical findings from the neurosciences. Neurobiological insights about neuronal areas implementing our mindreading abilities could not challenge it unless those areas could be interpreted as representing a theory of relevance, an interpretation that is rather implausible if one accepts the argument from the essential contextuality of thoughts as reasons.

Yet a theory theorist could still argue that the argument so far does not show that no theoretical inferences are causally involved in a central manner in our folk-psychological interpretation of other people. Various theory theorists have granted some involvement of simulation in response to Heal's argument (Botterill 1996; Botterill and Carruthers 1999; Nichols and Stich 2003). But they insist that simulation merely provides necessary information that is processed by theoretical inferences which utilize theoretical knowledge, particularly knowledge of folk-psychological generalizations such as the central action principle.[20] Certainly one can grant that to predict Linda's behavior, we need to recognize that there is an epistemic tension in her belief system and that such a recognition is possible only if we make use of our own cognitive capacities. Nevertheless, a theory theorist might suggest, to predict or explain Linda's subsequent behavior we also must make use of psychological generalizations such as that people will do A if they desire x and they believe that A is a means for achieving x. In this case we would use this generalization to explain Linda's readjusting her belief system because she wants to resolve an epistemic tension among her beliefs, she believes that there is such a tension within her belief system, and she believes that her revisions will resolve that epistemic tension. The argument so far does not seem to have excluded the possibility of such a hybrid theory-theory position. To decide this specific question further empirical research seems to be necessary.[21]

Heal herself might not be bothered by this response since she tends to think that theory theory denies any involvement of simulation and that it imperialistically claims that "everything comes from theory theory" (2003a, 67). I regard this imperialistic claim indeed to be refuted by the above argument. Yet I do not think that such a characterization of the theory-theory proposal is fair to practicing psychologists who as we have seen have no problems in accepting the involvement of some nontheoretical capacities in mindreading. In my characterization of the debate I have understood the simulation theorist to be committed to the more interesting thesis that folk psychology, as far as it is concerned with understanding rational agency, depends centrally on simulation as outlined above. On my reading, it would be admitting defeat if the simulation theorist were to acknowledge that simulation only provides information that is then processed by further theoretical processes.

Nevertheless, the above a priori arguments have to be understood as putting the theory theorist under justificatory pressure. It forces the theory theorist to explain why we should assume that any theoretical inference is causally involved in the production of predictions or explanations of individual behavior, if "rationalizing explanations" in terms of an agent's reasons require that I can imagine the other person's beliefs and desires as being my reasons for acting if I were in a similar situation. Notice that in this context we are merely concerned with the question of how folk-psychological explanations are *causally* produced, particularly singular causal explanations such as, for example, "he stood up because he wanted to get a beer." We are not concerned with the *epistemic* justification of such explanations. Although, as I will argue in the next chapter, it is quite plausible to assume that the epistemic justification of such explanations requires reference to generalizations, admitting such generalizations in the epistemic context does not imply that they are also causally involved in the production of singular causal explanations. As we have seen, the simulation theorist can admit that we have psychological knowledge and even that some such knowledge is required for getting the simulation started.[22] Understood in this manner, the above a priori considerations change the argumentative balance prima facie in favor of proponents of empathy by theoretically establishing empathy as the default position for our ability to understand rational agents within the folk-psychological context. It challenges the theory theorist to come up with specific empirical evidence to the contrary or otherwise admit the central claim of simulation theorists.

In addition, the above a priori claims allow us to recognize that the theory theorist faces a rather Herculean task. First, the theory theorist has to show for each and every folk-psychological principle (such as the *central action principle* or the *principle for changing a perceptual belief*, mentioned earlier in our explication of the theory theory position) that such principles are represented by each person from a very young age onward. That somebody could pass the false-belief task with the help of such principles would not prove that these principles are also internally represented by each child. I do not want to dwell on this problem, as I am prepared to accept that humans acquire some psychological knowledge early in their lifetime. But more importantly the theory theorist has to prove that knowledge of such generalizations is causally involved in the production of folk-psychological explanations and predictions. It does not appear plausible that such a demonstration could be provided by neurobiological evidence alone. Neurobiological research alone cannot decide whether or not activation of certain neuronal area should be interpreted as involving theoretical knowledge of psychology used in the manner suggested by the theory theorists. To be a bit more concrete, it has for example been found that when subjects read and answer questions about what psychological researchers call theory of mind (TOM) stories—because this involves the attribution successful application of such generalizations, it is required to know when all things are indeed equal. More significantly, in the realm of rational agency we can distinguish between two types of interfering factors. Factors of type I include conditions such as mental illness, tiredness, drunkenness, and absentmindedness. The existence of such interfering factors can be objectively established solely from the third-person perspective. Knowledge of such interfering factors for the proper functioning of our rational processes can be seen as theoretical knowledge. In core cases of explaining why folk-psychological principles such as the central action principle fail to apply, however, we refer to factors of type II. Particularly, we mention that the agents had overriding reasons, that is, beliefs and desires that are in some sense stronger and incompatible with the ones cited in the generalizations. We explain, for example, why somebody did not eat the bread in front of him, even though he is very hungry and thinks that bread would nourish him and satisfy his hunger, by pointing out that he also thinks that this particular bread is poisoned or infected by a fungus that would make him very sick. In this situation, his hunger did not constitute a sufficient reason for his action. But in order to thus recognize the others' thoughts as overriding reasons we would have to use our reenactive capacities—at least, I would be prepared to argue this claim in light of the arguments for reenactive empathy so far. If these statements are plausible, why should we assume that psychological principles play any causal role in folk-psychological explanation, and that simulation procedures or reenactive empathy merely provide information for further theoretical processing? It seems more reasonable to assume that putting ourselves in the shoes of the other person by taking sufficient care of relevant differences is primary for our understanding of others as rational agents. From this perspective, once I have evaluated another person's mental states as reasons for his actions, an appeal to generalizations would be completely superfluous (see also Collingwood 1946, 222–223).[23] Certainly some theoretical knowledge can be admitted in guiding this primarily empathetic procedure, such as knowledge that drunkenness reduces agents' capacities to act for proper reasons. But admitting such theoretical knowledge does not mean that folk-psychological generalizations are used in inferential procedures. To insist in face of these considerations on the essential causal involvement of theoretical inferences, as the theory theorist might, seems to be an ad hoc maneuver.[24]

Our discussion of the current theory of mind debate and the debate between simulation theory and theory theory has shown that it is best to distinguish between two forms of empathy, basic empathy and reenactive empathy. Mechanisms of basic empathy are probably implemented on the neurobiological level by systems of mirror neurons. Nevertheless, the evidence for basic empathy does not constitute an outright victory for simulation theory. Rather, basic empathy is the fundamental perceptual mechanism that allows us to directly relate to other human beings as like-minded and to develop intersubjectively accessible discourses using the folk-psychological idiom. It has been shown that the traditional assumption of both the Cartesian and behaviorist frameworks, according to which we primarily recognize only the physical behavior of another person, is wrong. Moreover, interpreting neurobiological evidence for the existence of mirror neuron systems as indicating mechanisms of basic empathy requires a critical evaluation of the nature of our grasp of folk-psychological concepts. Such an interpretation is possible only if one recognizes the shortcomings of a Cartesian account of psychological concepts and the blind spots of a theory-theory account.

If one accepts my understanding of basic empathy, it is still an open question whether our understanding of more complex behavior of other agents proceeds on the model of the theory theory and whether the appeal to theoretical knowledge is sufficient for this purpose. This question is particularly urgent for a proponent of the empathy view if one grants, as I am inclined to do, that we also possess some knowledge of how various mental states interact with each other. In this context, the arguments from the essential contextuality and essential indexicality of thoughts as reasons have proven to be crucial. Even though they do not establish with conceptual certainty that empathy is the primary strategy of folk-psychological interpretation, they dramatically change the argumentative landscape in favor of the simulation theorist and the proponent of empathy. They also suggest that it is very unlikely that a theory theorist is able to demonstrate empirically that folk-psychological generalizations are causally involved in folk-psychological mindreading.

I would suggest that empirical research into the underlying psychological mechanisms should no longer be conceived of as trying to provide evidence for either simulation theory or theory theory, since in conceiving of folk psychology in an engaged manner one has to admit empathy as centrally involved in our understanding of other agents. Instead, one should conceive of this research as providing us with an understanding of how our basically empathetic relation to other agents is implemented on the neurobiological level, and as providing us with a description of the conceptual sophistication and the conditions necessary for the acquisition of a conceptual repertoire such as is associated with our folk-psychological abilities. The increasing conceptual sophistication of a child should be seen as the development of a conceptual framework articulating the basic ontological categories for thinking about rational agency. Its primary purpose is not to provide us with psychological generalizations causally involved in the production of folk-psychological interpretations, as seems to be suggested by the detached conception of folk psychology. Following a suggestion by Perner (2004), a child's cognitive development should be primarily seen as proceeding from a conception of agents as objectively rational or goal-directed agents—an assumption supported by the earlier mentioned experiments of Gegerly and others—to a conception of persons as subjectively rational agents. Such conceptual sophistication helps us to make sense of the central ontological assumption of folk psychology that persons are rational agents who have a subjective perspective on the world. It also allows us to become aware of psychological aspects in respect to which agents can differ, a knowledge that is necessary for and further supports the use of our empathetic capacities in understanding complex social agency.

theory from the detached perspective did not address questions of underlying psychological mechanisms. Philosophers such as Sellars and Churchland adopted a theory conception of folk psychology because they felt, as we have seen, that only in this manner could one (i) account for the content of folk-psychological concepts and (ii) comprehend folk psychology as an explanatory practice.

Hempel (1965), for example, never objected to empathy as a causal procedure for coming up with interpretive hypotheses of other agents, particularly hypotheses for explanations of their behavior. His objections against empathy are not based on an analysis of the information each person internally represents and uses in order to be able to participate in our folk-psychological practices. His considerations are concerned with an *analysis of the information that is necessary and sufficient for a prediction or an explanation in the realm of human agency to be epistemically sanctioned.* Or, to say it differently, the epistemic analysis of our folk-psychological practices concerns the analysis of information that could answer questions about the epistemic status of one's folk-psychological interpretation, questions such as "why do you think that you are correct in predicting that Peter will marry Sue and in explaining that he voted for Kerry because he did not like Bush?" Hempel would indeed be able to live with the conclusion of the last chapter that empathy is centrally involved in the causal production of folk-psychological interpretations. For him this would mean simply that empathy is the central causal heuristic in the context of discovery. Pointing to the fact that we simulated Peter could answer factual questions of why we think that Peter will marry Sue. Yet Hempel would vehemently reject the claim that empathy can also be understood as a method for the justification of any explanatory and interpretive hypothesis within the folk-psychological realm. For him, pointing out that I simulated another person could never sufficiently answer why I think or why one should think that I am correct in my predictions and explanations. In order to do this we would have to rely on rich theoretical information and appeal to certain psychological generalizations. Unfortunately, these important epistemic concerns have been insufficiently addressed within the current philosophical debate over simulation theory.[1] Unless they answer these objections, proponents of the empathy view could find themselves in the philosophically unfortunate position of having won the causal battle against theory theory but being seriously in danger of losing the epistemic war.

Traditional proponents of empathy were aware of the epistemic framework of their arguments for empathy. Dray, the principal defender of Collingwood's reenactment view in the philosophy of history, insists explicitly in his defense of empathy against Hempel on its epistemically central function by declaring that "the point of the projection metaphor is...more plausibly interpreted as a logical one"—or as I would say an epistemic one. "Its function," he continues, "is not to remind us *how we come to know certain facts*, but to formulate, however tentatively, certain conditions which must be satisfied before a historian is prepared to say: 'Now I have an explanation'" (Dray 1957, 128). As I will argue in the following pages, Dray's remarks are right on target if they are interpreted in terms of a plausible account of the nature of explanation. But one has to be very careful in arguing for this claim. Dray himself tends to obscure his basic insight by associating it with the implausible claim that our explanations of ordinary action require us to think of causation in a very special sense. According to this line of reasoning, our notions of causation and explanation are fundamentally ambiguous, and we have to distinguish the concept of what one could call "natural necessity," to which we appeal in explaining the occurrence of natural events, from a notion of "rational necessity" that underlies our causal account of agency (ibid., 154). Empathy is central only in the realm of rational necessity, a realm that is categorically separated from the realm of natural necessity.

In my opinion, this manner of arguing for the epistemic centrality of empathy is fundamentally misguided since it presupposes a problematic bifurcation in our notion of causation and causal explanation. I will defend the central epistemic role of empathy without relying on such a bifurcation. To assess empathy's role within the epistemic context, it will be necessary to distinguish carefully between the epistemic requirements associated with folk-psychological prediction and those associated with explanation. Objections like Hempel's are plausible only if applied to the topic of folk-psychological explanations, not to the issue of prediction. Yet even if one admits that knowledge of psychological generalizations is important for the epistemic justification of the explanation of action, one is forced to concede a special epistemic role for empathy as long as such explanations are reason explanations using the folk-psychological vocabulary of belief and desire. Belief and desire explanations count as proper explanations only if they can also be comprehended as reasons for an agent's actions. And this is possible only in view of our reenactive capacities. Said differently, what makes a folk-psychological explanation epistemically special is that the information relevant to it—even if, as Hempel quite correctly insists, this information includes knowledge of psychological generalizations—can be counted as an explanation only in light of our empathetic abilities.

I will develop my argument for this claim through a critical discussion of the Dray–Hempel debate about empathy's epistemic role. Hempel objects to empathy in light of his account of the nature of scientific explanation and prediction, which for a long time has determined the parameters of this debate (see for the following Hempel 1965, chaps. 9–10). As is well known, Hempel conceives of explanations as arguments of a certain form; these are the so-called *deductive nomological* and *inductive statistical* models. According to the deductive nomological model, an event is explained if and only if a sentence describing the occurrence of the event (the explanandum) can be logically derived from the explanans, that is, a set of true and empirically well-confirmed sentences containing singular statements asserting the occurrence of particular events and universal sentences representing deterministic laws of nature. Within the inductive statistical model, where the explanans contains laws of a merely probabilistic character, an event is explained if and only if the explanandum follows inductively with high probability from the explanans. Hempel's conception of explanation is motivated by the view that explanations address certain epistemic desiderata. They dissolve our puzzlement that leads us to ask "why did event *e* occur" by showing us that the occurrence of a particular event of a particular type was to be expected given the information provided in the explanans of an explanatory argument. Any given explanation is justified if and only if the information provided can be articulated in the form of one of the above arguments. Hempel allows for the fact, particularly in historical explanations, that we do not always mention all of the premises that are logically required for the derivation of the explanandum sentence. Such formally incomplete explanations are understood as "explanation sketches." Yet they can be regarded as explanation sketches only because they could in principle be turned into full-blown explanatory arguments involving appropriate lawlike generalizations.

Given his epistemic conception of explanation, it is no wonder that Hempel considered explanations and predictions to be structurally isomorphic. Since an explanation provides us with information that shows us that an event in the past was to be expected, it also supplies us with information for predicting the future occurrence of an event of the same type. The only difference between explanation and prediction is the fact that an explanatory argument derives a statement describing an event that has already happened, whereas a predictive argument derives a statement describing an event that has not yet occurred. The structural isomorphism of explanation and prediction implies the following two claims: "(i) that every adequate explanation is potentially a prediction" and "(ii) that conversely every adequate prediction is potentially an explanation" (Hempel 1965, 367). From an epistemic point of view, the differences between explanation and prediction are negligible, although it should be noted in passing that Hempel was firmly committed only to the first of these two theses (1965, 376).

From this perspective, empathy can be granted only a causal role in our devising specific explanatory hypothesis. It cannot be understood as contributing anything in the epistemic context. Otto Neurath has memorably articulated this Hempelian judgment by stating that "empathetic understanding (*Verstehen*) and the like may help the research worker, but they enter into the totality of scientific statements as little as does a good cup of coffee which also furthers the scholar in his work" (1973, 357).[2] Our empathetic abilities might allow us to articulate a causal hypothesis about the causes of a person's behavior, such as "Peter went to the kitchen because he wanted a beer and thought that it was in the refrigerator in the kitchen." To point out that I believe that this is so because I would have done the same thing in his situation might indeed explain causally why I thought of this folk-psychological hypothesis. Hempel seems even to allow that empathy might justify why we should try to find further evidentiary support for this hypothesis instead of the hypothesis, say, that I went to the kitchen because I thought that $2 + 2 = 4$. Yet my causal hypothesis can be justified only in light of lawlike generalizations. Recognizing that I would have done the same thing as Peter does not dissolve the puzzlement that motivated us to ask the above why-question in the first place with sufficient generality. It immediately invites the question of why I acted in this situation in the same manner as Peter. Justifying an explanatory hypothesis in terms of the mechanism that caused me to articulate the folk-psychological interpretation is like answering the question of why the window broke when Peter threw a baseball at it by pointing out that it would also have broken had I would thrown the baseball.

Hempel's epistemic conception of the function of explanations and his understanding of explanations as arguments with specific logical structures have for a long time been regarded as philosophical orthodoxy. In recent years, though, his view has fallen on hard times. As has been conclusively shown, his deductive nomological model and inductive statistical model articulate neither necessary nor sufficient conditions for what we intuitively accept as an explanation within ordinary and scientific contexts. (For a survey see Salmon 1989 and Ruben 1990.) Here is not the place to bore the reader with an extensive repetition of the persuasive counterexamples against Hempel. For our purposes of evaluating the epistemic role of empathy it is important to emphasize that with the rejection of Hempel's model of explanation we also discard the view that explanation and prediction are structurally isomorphic and epistemically on a par. As the well-known barometer example shows, we certainly can use the information about the lawful correlation between a barometer's needle falling and a storm approaching in order to predict that a storm will occur. But this information is insufficient for explaining the occurrence of the storm. In addition, explaining an event does not require information that would enable us to justifiably predict its occurrence. Even if, as the paresis example illustrates, it is not likely that somebody with a syphilis infection will develop paresis (its tertiary state), we still explain its factual occurrence in a person by citing the syphilis infection. If we reject the thesis about the epistemic symmetry between prediction and explanation associated with Hempel's model of explanation, then we also have to provide separate models for analyzing the criteria by which we implicitly judge the epistemic adequacy of a prediction and an explanation. Arguments against empathy that have been developed in a context focusing for the most part on questions of explanations do not automatically carry over to objections against empathy's role in predictions as has been assumed in the traditional debate in the philosophy of social science. The epistemic evaluation of empathy has to distinguish strictly between its function in the context of folk-psychological prediction and its function in the context of folk-psychological explanation.

5.1 Empathy, Folk-Psychological Predictions, and Explanations

Rejecting the epistemic symmetry between prediction and explanation does not imply, however, that predictions are never justified in terms of information that would be sufficient for explanatory purposes. Even though not all explanatory information allows us to justify to a sufficient degree a prediction that a particular event will occur, there certainly are some explanations that do correspond to Hempel's model. In such a case we seem to be able to use the information in an analogous fashion for predictive purposes. Indeed scientific predictions to a large extent seem to conform to this model, since scientists tend to make use of their causal explanatory theories for predictive purposes using the same lawlike generalizations that they use to explain events in order to derive certain conclusions about the likelihood of the occurrence of future events. Such predictions could therefore be justified only in light of rich theoretical knowledge.

The fact that we do at times require rich theoretical knowledge in order to back up predictions should not make us overlook that not all predictions demand such a rich theoretical background. I would like to suggest that rich theoretical knowledge is required to back up a prediction only in specific contexts, certainly when a theory is used as a tool for predictive purposes. But theories are not our only tools for prediction. Often we base a prediction on readings from various instruments that have proven to be reliable indicators of states of affairs in the world. I predict the weather in the near future by looking at a barometer. I could justify my prediction that it will rain in the near future by pointing out that the barometer says so. In justifying my weather prediction in this manner I certainly assume that the barometer is in working order and that barometers that are not broken tend to be reliable indicators of weather in the near future. My inference from reading the barometer to the prediction that it will rain can be seen as epistemically mediated by a general belief about the reliability of barometers. Yet these generalizations in no way constitute a rich theory about how the barometer works internally and to what properties in the world it is sensitive in order to "calculate" that it will rain tomorrow. Such knowledge definitely would provide us with a deeper understanding of the working of the barometer by explaining why it is such a reliable tool. One might also concede that having such an explanatory theory would increase our epistemic justification for using the barometer. Ordinarily, however, we do not require that we are in possession of such a theory in order for our predictions to be justified. Even if one is an epistemic internalist, it seems too high a requirement for the justification of a prediction based on the use of certain instruments to require knowledge of a full-blown theory about how the instrument works. Possession of such a theory is not the only manner in which we can acquire reasons for believing in the reliability of instruments; assumptions about the reliability of a predictive tool can also be defended on an inductive basis in light of its past predictive success. I might for example have noticed that certain changes in how my joints feel are reliable indicators of changes in the weather. I can thus predict that damp and rainy days are approaching based on the fact that my arthritic joints are acting up. There certainly is (even though I am not familiar with it) a complex meteorological and biological theory that is able to explain why my joints act up in this manner, and such a theory would also enable us to provide weather predictions independent of my joints acting up. But weather predictions based on the feeling in my joints would still be justified, even though they could provide only a very limited, local, and not very long-lasting method of weather prediction. The fact that we do not trust the phenomenal qualities of a person with arthritic joints for predicting the weather has nothing to do with a lack of theory, but rather with the fact that such feelings tend not to be sufficiently reliable indicators of the weather.

In predicting another person's behavior using empathy and simulation, I use myself in a very specific manner as a predictive tool. As in the case of any other predictive tool, in taking my prediction to be epistemically justified I presuppose that my simulating your thought processes is a reliable tool for the prediction of your behavior. It also should be granted that this assumption minimally presupposes that I am *psychologically similar in the relevant respects* and that my cognitive system mirrors the functioning of your cognitive system, since such presuppositions would easily account for my being such a reliable predictor. But, at least in ordinary contexts, it is not the case that the only way to justify this "minimal theoretical background assumption" (Davies and Stone 2001) is by reference to a rich psychological theory detailing the exact functioning of the human mind. Instead, the assumption of psychological similarity could also be justified inductively by pointing to the past successes of our simulative procedures. As far as mechanisms of basic empathy are concerned, one can for example point to the fact that human beings are quite good at recognizing emotions—at least the basic emotions (Ekman and Davidson 1994)—from facial expression alone. Inductive evidence for reenactive empathy appears to be provided by our ability to follow rather complex arguments and conversations in ordinary contexts. In this context, one thought or utterance does not merely causally follow another. Rather, being able to follow a conversation in this manner requires an ability to grasp the inherent reasons for various utterances made (Harris 1996). The fact that human beings engage cooperatively in practices that are normatively structured can be regarded as evidence for the assumption that simulation is a reliable procedure for understanding the thoughts of others and that human beings are psychologically similar in the relevant respects.[3] A proponent of the empathy view is thus not forced to grant that viewing folk-psychological predictions as epistemically justified depends on implicitly admitting the truth of specific folk-psychological generalizations that outline the interaction of various mental states. Even in the epistemic context of justifying a specific explanation, empathy cannot be regarded as a mere causal heuristic.

The situation regarding folk-psychological explanation is more complex, since there are good reasons to think that causal explanations do implicitly depend on or presuppose the truth of specific kinds of empirical generalizations, regardless of whether one agrees with Hempel's specific logical analysis of the structure of explanation. Here I do not want to engage in a survey of the various conceptions that have been developed in response to the difficulties facing Hempel's model. I take it as an implication of this debate that causal explanations of an event e are best viewed as answers to why-questions that provide information about causally relevant aspects of the world "involved" in bringing about e. It is a necessary condition that causal explanations of the occurrence of e mention its cause c. But merely mentioning and identifying the cause of event e is not sufficient for providing an explanation for its occurrence. Information about causal relations also needs to use specific conceptual resources in identifying causes in order for such information to have any explanatory import or to count as an answer to a why-question (Kim 1999; Davidson 1980). These intuitions are best illustrated by analyzing the difference between singular causal statements (SC statements), such as "The event that was described on the front page of the *New York Times* caused the event described on the front page of the *Frankfurter Allgemeine*," and singular causal explanatory statements (SE statements), such as "A major fire started in a Texas oil refinery because an oil storage tank exploded." SC-type statements provide information that a certain event c caused another event e. They do not satisfy our curiosity as to why event e occurred. The reason for this has to do

always susceptible to interferences from outside of its domain. Psychological processes described in mental terms, for example, assume the normal functioning of the brain and the invariance of other physical factors such as a certain range of external and internal temperature. Any amount of deviation in this respect might affect the conditions under which the ceteris paribus generalizations apply. It is particularly troublesome that we seem to be practically unable to specify the almost infinite number of these potentially interfering factors. Without such knowledge, we cannot know whether all other things are indeed equal. If the above claims would indeed be true of ceteris paribus generalizations, they would seem to be too vague to be of any great scientific or explanatory use (Schiffer 1991).[4] We would have no practical way of empirically confirming or disconfirming them since we cannot know whether a particular instance is genuinely disconfirming the asserted regularity or instead is due to the fact that other things are not equal (for an overview see Henderson 1993; Pietroski and Rey 1995; Rosenberg 1995b). Moreover, it is unclear how ceteris paribus generalizations could ever support explanations, because in order to accept an account of events in terms of ceteris paribus generalizations as an answer to a why-question we would need to first know whether other things are indeed equal.

Requiring that explanations have to be underwritten by laws in the traditional sense exerts pressure on us to find ways of fixing these perceived shortcomings of ceteris paribus generalizations (cp-generalizations). Otherwise, our only option is to declare that even highly respected special sciences like biology are unable to provide any explanations. After the decline of logical positivism, such a conclusion is generally regarded as outright preposterous. Contemporary philosophers regard a philosophical analysis of the nature of explanation acceptable only if it is based on an analysis of actual scientific practice; they would never declare a scientific practice to be void merely because it does not correspond to their favorite philosophical theory. Motivated in this manner, Pietroski and Rey (1995) have suggested that cp-generalizations within the special sciences could be granted the status of explanation-supporting nonvacuous cp-laws as long as one can conceive of cp-clauses as "cheques written on the bank of independent theories" (1995, 89). Such checks are promises for future characterizations of the conditions under which a certain generalizations holds. They also enable us also explain why the behavior of a system deviates from predicted behavior in terms of such interfering factors. Cp-generalizations of the form "If x is G, then ceteris paribus, x is F" can thus be viewed to be nonvacuous. If true, they can support explanations since they promise that they can be transformed into exceptionless laws of the form "In condition C, if x is G then x is F," where the vocabulary used to characterize C does not have to be limited to the vocabulary of the special sciences. Pietroski and Rey mention Boyle's ideal gas law, $PV = nRT$, as an example of such a ceteris paribus law. It supports explanations, since any exception to it is explicable in principle in terms of interfering factors such as electrical attraction between the molecules and others (ibid., 89–90). Pietroski and Rey, however, emphasize that their view commits them only to viewing cp-laws as implicitly postulating the existence of theories that characterize the relevant conditions. They do not require that we know exactly how to transform ceteris paribus generalizations into exceptionless laws that describe in detail the conditions when certain systems will fully conform to its generalization (ibid., 93). Since typically we are not able to do this in our existing scientific practices, requiring such ability would indeed seem tantamount to declaring much of our existing scientific practices to be explanatorily void.

Implicit in the above conception of cp-generalizations is the contention that explanations in light of fully characterized conditions are always explanations in a fuller sense than explanations that leave such characterization as an open promise. Explanations in the special sciences would still not be granted the same status as explanations in the basic sciences such as physics, assuming for a moment that one can find strict and exceptionless laws within this realm. Philosophically speaking such explanations can only be regarded as explanatory promises; though we have some reason to believe that these promises will be kept since our special sciences are rather successful. I view the position that the explanations in the special sciences are not complete explanations to be counterintuitive. I agree with Woodward (2000, 2003), who considers the presupposition that explanations in the special sciences require exceptionless laws to be fundamentally misguided. In explaining certain economic facts in terms of various economic factors—for example, explaining the rise of the prize of oil in terms of demand and supply—one appeals implicitly to various cp-generalizations. Yet the value of an SE-explanation does not seem to increase if we mention factors that characterize the cp-clauses of such generalizations, such as the fact that the human brain is organized in a certain manner, and so on. My SE-explanation of why Peter went to Boston by car rather than by train does not improve if I mention not only the relevant beliefs and desires—he wanted go to Boston the fastest way—but also the conditions under which folk-psychological generalizations hold. My explanation is not strengthened if I bring up the fact that Peter's internal body temperature was under 104° Fahrenheit, even if it is the case that the relevant folk-psychological generalizations hold only if a person's body's temperature stays under 104° Fahrenheit for a certain period of time. Mentioning such factors, which would have to be included in our characterization of background conditions, does not increase the explanatory value of a given SE-explanation because these factors are compatible with a variety of economic states or psychological states, some of which would have led to very different economic outcomes or to very different behavior on Peter's side. Mentioning those factors is irrelevant to answering specific why-questions regarding a specific economic fact, a particular mental state, or a specific action. At most, describing such factors would be important for answering a different why-question such as why we should expect that the implicit generalization appealed to in this context can be expected to hold (Woodward 2000, 2003).

One is easily tempted to regard all factors characterizing background conditions as implicitly supporting our explanatory practices if one insufficiently distinguishes issues of ontology from issues of the epistemology of explanation as far as the special sciences are concerned. Ontologically speaking—at least within the framework of contemporary physicalism—the macroscopic properties appealed to in the practices of the special sciences have to be regarded as in some sense dependening and supervening on microphysical properties (Poland 1994). Given this ontological commitment, one can assume that the scope of a special science can be circumscribed in terms of the vocabulary of the lower sciences. One has reason to expect that ceteris paribus generalizations in the special sciences are in principle completable in terms of interfering factors, some of which will have to be described in the vocabulary of the lower sciences.[5] The existence of the supervenience base is a general ontological precondition for the existence of the macroscopic properties in light of which the special sciences constitute themselves and define their explanatory interests. It does not imply that knowledge of such exceptionless generalizations—outlining the boundary conditions of such ceteris paribus generalizations in terms of supervenience properties—are of greater explanatory worth within the scope of the special science itself, since within its scope we are primarily interested in answering specific why-questions formulated with its conceptual resources. Each and every one of its explanations has as its implicit ontological presupposition that we are within the respective domain of the special science and its particular conceptual resources. This ontological presupposition is made already in taking up the perspective defined by the conceptual resources of a special science itself. It does not enhance the credibility of a particular explanatory hypothesis as an answer to a why-question formulated with the help of those conceptual resources if one explicitly mentions properties from the supervenience base that are ontologically constitutive of the macroscopic properties appealed to in the special sciences (see also Stueber 2005a).

Thus I regard the requirement that explanations be supported by laws in the traditional sense to be a red herring.[6] Nevertheless I regard the intuition that SE statements are supported by generalizations to be sound, and I am very sympathetic to Woodward's account of explanation (Woodward 2000, 2003; Woodward and Hitchcock 2003).[7] In the following I will use Woodward's position as the framework within which I will discuss the epistemic function of empathy in folk-psychological explanation. Woodward escapes the above conundrum about the status of ceteris paribus laws by suggesting that it is not lawfulness in the traditional sense that distinguishes an explanation-supporting generalization from an accidental one but invariance for a particular explanatory domain. More specifically he conceives of an invariant generalization as a generalization that allows us to understand certain "counterfactual dependencies" among properties of the systems in question. He defines a generalization to be invariant "if it continues to hold under an appropriate class of changes involving interventions on the variables figuring in that generalization" (Woodward and Hitchcock 2003, 2). Without getting too technical, we may say an intervention on a variable of a generalization is taken to be any change in the antecedent variable X in a situation where any subsequent alteration in the consequent variable Y occurs only because of the modification in the antecedent variable and not because of any causal factors Z that are independent of X. An example of such intervention is the manipulation of various variables in an idealized experimental situation where one tries to make sure that the observed changes in Y are due only to manipulated changes in the value X and not some other extraneous factors independent of X (Woodward 2003, chap. 3). To use a well-worn example, the generalization "If you take a common antibiotic (X) it will cure the cold (Y)" is not an invariant generalization, even if after taking the antibiotic for two weeks you find that the cold is cured. Merely doing nothing for two weeks (Z) will also most likely cure the cold and will do so independent of X. Invariant generalizations let us not only expect the occurrence of a particular event, a feature Hempel stressed in his account of explanation. They also explain the occurrence of an event by enabling us also to answer "a range of *what-if-things-had-been-different questions*" (Woodward and Hitchcock 2003, 4).

Universally valid and exceptionless laws are invariant generalizations, yet for a generalization to be invariant and to have explanatory value it need not be invariant in all possible situations. Rather, invariance has to be understood as relativized to a particular domain or set of background conditions.[8] Following a suggestion by Henderson (2005), who uses Woodward's model to account for the explanatory role of norms in the social sciences, political scientists can explain why most Americans drive on the right side of the road by pointing out that it is a law to drive on the right side of the road. One thereby implicitly appeals to a generalization such as "If X is a law in America, most people tend to conform to X." Such generalizations are not universal laws in the traditional sense. Rather it is an invariant generalization relative to a domain characterized by a particular political system, a system of making, publicizing, and enforcing laws in the absence of war, and so on. Within this domain, changing the law of which side of the road to drive on would also change the behavior of drivers in America. For reasons similar to the one I explicated above, Woodward, however, regards the domain of the generalization as not itself part of the generalization (2003, 273–274). As long as the situation and explanandum that we are concerned with are within the domain of the invariance, we are able to explain the occurrence of a particular event in terms of the variables of the generalization. In this situation, adding a description of the domain to the explanation does not increase the explanatory value of the given explanation, since a description of these properties characterizing the domain does not allow us to answer any *what-if-things-had-been-different question*. Pointing out that we are not within the domain of an invariant generalization is equivalent to rejecting a certain explanatory perspective and directing us to use a different explanatory scheme. Yet recognizing that we are outside of the domain of a generalization does not automatically provide us with an alternative explanation for the explanandum.

The upshot of all of the above considerations is that even if one rejects Hempel's specific model of explanation, his general objection against empathy in the context of explanation still seems to apply. If folk psychology is in the business of explanation, and explanations demand invariant generalizations, then it is no longer so clear what, if any, epistemic role empathy or reenactment plays within this context. Folk-psychological explanations would seem to imply a heavy dose of psychological theory as proposed by the theory-theory position, even if these generalizations are not causally involved in the production of singular SE statement using the folk-psychological idiom. Even though folk-psychological generalizations certainly cannot be regarded as strict and exceptionless laws of nature, prima facie they do satisfy the condition of being invariant generalizations in the above sense. I explain why Peter drove over the bridge rather than take a boat to reach the other side of the river by pointing to his desire that he wanted to reach the other side and he thought that taking the bridge was the most reliable way of getting to the other side. I hereby presuppose a generalization that comes close to something like the central action principle. This principle appears to be invariant for a certain domain that we will characterize a bit more later on. If I intervene in this situation—holding Peter's desire steady (and his various other beliefs and desires) by changing his belief in suggesting to him that the bridge will collapse under the weight of his car, I will in all likelihood also have changed his behavior. Certainly such a prediction is prima facie empirically testable.[9]

Showing that empathy is central even within the epistemic context of justifying a folk-psychological explanation would require additional arguments. Such attempts to argue for empathy principally take two forms. One can try to argue for empathy in accepting the above account of explanation, or one can try to argue for empathy by rejecting it for the realm of action explanation. Traditionally, followers of Collingwood like Dray have unfortunately chosen the second option. Dray objects to the above account of explanation as irrelevant to the realm of action explanation. He would also deny that action explanations are supported by empirical generalizations.[10] For Dray, the fact that action explanations rather than other event explanations account for a person's behavior in terms of his reasons implies "a distinction between explanation types, a distinction between representing something as the thing generally done, and representing it as the appropriate thing to have done" (1957, 128). Accordingly, Dray maintains that our notion of causation is fundamentally ambiguous. He distinguishes what one could call "natural necessity," to which we appeal in our explanations of natural events, from "rational necessity" that underlies our causal account of agency. Dray admits that reasons for actions possess a kind of universality that can be explicated in terms of general principles such as when in "situation of type C1 ... C*n*, the thing to do is *x*." But these general principles should not be confused with empirical and descriptive statements about how people in general will act in certain situations. Rather they are to be seen as normative "principles of actions" that are not falsifiable by negative instances (Dray 1957, 132).

Yet, as Hempel has pointed out, Dray's conception cannot in any charitable sense be understood as providing a causal explanatory account of another person's actions. In appealing to normative principles of action, one would at most explain "why it would have been rational for *A* to do *x*," not "why *A* did in fact do *x*" (Hempel 1965, 471). Hempel suggests that in order to provide a causal explanatory account of rational agency it is insufficient to merely appeal to normative principles explicating what would be the rational thing to do in a particular situation; we also need the further assumption that agents are as a matter of fact rational and that such principles therefore also do describe the causal dispositions of these agents.[11]

It is therefore useful to look more closely at some of Kim's brief observations about reason explanations, since they are best understood as an explication of a position (hinted at by Dray) that does not suffer from the above shortcomings. In current philosophy of mind, Kim is best known for his contribution to the debate over mental causation in articulating the powerful causal explanatory exclusion argument (Kim 1993, 1998b; see also Stueber 1997b, 2005a). In two of his lesser-known articles, Kim directly addresses the nature of rational action explanation by suggesting that beliefs and desires conceived of as reasons do not play a primary role within the "causal-predictive" framework of accounting for an agent's behavior and his "overt physical and bodily movements" from the third-person perspectives (Kim 1984, 316, 319; 1998a, 85). Rather, rationalizing action explanations are concerned primarily with accounting for a different explanandum that involves essentially the first-person perspective. We appeal to reasons in explaining why the agent formed certain intentions and made decisions. Kim bases his suggestions about rational action explanations on considerations about the nature of agency similar to those we explicated earlier. Beliefs and desires cannot be understood as merely internal events whose occurrence allows me to predict with a certain probability what I will do next in the manner that being aware of an itch in my throat allows me to realize that I will cough soon. Rather, from the first-person perspective beliefs and desires function as reasons "on the basis of which I chose, or decided, to do this action" (Kim 1998a, 77). Kim rejects the idea that a principle assumed to be involved in action explanations such as the central action principle can be conceived of as an empirical generalization because such understanding fails to recognize it as a "principle that underlies the self-understanding of actions" (ibid., 74). Conceiving of the central action principle as an empirical generalization on par with other explanation-supporting principles would treat beliefs and desires as internal events that lead only with a certain probability to decision and action. In treating the central action principle as primarily belonging to the "third-person causal predictive stance," we fail to account for the role of beliefs and desires as reasons for decisions within the first-person deliberative stance. Within the first-person deliberative stance reasons cannot be understood as mere causes that "naturally necessitate" my action independent of my recognizing them as my reasons. The central action principle is thus better understood as a "normative constraint on decision making and intention formation" (Kim 1984, 318; see also 1998a, 77). Accordingly, rationally explaining the actions of others requires us to treat them as agents who deliberate about their actions and decide to act based on their reasons. Treating other agents in this manner implies, however, as our considerations regarding the essential indexicality of rational thought have shown, conceiving of them as possessing a first-person perspective. On those grounds we can agree with Kim that it requires us to project "to them the way we understand our own actions" (Kim 1998a, 84; see also 1984, 319).

Like Dray, Kim regards our notions of explanation and causation to be fundamentally ambiguous. Rationalizing explanations involve a normative element. They do not appeal to nomological causation or "natural necessity"; rather they constitute a form of justificatory explanation and appeal, as Dray suggests, to a type of rational necessity. Yet by linking reason explanation directly to the moment of reflexive awareness on part of the agent,

Kim, in contrast to Dray, is able to account for the epistemic difference between rational action explanation and event explanation. Empathy is required because only in this manner are we able to see others as agents who struggle to gain a consistent view of themselves. Yet Kim's position still falls short of providing an account of the explanatory force of reason explanations even if we agree with him that reason explanations account only for the intentions and decisions of agents and do not explain their actions. Hempel's objection to Dray can be easily reformulated on this level. Given our explication of the nature of explanation, explaining why somebody formed certain intentions and made decisions in a certain manner still requires implicit reference to invariant generalizations. Pointing to the fact that the central action principle is understood from the first-person perspective as a normative principle only tells us why somebody should think that a certain decision would be rational in a certain situation. It does not tell us why that person actually made that decision.

Certainly we can agree with Kim that in relating to other agents on the basis of empathy we somehow understand them as agents having a first-person point of view. What he fails to explain, however, is why relating to others in this manner should also count as an explanation of their decision without requiring reference to empirical generalizations and theoretical knowledge. In limiting reason explanations to the domain of intentions and decisions, we seem to be forever banned from conceiving of reason explanations as explaining the behavior that agents perform because of their decision. Such conception of reason explanation leads to a highly revisionary account of our folk-psychological practices. It seriously undermines our conception of ourselves as agents who can be held responsible for our actions since we act because of our decisions or intentions. For Kim, reasons, however, cause decisions in a manner radically different from the way that physical events cause each other. Yet for decisions to be conceived of as mental events that cause further bodily movements, they would have to cause actions in an ordinary sense, in the manner that physical events cause other physical events. Decisions would thus have to be conceived of as being causes in a very different sense than reasons for such decisions. Such a bifurcation of mental causation is deeply counterintuitive and not supported by our ordinary explanatory practices. At a minimum, such a position constitutes a radical revision of our ordinary explanatory practices, in which we normally refer to beliefs, desires, emotions, and other mental states not just to explain decisions but also to explain the ensuing actions.

According to our ordinary understanding, mental states such as pain and more complex emotions can cause our behavior in a direct manner, thereby circumventing our deliberative and reflective capacities. If such mental states can cause events in the ordinary sense, why should this not be possible for beliefs and desires? Moreover, Kim not merely bifurcates our notion of causation, he also bifurcates our ordinary understanding of our concepts of belief and desire. Whereas he situates our understanding of belief and desire in his 1984 article exclusively within the first-person perspective, he allows in his later article for the possibility that the central action principle can also serve as an empirical and descriptive principle for the prediction of action from the detached third-person perspective (Kim 1998a, 82, 79). These two stances have to be strictly distinguished since from the third-person perspective, where we appeal to empirical generalizations, beliefs and desires cannot be understood as reasons for a decision and as the basis for the agent's self-understanding. They are conceived of merely as internal causes that have certain external and bodily effects. In treating beliefs and desires in this manner we treat them similarly to any other theoretical entities of a comprehensive theory in a particular domain, and not as reasons directly accessible to the agent.

Kim is unable to explicate one of the central presuppositions of our folk-psychological practice, that is, that we causally explain human agency by appealing to agents' reasons for their actions. Kim's position encounters the following conundrum. If we think of belief and desire as explaining action or decision making in the ordinary sense, requiring reference to empirical generalizations, then we do not explain the agent's actions in terms of his or her reasons. But if we appeal in a projective or empathetic mood to an agent's reason without referring to any empirical generalization, it is not at all clear why we should regard such an account to have any explanatory power at all. Kim, however, fails to realize that within the folk-psychological framework the explanatory third-person stance cannot be neatly separated from the first-person stance. What Kim fails to notice is that one can explain an action in terms of belief and desire only if we at the same time recognize those beliefs also as reasons for the other person's actions. If we cannot do this, any appeal to belief and desire and folk-psychological generalization tends to lose its explanatory force. An example by MacIntyre (1986, 73) might be useful in this context. MacIntyre discusses the case of a scientist who snatches and eats the only specimen of a hybrid fruit that he knows has been developed to allow people to survive in a particularly poverty-ridden and famine-endangered section of the world. MacIntyre is quite right to suggest that pointing out that the person ate this fruit because he was hungry and he likes fruit fails to render this action intelligible to us. Given that he otherwise seems to be a "normal" person, he would have all the reasons in the world not to eat this particular piece of fruit. In order to understand how such beliefs and desires are his reasons for his action we would minimally have to know a lot more of his other beliefs and desires that would allow us to understand those beliefs and desires as his reasons. I would like to suggest that pointing to such desires and the appropriate belief set in the above manner without enabling us to conceive of them as reasons for his actions not only fails to make his action intelligible; it also undermines our attempt to provide an explanatory account of his behavior. The reason for this explanatory failure has nothing to do with the fact that folk-psychological generalizations do not have the status of laws. As I have argued, following Woodward, explanations do not necessarily require laws. Rather, one should think of the failure of the cited belief and desire pair to explain the action analogously to the failure of any explanation in terms of a vocabulary that is being applied outside of its proper domain. Or to say it slightly differently, we cannot accept the above belief/desire explanation because we have grave doubts about whether it is being applied within its proper domain.

After all that has been said, it should be obvious that I regard rational agency as the proper explanatory domain for our folk-psychological vocabulary. Further empirical research will certainly allow us to circumscribe the scope of this domain more precisely either in terms of underlying neurobiological mechanisms or even in terms of certain cognitive tests such as the IQ test. Yet we recognize whether we are within the folk-psychological domain by whether we are able to relate to other persons in terms of mechanisms of basic empathy and reenactive empathy. It is an essential attribute of the domain of folk-psychological explanations that we can accept them only as long as we are also able to grasp how the cited beliefs and desires can be reasons for one's actions in a particular situation. Given our understanding of the rationality assumption within the folk-psychological realm, we can explain the action of an agent in terms of his beliefs and desires only if we are simultaneously able to see his beliefs and desires in the situation that the agents finds himself as his reasons for his actions. We for example explain Bismarck's slightly editing and publishing a telegram sent to him by the Prussian King—the so called Ems telegram—in terms of his desire to start a war between France and Prussia, his hope that publishing the telegram would give the impression that the French emissary was badly treated by the Prussian King, and his belief that this might lead France to declare war with Prussia (for the full example see Hempel 1965, 479–480). Notice, however, that in my account of folk-psychological explanation, in granting any explanatory force to the above account of Bismarck's behavior we are committed to the claim that, given this situation and the invariance of any of his other psychological states, Bismarck, or any other person with his psychological states, would have acted differently if he had not had the cited beliefs and desires. It is for this reason that we regard folk-psychological generalizations such as the central action principle as being implicitly appealed to in the folk-psychological context. But they are able to back up the specific explanations only if we are not in doubt that we are within the proper domain of folk psychology—that is, as long as we are able to reconstruct the cited beliefs and desires also as reasons of a particular person to act in specific circumstances.

Given my reconstruction of the nature of explanation one can therefore admit that we refer at least implicitly to generalizations in providing folk-psychological explanations of behavior. As far as the epistemology of folk-psychological explanations is concerned, one has to admit that folk psychology cannot be as knowledge poor as suggested by simulation theorists who focus mainly on questions of underlying causal mechanisms. Nevertheless, a proponent of the empathy view can happily concede all of the above since it does not follow that we have to view empathy as playing merely a heuristic role within the context of discovery. The arguments from the essential contextuality and indexicality of rational thought not only allow us to reject theory theory as an adequate interpretation of the underlying causal mechanisms of our folk-psychological practice. They also allow us to assert empathy's epistemic role in the evaluation of explanatory proposals within the folk-psychological context. If the arguments from the essential contextuality and indexicality of thought hold up, then it is only in light of our capacities of reenactive empathy that we are able to judge or raise doubts about whether or not we are within the proper domain of folk psychology dealing with the explanation of rational agency.

6   The Limits of Empathy

Philosophers of social science have objected to the notion of empathy not only because they see our understanding of other agents primarily as a theoretical enterprise. Philosophers from the hermeneutic and Wittgensteinian traditions agree with proponents of empathy that interpretation in the human realm cannot be conceived of on such a theoretical model. Yet they have given up on the concept of empathy as well and generally adopted the concept of understanding to express their opposition to conceiving of the interpretive project in the human realm on the model of the natural sciences. Hence to point to empathy as the basic epistemic means of interpretation in the human sciences is the wrong way to argue against the assumption of methodological monism in the philosophy of social science. To thus rely on empathy expresses a Cartesian quest for certainty that is impossible to achieve, especially in the realm of human history and human affairs. In the end, the proponents of empathy can only be understood as opposing methodological monism by sharing some of the basic assumptions of the positivist position that they oppose, for example, the misguided empiricist presupposition that there is such a thing as theory-free perception. In this vein, Gadamer accuses Collingwood of striving for a "cognitive ideal familiar to us from the knowledge of nature, where we understand a process only when we are able to reproduce it artificially" and "as having not fully made the transition from the narrowness of psychology to historical hermeneutics" (Gadamer 1989, 373, 513).

Whereas the debate between simulation theorists and theory theorists in current philosophy of mind and the discussion between Dray and Hempel in philosophy of social science focused on the role generalizations play in the interpretation of other agents, the critique of empathy from a hermeneutic and Wittgensteinian perspective is best understood as concentrating on the question of whether we are able to account for the relevant differences between interpreter and interpretee in the manner suggested by contemporary simulation theory (Makkreel 2000; Kögler 2000). This topic becomes particularly methodologically virulent in the human sciences when we apply our ordinary folk-psychological techniques in a context of greater historical distance and more extensive cultural differences between interpreter and interpretee. Unless we can respond to these worries, we cannot assume that the information gained in the simulation phase allows us to understand the actions of the other person in those circumstances.

6.1 Objections and Misconceptions in the Philosophy of Social Science

Critics of empathy tend to be united in claiming that making sense of agency requires taking into account larger cultural background conditions. They also claim that differences in these conditions cannot be adequately dealt with on the basis of empathy. Whereas I am more than willing to admit that this topic has not received the attention it deserves in the current debate, the critique of empathy from this perspective is not as philosophically devastating as commonly thought within hermeneutic circles. Philosophers of social science tend to assume, falsely, that proponents of empathy are committed to a Cartesian view of the mind. Nonetheless, addressing the objections will force us to characterize more precisely the proper scope of the "method" of empathy. It will also force us to acknowledge certain epistemic limitations in using empathy to interpret agents who are from very different cultures. In such situations, our attempt to make sense of other agents by trying to reenact their reasons for their actions has to be supplemented by further cognitive strategies and different theoretical considerations. Still, even if one has to appeal to supplemental strategies, empathy has to be regarded as epistemically essential for judging the plausibility of any interpretive hypothesis. It has to be understood as the central epistemic default method in our relations to other agents since it is only in light of the difficulties that we face in grasping another person's reasons for his actions that those supplemental strategies can be viewed to be explanatorily relevant.

Before I address these specific concerns, I would like to guard against possible misunderstandings of my defense of empathy that might arise if one misleadingly reads it in light of the nineteenth-century defense of empathy as the unique method of the human sciences. I do not claim that it is the unique and only viable explanatory strategy to account for human affairs. My defense of empathy is limited to its being of central epistemic importance to interpreting individual and rational agency. Empathy is epistemically important within the context of the human sciences as long as such sciences view an account of individual agency as central to their purposes. Whether or not they necessarily have to do so has been the topic of a wide-ranging debate within the philosophy of social science that I do not have space to adequately address in this context (see Rosenberg 1995a; MacDonald and Pettit 1981; Pettit 1993). I am prepared to argue that the explanatory strategies in the human and social sciences have at some point to connect with or take notice of our folk-psychological account of individual agency. Yet I agree with hermeneutic theorists such as Gadamer (1989) that we must reject the purely psychological conception of the interpretive process as proposed by the early Dilthey. The task of the historian is not exhausted by accounting for actions of individual agents at a particular time and place, and it is not bound by the agent's perspective. Rather, historians also have to construct a narrative of a particular time-span that integrates various strands of intersecting causal chains seen as having particular significance for the construction of this narrative. Even in the historical sciences, empathy cannot be conceived of as exhausting the means with which we grasp various phenomena of significance. Still, I would insist that part of the proper account of grasping the larger historical significance of various individual actions includes understanding those intentions of the agent for which they as a matter of fact did act. I regard a wholehearted rejection of an agent's intentions as proper objects of interpretation to be implausible because it leaves us without any convincing account of human agency (Stueber 2002a, 2004).

Similarly, I do not take my defense of empathy to imply any particular position regarding the correct interpretation of texts, literary or otherwise. In particular I do not see my view as associated with the traditional claim that one can correctly interpret a text only in light of the intentions of its author (Hirsch 1967). Indeed I tend to agree with Gadamer (1989) that texts such as classical literary works, legal documents, or religious tracts possess a dimension of meaning and significance that is autonomous from the intentions of their authors (see the introduction to Kögler and Stueber 2000). But I am also a bit skeptical of Gadamer's claim that every aspect of textual meaning can be understood as independent of the author's intentions (see Skinner's contributions in Tully 1988). How important one regards the author's intentions for the interpretation of a text depends on the nature of the text at hand. For an interpretation of the Bible or Shakespeare's plays, recovering the author's intentions is probably less important than for the interpretation of a political pamphlet. Nevertheless, empathy is crucially involved in our understanding of fictional texts if those texts depict the actions of individuals. Since empathy is central to understanding individual agency it will have to play a role in grasping the intentions and actions of even fictional characters (see Harris 2000; Currie and Ravenscroft 2002; Walton 1997).

Both of the above topics are marginal to the interests of this book, even though they have played large roles in the rejection of empathy in the hermeneutic tradition. Within the philosophy of the social sciences, though, empathy was rejected not only because the traditional object of an empathetic reenactment was deemed to be unimportant for the human and social sciences; rather, the method of empathy has also been rejected by philosophers who think that the reconstruction of an agent's or author's intentions and his or her particular ideological perspective on the world is indeed a central interpretive task in the human sciences. To quote a few representative examples, Quentin Skinner emphasizes strongly that understanding texts requires "to recover the intentions with which they are written." He hastens to add "that this is not the mysterious empathetic process that old-fashioned hermeneutics may have led us to suppose" (Skinner in Tully 1988, 279). Similarly, Anthony Giddens contrasts empathy as "'reliving' or 'reenactment' of the experiences of others" with understanding as "a semantic matter" (Giddens 1976, 19–20). More recently, Mark Bevir, mentioning Collingwood explicitly, accuses commitment to reenactment as relying on an outdated conception of objectivity that is dependent on the idea of "pure perception" (Bevir 1999, 157–158).

I am not interested here in engaging in close textual exegesis of the writings of various authors opposed to empathy. Instead I am interested in distilling what I regard as the common thread in the counterarguments that could prima facie be applied to my defense of the epistemic centrality of empathy. Regardless of whether it is expressed in more Wittgensteinian or Heideggerian terminology (see Dreyfus 1991), any version of the opposition to empathy tends to be united with the rest in its claim that each agent's perspective is culturally and socially mediated in such a way that it is impossible for individual agents to abstract from deeply ingrained social and cultural presuppositions constitutive of their way of seeing the world. For that reason, it is impossible for anyone to enter directly into the mind of another person. From this perspective the interpretation of another person's action cannot be understood in merely psychological terms as a relation between two individuals; rather, one has to conceive of the interpretive act in a manner that acknowledges the cultural and social embeddedness of each individual.

Skinner's and Giddens's hostility toward empathy or reenactment as a mental act of understanding is directly influenced by Wittgensteinian considerations about the public or social constitution of mentality and mental concepts and by Wittgenstein's rejection of Cartesianism.[1] Accepting these Wittgensteinian premises and rejecting Cartesianism implies for the above philosophers that the interpretation of other agents in the folk-psychological framework must account for the significance and intelligibility of individual behavior within the wider public and social realm. The correctness of such an interpretation depends on the degree to which such a mentalistic redescription allows us to view individual behavior as being embedded in a larger external, social, and cultural context. Accordingly, mentality has to be understood as being constituted not by our intrinsic but by our relational properties to our environment broadly conceived, including natural, cultural, and social components. Thus conceived, understanding other minds is a purely public affair. To use Skinner's example, in order to understand a man's hand-waving as a warning, I have "to understand the intentions with which he is acting." "But," he continues, "to recover these intentions is not a matter of identifying the ideas inside his head.... It is merely a matter of grasping the fact that arm-waving can count as warning.... Nothing in the way of 'empathy' is required, since the meaning of the episode is entirely public and intersubjective" (Skinner in Tully 1988, 279).

Even if one agrees with Wittgensteinians in their rejection of Cartesianism, as I certainly do, it is still legitimate to wonder how it is possible to interpret a certain behavior such as an agent waving his hand as that agent's trying to warn another person unless we can also grasp that the agent has *reasons* to warn the other person in this particular situation. And if my considerations in this book are right so far, to grasp such reasons involves our empathetic abilities. Or, to put it differently, even if we agree with Skinner that such reasons or that the meaning of physical behavior is an inter-subjectively accessible fact that is not hidden in a private Cartesian realm, we could still legitimately ask how or by what mental process an interpreter might grasp such a public fact as that a hand-waving constitutes a warning. Yet such "natural" questions about how to conceive of the interpreting process are usually not addressed within the philosophy of social science influenced by either Wittgenstein or Heidegger. Such questions are regarded to be suspect, since they lead us onto a slippery slope that entices us to have a favorable impression of the discarded Cartesian position according to which minds are privately constituted and are not necessarily publicly and intersubjectively accessible entities. Within the Cartesian framework, empathy or reenactment indeed would have to be understood as a direct meeting of minds—a mystical union of souls—that is independent of and unaided by these minds' being embedded in a broader environment. For Cartesians such empathetic mindreading would also be possible in a world in which only mental substances exist.

I certainly agree with contemporary philosophers of social science that we should reject empathy if it commits us to a Cartesian conception of a mind. Empathy would indeed seem to be too mysterious an ability to be of use for serious philosophers and epistemologists, since we would not be able to justify our at times elaborate folk-psychological account of another person in any discursive manner. I would also admit that some formulations of "old-fashioned" hermeneutic philosophers, as Skinner refers to them, particularly of the nineteenth century, could mislead us into thinking that empathy has always been thought of in this mysterious and mystical fashion. Droysen, for example, distinguishes between the "logical mechanisms of understanding" and the "act of understanding" and describes the latter as "immediate intuition [*unmittelbare Intuition*], wherein soul blends with soul, creatively, after the manner of conception in coition" (Droysen 1893, §11). Yet such quotes should not be viewed out of context and have to be read together with Droysen's insistence that a historian has also to engage in the painstaking process of critically evaluating available sources, researching the various linguistic and social conventions, and so on.[2] Independent of whether some "old-fashioned" hermeneutic philosophers have conceived of empathy in an objectionable manner, neither my conception of empathy, nor Collingwood's conception of reenactment, nor any of the positions of contemporary simulation theorists is tied to an objectionable conception of empathy or to the Cartesian conception of the mind. In rejecting empathy on the above elaborated grounds, Wittgensteinians conflate two essentially separate issues. They confuse questions about whether minds are individualistically/atomistically or externalistically/socially constituted with questions about how minds understand and relate to each other. The Wittgensteinian critique of empathy therefore confuses questions of ontology with questions of epistemology. Whether or not empathy is important for our ability to understand other minds or important for a historian's understanding of past agents is an epistemological question. Even if our minds are socially constituted, this does not automatically answer the question of how we use such a socially constituted mind in understanding other agents.

My defense of empathy also does not entail that we grasp the reasons for another person's action independently of situating him at the same time in a complex environment. In this I am in agreement with Collingwood and contemporary simulation theorists, who emphasize that in simulating another person's thoughts we are not oriented toward the mental realm to the exclusion of viewing the person as embedded within a particular social and physical environment. We are trying to understand agents as being engaged with and as responding to the demands of an environment-as-they-conceive-of-it.[3] An agent is not rational primarily because he lives in a frictionless world in which anything goes and nothing is important. An agent is rational because the world allows him some choices between alternatives, choices that he has to evaluate as better or worse given his values, the conventions of his society, how he perceives the consequences of his action, and how limited his available resources are for implementing his decisions. To use Collingwood's example, in understanding the Theodosian Code, "we must envisage the situation with which the emperor was trying to deal, and we must envisage it as that emperor envisaged it. Then he [the historian] must see for himself, just as the emperor's situation were his own, how such a situation might be dealt with" (Collingwood 1946, 283).

Collingwood as a practicing historian was keenly aware that putting ourselves into the perspectives of agents from different historical and social contexts can be a rather difficult and laborious task. It cannot be accomplished without further knowledge about the constitution of an agent's social surroundings required for making appropriate guesses about relevant differences between us and the interpretee. As Collingwood's famous comparison of the work of a detective trying to solve the murder of John Doe with the work of a historian illustrates, reenactment cannot be conceived of as a method of "pure perception" that allows us to directly perceive mental facts (Collingwood 1946, 266–268). Rather, historians have to interpret the underlying thoughts and intentions of past agents and judge the correctness of their interpretation in the same manner that a detective tries to judge the reliability of a person's testimony and tries to determine the reasons for their testimony by determining whether it coheres with the other available evidence about the case. Reenacting the thoughts of the agent then presupposes that one reconstructs his situation from the available evidence, physical and otherwise. It also requires one to determine how the agent would have viewed his position by taking into account what he could have known about it, given his situation and the knowledge and conventions of his time. Only in this manner is the detective in Collingwood's example able to discount the confession of the murder by the "elderly neighbouring spinster," who was physically incapable of committing the deed, and interpret it as being motivated by the desire to save the real murderer.

There is no reason to claim that a defender of the epistemic centrality of empathy is committed to viewing empathy as a self-verifying act of pure perception. As we have already seen, contemporary simulation theorists are free to admit that some propositional knowledge plays a role in one's entering the correct initial state for simulation without repudiating their assertions that simulation is of central causal importance to our folk-psychological understanding of other agents. Similarly, the epistemic centrality of empathy is not diminished by admitting that we can make final decisions about the correctness of an interpretation only in light of additional evidentiary information, unless appeal to such evidence would make the need for empathy epistemically superfluous. Bevir (1999) objects to empathy for exactly these reasons. For him the use of empathy is methodologically inappropriate because it cannot objectively justify our choices among many plausible interpretive hypotheses. Did President Clinton, for example, sign the bill that ended welfare as we know it because he really thought it was a good idea or because he thought that signing the bill would rob the Republicans of a particular issue in the next elections? Both interpretations would allow us to understand him as rational, yet only one might be true. At most, one might argue, we should therefore grant reenactment a heuristic role in the context of discovery but it seems to play no role in the context of justification. For Bevir, the evaluation of the objectivity of intentional interpretations has to be conceived of in analogy to the evaluation of the objectivity of other scientific theories. Bevir views the attribution of intentional states to other agents like any other theoretical explication of natural phenomena, as an "inference to the best explanation" (Bevir 2002, 212).[4] Such an "inference" can be justified only by comparing it to rival accounts in terms of certain epistemic standards such as "accuracy, comprehensiveness, consistency, progressiveness, fruitfulness, and openness" (Bevir 1999, 125).

In response to Bevir's concerns, one has to admit that neither Collingwood's defense of reenactment nor the current discussion within philosophy of mind sufficiently takes into account the possibility of a plurality of intentional interpretations.[5] This is unfortunate since some of the central historical debates about how to interpret agents in folk-psychological terms arise because the evidence allows for different ways of reconstructing the context in which a particular agent acted. For that very reason, one can also attribute very different motives to particular agents. Chris Lorenz, for example, mentions the central debate in German history about how to interpret the September Memorandum by German Chancellor Bethmann Hollweg in 1914, which was written one month after the start of the First World War and in which he lists the occupation of half of Europe as a German goal (Lorenz 1997, 100–103). Historians differ in their judgments of whether the memorandum reveals Bethmann Hollweg's prewar imperialistic and aggressive intentions, or whether it should be better understood as expressing more defensive or moderate intentions given that the political right in Germany had even grander advances in mind and given the aggressive English plans to curtail Germany's access to the world's oceans. Lorenz points out that how one interprets the intentions of the author of the memorandum depends on how one views the context in which he acts. Which interpretation one views as correct depends on which reconstruction of Bethmann Hollweg's situation one finds to be better supported by the evidence.

However, admitting that choosing the correct interpretation from a plurality of plausible interpretations in folk-psychological terms requires further factual knowledge about an agent's situation is not equivalent to

admitting that empathy is epistemically irrelevant in such contexts. Analogously to my reasoning against Hempel in the last section, one has to recognize that our empathetic capabilities remain of central importance even
in this context since it is only in light of such capacities that we can recognize whether an interpretive hypothesis in the folk-psychological idiom is a
plausible contender for being the correct one in the first place. In this case
historians disagree with each other of how they should describe the political dilemma that Germany faced in the eyes of Bethmann Hollweg and for
which he tried to outline a rationally compelling solution in his memorandum. But in order to recognize the external context as a political dilemma
for Bethmann Hollweg we need to look at the situation through his eyes
using our reenactive or simulative capacities. The only reason for Bevir—
who emphasizes the importance of intellectual dilemmas for explaining
why a particular person changed his belief system or why a political author
develops a specific theory—to discount empathy (Bevir 1999, chap. 6) is
that he continues to think of it as being necessarily committed to the discarded empiricist conception of pure perception and the Cartesian conception of the mind.[6] Once we recognize that empathy does not have to be
conceived of in this manner, we must admit that reenactment might not
be sufficient to decide between different interpretive accounts. Yet, we also
have to insist that reenactment is still essential in judging the intrinsic
plausibility of each of the interpretive proposal as a reconstruction of rational agency. Only in this manner are we able to grasp the rationality of the
agent's deliberation. And this is a necessary precondition for any interpretive proposal to be counted as a contender for providing a correct account
of the agent's behavior. Empathy, particularly reenactive empathy, is essential also in the context of justification and for evaluating the objectivity of
an intentional interpretation.

6.2   Empathy and the Prejudicial Nature of Understanding

There is a much stronger argument against empathy within the context
of the philosophy of the social sciences, one that is not easily countered
by admitting that empathy or simulation needs to appeal to additional evidence in the first and the second phases. This objection is based on the
claim that proponents of empathy fail to sufficiently reflect on what in the
hermeneutic tradition has been called the "prejudicial structure of under-

standing" (Gadamer 1989). They fail to understand that grasping the content of an utterance or a thought requires it to be integrated into our own culturally and historically contingent perspective on and conception of the world—including our preconceptions regarding the world of the interpretee—from which we as interpreter are never able to abstract. Understanding another person's reasons for his actions or grasping his thoughts cannot merely be understood as reenactment or as a form of inner imitation because the manner in which we "think" that thought is always already—to use one of the signature phrases of hermeneutic thinkers—colored by our system of beliefs and values, which can differ considerably from that of the interpretee. To express this point in more general terms, it is denied that mere biological similarity among humans confers a sufficient degree of psychological or cognitive similarity that would allow us to reenact another person's thought, especially in case of great cultural differences.[7]

As far as I can see, two aspects have been closely associated in the literature with the above critique of the empathy strategy based on the presupposition of the prejudicial nature of interpretation.[8] First, the critique points to an inherent danger of insufficiently recognizing the relevant difference between myself and another agent. If it leads me to see other agents as too much like me, I would like to call it the danger of projectionism or what historians call anachronism. Using the egocentric strategy of pure empathy might lead to merely projecting one's own centrally held beliefs and attitudes onto the other person. More precisely, the danger consists in conceiving of the other person as more like me than he is and in overlooking relevant evidence that would force me to acknowledge relevant differences between me and the other person. Emphasizing the prejudicial nature of interpretation points also to the possibility of the exact opposite mistake, what one could call the danger of nonprojectionism, since interpretation is also influenced by our preconceptions and prejudices about other cultures and other persons as foreign. As various discussions in the history of anthropology suggest, the danger here consists in conceiving of the other as not being sufficiently like us, perhaps because we conceive of the other as belonging to a more primitive culture not capable of a particular degree of conceptual sophistication or certain ways of thinking. In a recent anthropological debate about "how the natives think about Captain Cook, for example," this is exactly the objection that Obeyesekere (1992) makes against Sahlins (1995). According to Obeyesekere, Sahlins interprets the "natives" from a merely Eurocentric perspective as being primarily driven by a "mythico-practical" conception of the world. For that reason he does not recognize that the "natives" are driven by the very same instrumental concerns that we have.

Proponents of empathy and simulation should in my opinion freely admit the above dangers (see also Stein 1917, 98). However, if the hermeneutic emphasis on the prejudicial structure of interpretation would be nothing more than pointing out the dangers of projectionism and non-projectionism, its critique of the empathy view would indeed not reach very far. It would only describe more precisely how we can be led astray in our interpretations of other agents within the folk-psychological perspective, particularly because of difficulties we encounter in what I have called earlier the matching phase of the simulation procedure. The above critique would merely point out that the interpretation of other agents is fallible and that the knowledge gained by empathetic strategies is in this respect on par with other forms of human knowledge. These concerns would not touch my conception of the epistemic centrality of empathy since I have already admitted that interpretation based on empathy is not self-verifying. It has to be justified against its interpretive competitors in light of further knowledge and evidence about differences between the interpreter's and interpretee's biographical and cultural backgrounds. As far as the interpretation of individual agents is concerned, the methodological lessons drawn from the above observations would not consist in abolishing any attempt to empathetically reenact the thoughts of other agents, since this is not possible if we intend to grasp others' reasons for their actions. Instead the lesson learned would be to make sure that these attempts are supplemented by or implemented in the context of rigorous research that aims at precisely defining the difference between interpreter and interpretee through judicious use of relevant evidence. The correct inference to draw from all of the above considerations is not that one should neglect empathy but that it has to be applied carefully in a methodologically sound manner.

A stronger reading of the critique of empathy is possible, though, that I take to be part of the intended meaning of this hermeneutic thesis on the prejudicial structure of understanding. (See, e.g., Gadamer 1989; Hahn 1997, 55.) In this form, it points to some real limits of the empathy strategy as we have presented it so far.[9] The claim about the principal limits of the empathy strategy is closely associated with the recognition of the holistic constitution of thought, which we have also acknowledged in our analysis of radical interpretation. Reenacting another person's thoughts requires keeping in mind differences in our central background assumptions, since those background assumptions might influence our inferential behavior, which aspects of a situation we count as salient and relevant to our practical deliberation, and what reaction we would regard as appropriate. One might think of the differences between a person with a modern scientific outlook and a devout religious believer, between a political conservative and a liberal, or even between persons from different disciplinary backgrounds who are committed to very different explanatory paradigms. It follows that the practical difficulty of reenacting the thoughts of another agent would increase exponentially the greater the cultural distance between the interpreter and the interpretee and the smaller the set of centrally held beliefs and background assumptions they share.[10] It certainly is possible without great difficulty to pretend that the banana is a telephone or that I am a waiter in a restaurant. In this case I merely have to imaginatively "add" or "drop" a few beliefs from my normal way of looking at the world. But reenacting the thoughts of an Azande, as described by Evans-Pritchard (1937), for example, would entail holding a whole book of anthropological research in my head in order to make sure that my views of the world are appropriately quarantined and will not unduly influence my deliberation within the simulation phase. The larger the relevant differences between interpreter and interpretee, the less reliable we can regard the reenactment procedure. The interpreter will likely be unable to guard against inappropriate interferences that follow from his own ideological outlook on the world in the very process of attempting to reenact another's thoughts.

The above critique of empathy does not focus on the mere fact that the reenactment of an agent from a different cultural environment has to proceed carefully in order to count as epistemically reliable. It is instead concerned about limitations of our cognitive capacities to actually use our imagination for the purpose of entertaining another person's thoughts, while quarantining our own at times strongly opposed, strongly held, and well-entrenched views of the world from interfering in the reenactment process itself. These worries are further supported by the recognition that what distinguishes members of other cultures cannot be merely accounted for in terms of their explicitly held or even tacit beliefs. It also concerns differences in some of the norms according to which beliefs and desires are evaluated, and differences in well-entrenched habits of thoughts and behavior that correspond to those differences of normative evaluations. As the anthropological debate about rationality (see Wilson 1970; Hollis and Lukes 1982) and the interpretive problems associated with examples of apparent irrationality encountered by anthropological field workers have made clear, differences between agents from different cultures are not merely differences in beliefs about the fundamental organization of the world. They also involve differences in the evaluation of these beliefs in view of conflicting evidence. The problem of interpreting the Azande consists not merely in realizing that they believe in witchcraft. One also has to make sense of the fact that they continue to hold onto such a belief system that—from a perspective of a "Western" mind trained in the modern scientific methods and committed to norms of scientific conduct—is riddled with obvious inconsistencies. What was particularly puzzling to Evans-Pritchard (1937, 24–26) was not so much that they had beliefs about witchcraft which he regarded to be obviously false but their at times strange inferential behavior. As he tells it, the Azande were not interested in drawing the "obvious" conclusion that all men of a clan are witches even when it was shown by a postmortem investigation that one man of the clan is a witch and it was assumed in addition that witchcraft is inherited by the son from his father and by the daughter from her mother. The Azande in general had no problem of treating only one man of a clan as a witch while at the same time maintaining normal contact with the other members. The shortcomings of the Azande, as described by Pritchard, are not shortcomings of logical capacities. It seems that they could abstractly recognize the apparent inconsistency in their belief system if prompted to do so. Yet they were not bothered to change any of their beliefs regarding witchcraft even when the inconsistency was pointed out to them.

In this respect, one should agree with social theorists like Pierre Bourdieu for whom normative social practices rest on an embodied but nonrepresentational sense of the "feel for the game," which allows agents to act appropriately in their social world. Bourdieu uses the notion of a "habitus" to refer to an agent's embodied and practical know-how, which enables him or her to participate in social practices. The habitus is the "set of structured and structuring dispositions" (1990, 53) that provides us with schemes of perceiving the world and also with the appropriate emotional reactions to the world in its infinite variety. As Bourdieu stresses, the acquisition of such a habitus should not be seen as the outcome of explicit theoretical instruction but is primarily acquired in growing up in and becoming practically familiar with social practices through trial and error, imitation and mimicry of the competent players of the game (see also Turner 1994, 2000). As concrete examples of such embodied practical know-how, one might think of our ability to stand at the proper distance from our partner in conversation, to know what clothes to wear for particular occasions, or to know how to engage in small talk at a dinner party. More significantly, one could also think of a whole range of what Strawson calls our reactive attitudes towards others, such as being angry, being insulted, feeling ashamed, or being proud in the appropriate situations. In my opinion, it is especially important to emphasize the emotional attunement and attachment to various social norms in this context. We do not merely recognize abstractly the incorrectness of a person who is coming too close to us. Instead we recognize it as being incorrect by starting to feel uncomfortable talking to such a person. We do not realize behavior as bad manners and as a violation of some norms from a detached perspective. Rather, we get angry about it. More generally, the whole range of our reactive attitudes toward other agents seems to be closely tied to the norms and rules that we regard as central to the well-being of a society. I would suggest that the degree of emotional reaction in this regard indicates the degree to which certain of these norms are important to our own social identity. They reveal something about ourselves by revealing what we care about, how we implicitly view ourselves, and how we implicitly think of the appropriate relation between self and other.[11]

The purpose of the above brief analysis of Bourdieu's notion of habitus is not to advocate the correctness of his analysis of social practices. (For a critical view see Stueber 2005b.) Rather, the goal of the above reflections was to emphasize a possible limitation of the empathy strategy as we have discussed it so far. Phenomenologically, these reflections can also be illustrated by the following example. Even after having lived in the United States for an extended period of time and even though for years I understood abstractly the rules of baseball—the reader is welcome to substitute this example with his or her "favorite" game he or she did not grow up with—I did not see any point to it. Only after my son started enjoying playing the game was I able to get a better sense of the game. If all of this is right, then it seems unrealistic to assume that we can account for relevant differences between agents from very different cultural contexts merely by imaginatively entertaining a few of their beliefs and desires. Even if one does not follow Bourdieu and others who claim that the difference between agents has at times to be analyzed in terms of an embodied, nonpropositional, and irreducibly practical know-how, and even if one insists on analyzing the above difference as a difference in evaluative propositional beliefs, one should acknowledge that a difference in evaluative beliefs also concerns a difference in how such beliefs are integrated with our emotional responses to the world. It should also make us skeptical about our ability to recognize which aspects of a situation another person might find salient by placing ourselves in the other person's shoes and imagining it from his perspective, since we cannot easily shed and quarantine our own emotional attachment to at times very different normative standards of appropriate behavior. Adding a different evaluative belief in the pretense mode or imaginatively entertaining such a belief does not automatically enable us to reenact that belief in a manner that would also mirror the emotional integration of that belief in the mind of the other person, especially as far as the emotional attachment to specific social norms is concerned. Such emotional integration of evaluative beliefs is the result of a complex process of social conditioning.

In saying this I do not want to deny that we can be trained to look at the world in a manner that incorporates these new standards of evaluation as the automatic default standards and the standards in light of which we are emotionally attuned to the world. We certainly can acquire such new habits of thoughts by immersing ourselves in a different culture over an extended period of time. Yet it is implausible to assume that our cognitive system is flexible beyond restraint. And immersing oneself into another culture is very different from the empathy conception of interpreting other agents that I have argued for. I have presented empathy as an act of the imagination, that is, an act of using our own cognitive machinery as it is defined right here and now, in order to interpret other agent's behavior in folk-psychological terms and to gain information about another person's mind. Retooling our mind by actually living in a different social environment is a very different project.

For the above reason, there is some validity to Peter Winch's critique of Collingwood's claim regarding the centrality of reenactment to our understanding of other agents as being an "intellectual distortion" (Winch 1958, 131)—a claim that is echoed by Bourdieu's rejection of empathy as a "psychic reproduction" of "lived experience" in Dilthey's sense or any other "sophisticated versions of the spontaneous theory of understanding as 'putting oneself in somebody's else's place'" (Bourdieu 1990, 19, 58) as a method of the social sciences. But rather than conceding to Winch and Bourdieu that empathy has no principal role to play in understanding other agents, one should view the above observations as pointing out that empathy as a strategy for grasping another person's reasons for his actions is indeed limited and has at times to be supplemented by various theoretical approaches (see also Henderson and Horgon 2000; Stueber 2000). Yet even in interpretive situations where further theoretical tactics are involved, the attempt to grasp in the empathic mode the agent's thought as his reasons for action remains the basic interpretive default method. In fact, conceiving of a problem in understanding other agents as an interpretive problem is possible only if one encounters difficulties in reenacting the other person's thoughts and deliberations in one's own mind. The supplemental strategies that I will speak of cannot be understood as completely replacing empathy. They should be seen as implicitly affirming the centrality of empathy in our relation to others since these strategies are used only if interpreters have difficulties of making sense of another person in the empathetic mode.

Crucial to this point is the fact that, as I have elaborated in the second chapter, folk-psychological interpretation has to proceed under the tutelage of the principle of charity understood in a global manner. I reject assertions about radically different forms of rationality and the claim that we could be different in all of our habits of thoughts, as Winch (1964) at times has suggested. If charity has to be seen as a central principle of interpretation without providing us with an algorithmic procedure then we are in need of some mechanism that allows the interpreter to fill out the details of his interpretation. Putting oneself into the shoes of the interpretee is indeed one of the methods that guide the interpreter in attempting to find a plausible interpretation. Not only is it a plausible method but a necessary one, since it is only in this manner that the interpreter can suitably guess what a person might find salient in a particular situation and what his reasons could be for acting in a certain manner when he faces that situation. If we are not even able to understand some of the reasons for another person's actions in an empathetic mode we are not able to understand him as an agent interpretable in the folk-psychological idiom. That is why I think that Quine is right that "practical psychology is what sustains our radical translator all along the way, and the method of his psychology is empathy: he imagines himself in the native's situation as best as he can" (Quine 1990, 46). Only if we are able to grasp the reasons for actions to a large degree are we indeed able to identify specific interpretive problems in localized circumstances that seem to resist the power of empathy and our imagination.

I would like to illustrate these claims by an example from a recent dispute in German history, specifically the debate between Christopher Browning (1992) and Daniel Goldhagen (1996) about how to account for the behavior of "ordinary" men of Police Battalion 101 during World War II. Although I personally find Browning's interpretation more plausible, here I am not interested in contributing to the historical debate itself. I am interested in the debate as an illustration of how interpretive disputes are essentially tied to our folk-psychological ability to cognitively empathize with other agents and in order to show how various "theoretical" strategies can be used to overcome empathy's limitations in localized circumstances. The explanatory problem for Goldhagen and Browning consists in explaining why most of the men of Police Battalion 101 participated rather willingly in the extermination campaign against Jews in Eastern Europe, even though they could not be regarded as particularly ideologically committed Nazis, and even though they did not face severe punishment like the death penalty if they excused themselves from participating in various forms of genocidal activities. As particularly Goldhagen points out, the participants are at times rather open about their activities; they do not seem to be particularly ashamed or try to hide their activities. They even take the time to photograph their involvement and can be seen smiling in such photographs as if they were taking pictures during vacation.

The interpretive problem for Goldhagen and Browning does not arise because they are completely unable to conceive of the members of the police battalion as rational agents acting for a reason. Rather Browning and Goldhagen identify them as ordinary men who grew up in the pre-Nazi period and could therefore be assumed to be accustomed to normal moral standards. We can fully understand their ordinary reasons for joining the police battalion when they did not know what kind of task was waiting for them. The problem of understanding arises because we conceive of them as ordinary men, human beings like you and me. It is for this reason that we are unable to imaginatively put ourselves in their position and fathom their reasons for going through with their assigned tasks rather than at least asking to be excused. Given their ordinariness—and their assumed knowledge of normal moral standards—we cannot understand how they could have not refused to participate in genocidal activities. Looking at these pictures, we do not merely judge such actions as morally wrong; we are also morally repulsed. In trying to put ourselves in the other person's point of view and trying to figure out what reasons somebody could have had to commit such acts we encounter a phenomenon of "imaginative resistance," a phenomenon already noted by Hume (Gendler 2000).

Such limitations of our empathetic capacities, in my opinion, have to do with the fact that some of our habits of thinking are closely tied to our emotional "attunement" to the natural and social world. On reflection we regard beliefs and norms that we are emotionally attached to as being essential to our own identity, our conception of ourselves as rational agents, and our conception of the fundamental parameters for our relation to the world and other human beings. We have difficulties in reenacting the deliberation process of another person if we are asked to reenact thought patterns that contradict our habits, because we are unable to quarantine them from our own deeply engrained intellectual and ethical customs. Consequently, I cannot understand the thoughts of the other person as his reasons on the model of empathy that we have discussed so far. In certain circumstances, I am unable to integrate the other person's thoughts into my cognitive structure in a manner that would allow me to understand them as my reasons for these actions and in a manner that would allow me to fully understand myself as an author of these actions. Such resistance of imagination, I would suggest, does not occur only when we differ in deeply held moral beliefs. Such limits of empathy are generally encountered when we are trying to reenact thought processes that contradict what we regard as important for our well-being as agents. We also encounter such limits, therefore, when we try to understand people who are clinically depressed or have unusual phobias.

Acknowledging these limits of empathy is not equivalent to denying the centrality of empathy to the ability to understand other agents. Instead it means having to recognize further supplementary explanatory strategies that we appeal to in order to deal with those limits. Goldhagen, for example, suggests that to account for the behavior of the people in Police Battalion 101 we have to conceive of ordinary Germans of that time as having a very different set of beliefs that he refers to as "eliminationist anti-Semitism" (Goldhagen 1996, chap. 3), a racist anti-semitic ideology for which extermination of the Jewish population is the only logical conclusion. Goldhagen's explanatory strategy appeals still to ordinary notions of belief and desire. In this manner he tries to account for the actions of ordinary men by providing an explanation that in some sense "rationalizes" their behavior. Yet it should be clear that merely being told that other persons have such a different worldview including very different moral standards does not sufficiently allow us to understand their reasons for actions as reasons that I could imagine acting on. We still seem to be unable to fathom how somebody could actually hold such beliefs and regard them as his reasons for actions, for the reasons given above.

Goldhagen's interpretive strategy, I would suggest, does not correspond to the model of reenactive empathy that we have considered so far. According to this model, information of the relevant differences between the interpreter and interpretee is used in order to enter the right initial stage for the simulation process and in order to help us quarantine our own beliefs or desires from the relevant considerations during the simulation process. On this model of empathy we can always understand the other person by reconstructing the same thoughts on the first-order level in our own mind. An interpretation of an agent is judged to be plausible if and only if we are successful in reenacting his deliberation process in our own mind. The reasons why Goldhagen's theory of eliminationist antisemitism seems to provide at least a prima facie plausible account of the actions of Police Battalion 101 has nothing to do with enabling us to get us into the initial stage of the simulation. Rather, it appeals to our second-order capacities of cognitive extrapolation (Stueber 2002a, 2004), that is, our abilities to extrapolate another person's reaction from my knowledge of how I would have reacted in such a situation and my knowledge of the relevant differences in our background assumptions. In this case, we still try to find a way of accounting for the other person's action as "rationally intelligible," but not by reenacting the other person's thoughts on a first-order level. Rather, we first project ourselves in his situation, notice our own reaction, and then calculate his reaction in light of the recognition that he holds a very different set of factual and evaluative beliefs to which he is emotionally attached. This strategy of cognitive extrapolation requires of us an implicit theoretical grasp of the causal efficacy and interaction of various mental states, since only in light of a detailed understanding of how minds work in general would we seem to be able to extrapolate the other person's reactions with the help of our knowledge of the differences in our background assumptions.

To a certain degree, understanding the reactions of another person in this manner can be compared to the model of folk-psychological interpretation that some theory theorists proposed in response to Heal's argument from the essential contextuality of rational thought. Recall that according to that model, simulation is needed only for providing certain information that is further processed by theoretical inferences. In this case, for example, we seem to use our own mind to draw logical consequences from an initial set of beliefs in the same way that we use our own mind in a logic class to judge intuitively whether an argument is valid. Being informed about the nature of the set of beliefs that according to Goldhagen characterizes eliminationist anti-Semitism, we seem to be able to grasp that certain recommendations for action do logically follow from such beliefs. Yet we need to appeal to further theoretical principles in order to explain how somebody could act on those recommendations. In contrast to theory theorists, I however do not regard such a theoretically informed interpretive strategy as the basic default procedure of folk psychology. Instead it should be seen as a supplemental strategy that is appealed to only when the attempt to empathetically grasp other persons' reasons for their action has failed. It is a method of trying desperately to hold on to our conviction that the other agents are rational in situations in which we can no longer comprehend how the agents could be the authors of their action and we cannot comprehend how they themselves can conceive of their beliefs and desires as their reasons for action.[12]

Whether or not Goldhagen's explanatory account is acceptable ultimately depends on whether the attribution of what he calls "eliminationist anti-Semitism" can be independently corroborated by further evidence from German history. Browning tends to be skeptical in this respect. Yet he does not see any suitable manner of reenacting or extrapolating the reasons of the agents. In contrast to Goldhagen he suggests that the behavior in question cannot be accounted for from the perspective of ordinary belief/desire psychology. Instead he adopts a purely third-personal explanatory stance by appealing to results from Milgram's obedience and Zimbardo's prison experiments (Milgram 1963; Zimbardo 1972); that is, he appeals to psychological theories about how situational factors might influence a person's behavior. In this situation it seems that our only option is to provide a merely causal account of the other person's behavior since we can no longer grasp the causes of the behavior in question as the agent's reasons for his actions.

We thus have to agree with critics of empathy in their insistence that empathy cannot be regarded as the only method for interpreting other agents. As my analysis of the dispute between Goldhagen and Browning has shown, empathy's scope is limited. To overcome these limits, we have to supplement the strategy of pure empathy with theoretical information within or outside of the folk-theoretical framework. I want to stress, however, that admitting limitations of the strategy of pure empathy does not at all diminish the central epistemic importance of empathy for our ability to understand other agents. As we have seen, contrary to widespread opinion, viewing empathy as central to our ability to understand other agents does not entail a Cartesian model of the mind or an epistemology of pure perception. Rather, reenactment is essential for understanding intentional agency because it is only in this manner that we are able to conceive of agents as situated in certain environments and as responding in a rational manner to the demands of this environment. It allows us to admit that justifying the attribution of intentions to other agents is constrained by evidence for reconstructing the agent's historical context without accepting that reenactment plays no role in the context of justification. Empathy has to be understood as the basic default mode of understanding other agents, and other theoretical strategies should be viewed as supplemental procedures. First, as I have argued, particular interpretive problems such as the one discussed above arise only because I typically am able to conceive of the reasons for an agent's actions in a variety of other circumstances. Second, the interpretive problem that one encounters is defined precisely by the failed attempt to reenact the reasons for another person's actions. It is just in this context that an interpreter might start wondering whether he has sufficiently taken into account the relevant differences between himself and the other agent and that he might consider the use of more theoretical strategies.

For the above reason, we must regard interpretation as an open-ended process: how an interpretation is finally structured—what information an interpreter finds particularly relevant to mention in the context of providing an account of other agents—depends crucially on the above difficulties that he experiences in his empathetic attempts. Any change in the background assumption on part of the interpreter is likely to affect the kind of difficulties he faces in attempting to empathize with the other person. The above account of interpretation as dialectical interplay between reenactment, cognitive extrapolation, and theory proper cannot be taken as providing an algorithmic procedure that determines when to use reenactment and when to supplement reenactment with various theoretical considerations. Such decisions—similar to scientific revolutions à la Kuhn—are in the end irreducible, practical decisions that depend on the degree of dissatisfaction felt with an interpretation of the agents, given the cultural perspective of the researcher, the historical evidence, and the availability of various theoretical resources. In light of different background assumptions, researchers might not even agree on which aspect of another person's behavior deserves special explanatory attention. A devout Christian, for example, might have a very different attitude toward the magical practices of the Azande than Evans-Pritchard, writing from a predominantly scientific perspective. A devout religious person would probably describe the practices of the Azande very differently because he proceeds from a very different "baseline," so to speak. Different bases require very different information either for entering the initial stage of simulation or for the purposes of cognitive extrapolation.

Seen in this light, Winch's objection against Evans-Pritchard's account of the Azande can be given a different reading. Rather than arguing for radically different forms of rationality, the objection is better understood as arguing that Evans-Pritchard fundamentally misconstrues the appropriate basis for interpreting their witchcraft practices. In his book Evans-Pritchard (1937) provides us with information that allows us to extrapolate the behavior of the Azande from the perspective of the modern scientist. Yet, as Winch argues, the Azande are better understood as engaging in a specific social ritual; that is, they are better understood from the perspective of a religious believer who is engaged in his own religious rituals. Needless to say, we would need very different information from that which Evans-Pritchard gives in order to accomplish such a task.[13] However, admitting the limitations in our use of the empathetic method and granting the open-endedness of interpretation does not justify the orthodox disdain that philosophers of social science have shown toward the empathetic method for the last few decades, since all such features of interpreting agency are centrally linked to our difficulties in using empathy to understand other agents as acting for reasons.

Concluding Remarks

In this book I have limited my claims for empathy to the question of whether or not empathy is central to our ability to understand other individual agents within the folk-psychological realm, which is also the current focus of the theory of mind debate. I agree that claims about empathy as the only method of the human and social sciences are exaggerations. But as I have shown, empathy must be regarded as of central epistemic importance and as the epistemic default mode in understanding other agents. In order to make that argument, the book has distinguished between basic and reenactive empathy. Basic empathy has been understood as a quasi-perceptual mechanism delineating perceptual similarity spaces encompassing both myself and the other person. It allows us to understand each other in a perceptually direct manner as "same-minded" and it allows us to develop the intersubjectively accessible conceptual framework of folk psychology. I have argued that evidence for the existence of mirror neurons from recent neurobiological research strongly speaks in favor of this thesis. It also allows us to avoid the shortcomings of Cartesianism and behaviorism in accounting for our grasp of psychological concepts that still seem to plague contemporary philosophy of mind.

One can grant the centrality of basic empathy to interpersonal relations while claiming that the explanation, prediction, and interpretation of an agent's complex social behavior requires knowledge of a folk-psychological theory as proposed by the theory theorist. As I have suggested in this book, to argue for the centrality of empathy on this level—or what I have called reenactive empathy—requires recognizing that folk psychology is not a conceptual and explanatory framework that has been adopted from the detached perspective. Rather, it has been adopted from the engaged perspective, in which we try to explain the actions of other rational agents who, like us, act for reasons. Given the arguments from the essential contextuality and indexicality of thoughts as reasons, the claim that mindreading is implemented by mechanisms of theoretical inferences is highly implausible. I have suggested that the empirical investigation in our mindreading abilities is best viewed not as deciding whether theory theory or simulation theory is correct. Instead it is better seen as investigating the nature of psychological mechanisms that implement our mindreading abilities, which we have to understand on the personal level as strategies of reenactive empathy.

In contrast to much of current philosophy of mind, this book has been conceived of in the conviction that empathy as an epistemically central strategy to understanding other agents can be successful if and only if it addresses genuinely normative concerns about empathy that have been voiced primarily within traditional philosophy of social science. Addressing the question of empathy within this normative context has compelled us to admit that theoretical knowledge is central to the justification of our interpretive hypotheses, particularly in regard to the justification of folk-psychological explanations of action. As I have shown in the last two chapters, however, it does not force us to understand empathy as epistemically superfluous within this context. Even if the justification of an explanation of action in terms of beliefs and desires has to appeal implicitly to generalizations, it is only in light of reenactive empathy that we are able to assess that we are still within the proper explanatory domain of such generalizations, that is, that we are in the domain of rational agency. Interpersonal understanding of other agents, whether in ordinary contexts or in more disciplined contexts of the human sciences, depends centrally on our empathetic abilities. As it turns out, proponents of the empathy method in the human sciences in the nineteenth century and early twentieth century were not as epistemically naive as they are sometimes made out to be. They at least were on the right track, even though they misconceived the structure of empathy. Our understanding of other agents must be epistemically distinguished from our understanding of the occurrences of other natural objects and events, since empathy plays an epistemically central role only in the domain of human agency.

Notes

Introduction

1. A recent one at least in the sense as I have defined this term. There is, however, an earlier and very different use of the term "folk psychology." It has been used to translate Wilhelm Wundt's concept of *Völkerpsychologie*, that is, the psychology of a people.

2. See Droysen 1977, 20; Dilthey 1961, vol. 1, 36; Lipps 1905, 1–31; Collingwood 1946, 213–214.

3. Within the context of German romanticism, the concept of "poetic" empathy is certainly widespread even if various authors do not use the exact same terminology. In this context Jean Paul and Friedrich Schlegel are often mentioned. Furthermore Schopenhauer plays an important role as a predecessor of the idea of aesthetic empathy. See Stern 1898, 4–5 and Makkreel 1996, 206ff.

4. "Introjection" is a term used by Avenarius in a derogative sense. See his 1912 (first published 1891).

5. See Lipps 1903b, 1ff. The attempt to explain aesthetic experiences and its intersubjectivity in terms of the psychological constitution of the subject has an obviously Kantian lineage. Here, however, I do not have the space to pursue this historical lineage further.

6. Stein 1917 (1980), 16–17. Scheler follows Stein in her interpretation, though he accepts *Einsfühlung* as a mass-psychological phenomenon of "primitive" cultures. Makkreel (1996, 2000) is also persuaded by Stein in this regard. For a slightly earlier discussion of this point see also Prandtl 1910, 50. Stein therefore prefers to speak of empathy as an experience *sui generis* (10), as a "non-originary experience that points to an originary experience" (14, translation Makkreel). However, while such characterization might be phenomenologically adequate, it does not provide any psychologically plausible explanatory account of how such an experience could be possible. Lipps is interested in precisely this project.

7. See also 1903b, 134–135. Stein's interpretation of Lipps would not allow us to make sense of what he calls "negative empathy" that forms the basis of our aesthetic experience of ugliness. In negative empathy, such as recognizing the arrogance of another person, I do not experience objectified self-enjoyment; rather, "it is the objectified feeling of the negation of me or the feeling of experienced and objectified negation of life" (1903b, 140). Such complex experience presupposes that I somehow distinguish between myself and the person with whom I "empathetically identify." Otherwise I would not be able to experience the other person's feelings, emotions, and thoughts while recognizing that they are not compatible with my own thoughts.

8. Unfortunately, Lipps himself tends to be too liberal in his usage of the term "empathy." Not only does he speak of intellectual empathy and aesthetic empathy, but he also distinguishes between general and specific empathy and apperceptive and empirical empathy. He thereby leaves behind the idea of "inner imitation" that was originally used to explicate the concept of empathy, and instead uses "empathy" to refer to any of the subject's contributions to the constitution of a recognizable world. What Kant would have called the synthesizing activity of the epistemic subject becomes a different kind of empathy in the hand of Lipps. He thus refers to empathy even when it is a matter of us counting a number of objects, making causal judgments about the world, or conceiving of an object as an object in the first place. He also appeals to empathy in the context of trying to explain certain perceptual illusions. See particularly his 1912–13, esp. 113, 216, and 1903b, chap. 6, 169ff.

9. See Stein 1917, 72. A precise explication of Husserl's conception of empathy is beyond the scope of this book, since my concerns are primarily epistemic. I am not so interested in what one might call a description of the intentional structure of the empathetic experience, something that is at the center of phenomenological interest. For a closer explication of Husserl and the phenomenological tradition, see Depraz 2001; Makkreel 1996; and Zahavi 2001.

10. Aristotle's logical work on the nature of propositions is therefore also called *peri hermeneias*. See Grondin 1994, 21. See also Boeckh 1886, 79–80.

11. Here one should think of the introduction of Christianity and the interpretive problem of how to correlate the Old and the New Testament, the debate about the proper role of the interpretation of the Bible in the aftermath of Luther's dictum of *sola scriptura*, the new importance attributed to the reading of classical texts of antiquity after the Renaissance, and the significance of philology for the German intellectual tradition particularly at the end of the eighteenth century.

12. Schleiermacher also refers to psychological interpretation as technical interpretation. The term psychological interpretation, however, became standard after his work.

13. People familiar with the contemporary debate about simulation theory should be reminded of Jane Heal's conception of simulation as co-cognition.

14. Droysen 1977, 22ff, 159–163. See also Dilthey 1961, vol. 5, 144: "Die Natur erklaeren wir, das Seelenleben verstehen wir." (Translation: We explain nature, but we understand the life of the soul.)

15. For the German version, see Droysen 1977, 423. For a more extensive explication of the same thought, see Droysen 1977, 22–28. In my translation I have mainly followed the translation of Droysen 1893 but have modified it where I thought it necessary to better capture the German original. For that reason, instead of using "utterance" in order to translate *"Äusserung,"* I have used the term "expression." For similar passages, see also Dilthey 1961, vol. 5, 249–150, and Spranger 1905, 88. For a brief explication of Droysen see also Lorenz 1997, esp. 91–91.

16. Dilthey 1961, vol. 5, 156–157 and vol. 1, 36–37.

17. Makkreel (2000, 182) suggests that Dilthey does not use the term *"Einfühlung"* because Lipps's explication of it—with its suggestion of a losing of the self into the object—is too narrow for his purposes. As we have seen, this interpretation of Lipps is incorrect. Nevertheless it might have been a common misunderstanding at the time, as Stein's interpretation suggests. I think a more mundane reason could also be found for Dilthey not using the term. At the time of his early writing, the notion of empathy was still not sufficiently established outside the realm of aesthetics. By the time it was, Dilthey had already abandoned his strongly psychologistic conception of the human sciences. For an explication of Dilthey's change in this regard, see esp. Ermarth 1978, Makkreel 2000, and the introduction of Kögler and Stueber 2000.

18. For both aspects, see, e.g., Dilthey 1961, vol. 5, 170–180; Spranger 1905, 95; 1930, 12.

19. For various references to the circular structure of interpretation, see, e.g., Schleiermacher 1998, 8ff, 230ff. See also Boeckh 1886, 139.

20. Dilthey 1961, vol. 5, 144, 170, but esp. 248ff. See also Dilthey 1961, vol. 1, 15, 37.

21. See Dilthey 1961, vol. 5, 263: "Hingegen sind die geistigen Tatsachen, wie sie sind, im Erleben gegeben; aus der Fuelle des eignen Erlebnisses wird durch eine Transposition Erlebnis ausser us nachgebildet und verstanden, und bis in die abstraktesten Saetze der Geisteswissenschaften ist das Tatsaechliche, das in den Gedanken repraesentiert wird, Erleben und Verstehen." See also p. 264.

22. It would be inappropriate, however, to call Dilthey's early position a Cartesian one. Whereas the emphasis on inner observation (*innere Wahrnehmung*) could be called Cartesian, Dilthey's emphasis on the experienced totality of mental phenomena as the primary unit of significance is not. Furthermore, as Ermath (1978, 108ff) has pointed out, Dilthey's category of lived experience (*Erlebnis*) is world-involving.

23. See 177, 263ff. After having rejected understanding as a psychological act on p. 96, Dilthey continues to speak of becoming aware of "a psychic state in its totality and its re-discovery through re-experiencing it" (164). For more references, see Ermarth 1978, 250.

24. Makkreel (2000), for example, suggests that the Dilthey disavows any allegiance to empathy in his later work. Spranger (1930) is clearer in this respect (see pp. 19–25, 410ff). He stresses that understanding has to be conceived of being "always more than putting oneself into the other's place" (410). This seems to indicate, however, that "putting oneself in the place" of the other person is still an integral part of understanding.

25. For a sympathetic presentation of Dilthey's conception of understanding, see Ermarth 1978, chap. 5. Dilthey's failure to sufficiently justify the usage of his psychological categories in the context of his later philosophical positions is certainly one of the reasons why his work has been closely associated with what has been regarded as an objectionably naive conception of empathy.

26. See, e.g., the entry "Empathic Accuracy" by A. Barbee in *Encyclopedia of Human Emotions*, vol. 1, 241. For a more detailed survey on research in this domain see Ickes 1997.

27. I thus strongly disagree with J. Strayer in her attempt to provide a definite definition of empathy as feeling into the affects of another person. See her essay in Eisenberg and Strayer 1987, esp. 236.

28. "No quality of human nature is more remarkable, both in itself and in its consequences, than that propensity we have to sympathize with others, and to receive by communication their inclinations and sentiments, however different from, or even contrary to our own. This is not only conspicuous in children, who implicitly embrace every opinion propos'd to them; but also in men of the greatest judgment and understanding who find it very difficult to follow their own reason or inclination, in opposition to that of their friends and daily companions. To this principle we ought to ascribe the great uniformity we may observe in the humours and turn of thinking of those of the same nation ..." (Hume 1739–40, 316). See also 1739–40, 577 and 1751, 42–51.

29. My reading of Hume and Smith has benefited from Wispe (1991, 1–17).

30. See also pp. 318 and 576: "As in strings equally wound up, the motion of one communicates itself to the rest; so all affections readily pass from one person to another, and beget correspondent movements in every human creature" (Hume 1739–40). Such "resonance however is not only limited to affective states but applies also to opinions" (365).

31. In contrast to Hume, Smith also links sympathy to a particular cognitive mechanism of taking the perspective of the other person or putting oneself imaginatively in

his situation. He particularly stresses that it is mainly in light of the view of the other's perspective (and not merely the recognition of a particular facial expression) that we are able to sympathize with another person. Smith seems to have thus generalized and clarified some of Hume remarks in the *Treatise* (1739–40) where he links our ability to recognizing the functional beauty of another man's house by imaginatively recognizing the pleasure that its owner would derive from it (Hume 363–364). Sympathy for Smith is an automatic by-product of perspective taking as the primary mechanism of gaining knowledge of other minds, at least insofar as the other person's emotions are concerned. It is not clear in Smith whether he would maintain that perspective taking is the primary epistemological means of knowing even nonphenomenal states such as another's beliefs. One also should not expect to find such a general thesis in Smith 1759 since knowledge of other minds is not a primary concern in that context.

32. Even though he also does not always sufficiently distinguish between the various senses of sympathy, Smith defines sympathy explicitly on the model of pity and compassion, which signify a "fellow feeling with the sorrow of others" as a general "fellow-feeling with any passion whatever" (Smith 1759, 5). In his 1872 (1998), Darwin speaks of sympathy as a "separate or distinct emotion" that has some related facial expressions.

Chapter 1

1. I will discuss the question of a proper account of psychological concepts in more detail when discussing simulation theory in chapter 4.

2. Churchland 1970, 221. Following Davidson (1980, 77), I have used a condensed version of Churchland's formulation. For a good schematic representation of the principles of adult folk psychology, see also Wellman 1990, 109.

3. Stich and Ravenscroft (1996) call the first understanding of the theory view of folk psychology the internalist account and refer to the second one as the externalist account.

4. Stephen Stich (1983) has been another prominent proponent of eliminativism. For an evaluation of his arguments, see Horgan and Woodward 1991. However, I will focus here only on Churchland, since Stich has since his 1996 expressed doubt about the validity of the eliminativist argument. In Nichols and Stich 2003, it is thus assumed that the "a well-known commonsense account of the architecture of the cognitive mind is largely correct, though it is far from complete" (13). For a summary of other possible eliminativist arguments, see chap. 1 of Stich 1996. Stich's recent doubts about the soundness of eliminativist arguments are derived from considerations about the appropriate theory of reference. It seems to Stich that in order to conclude that mental terms do not refer to anything at all one has to subscribe to a controversial description theory of reference that has been challenged by Kripke,

Putnam, and others. Stich furthermore argues that it is also very implausible that we will ever be able to devise a theory of reference that will articulate principles according to which we can objectively decide whether we should think of theoretical terms of an outdated theory such as "belief" and "desire" as referring to *nothing but* neuronal states or to *nothing at all*. In the end, such questions are decided only pragmatically. I tend to agree with Stich in this regard. However, Stich's insights do not answer the eliminativist worries. All he shows is that the eliminativist argument is not strictly a deductive argument, but an inductive one. It depends on the assumption that when all the relevant neuroscientific research is done, we will find folk psychology sufficiently similar enough to phlogiston theory or the humors theory in medicine that we will regard the terms of the replaced theory to be nonreferring in light of pragmatic criteria, such as the overall parsimony and simplicity of a theoretical enterprise.

5. Contrary to some earlier statement by proponents of the simulation theory (Gordon 1995, 71; Goldman 1995a, 93; Stich and Nichols 1995, 124–125), I think that Stich and Ravencroft (Stich 1996, chap. 3) are right in maintaining that the debate between theory-theory and simulation theory, understood primarily as a debate about the underlying causal processes of our folk-psychological abilities, is not relevant in this context. (For an early opposing view, see Harris 1995, 208.) First, as already noted, the detached conception of folk psychology is not necessarily committed to a psychologically realistic interpretation of its position. Second, it would be a rather curious fact that a debate about the underlying internal causal processes of our competence to use psychological concepts would also be able to insulate these very same concepts from a critique about their descriptive adequacy in regard to the external world. One of the main reasons that Paul Churchland views psychology as a theory is a rather widespread view about the *epistemology* of explanations (Churchland 1989a, 2), not a thesis about the *causal production* of particular explanations. Churchland himself, however, is not sufficiently aware of this distinction in his critique of simulation theory (1989b, 120). He also seems to be committed to the thesis that the internal representation of folk theory whether it represents psychological generalizations or stores "prototypes of the deliberative or purposeful process" (1989b, 124) also play a role in the production of our folk-psychological practices.

6. My considerations here have greatly benefited from Velleman 1989, 2000 and the first two chapters of Pettit 1993.

7. See particularly his "Freedom of Will and the Concept of a Person," in Frankfurt 1988. For an in-depth discussion of various aspects of Frankfurt's position and philosophical development, see Buss and Overton 2002.

8. Velleman (1989, 193, n. 5) describes this distinction as the distinction between "acting rationally" and "acting for a reason." However, I find the phrase "acting for a reason" still rather ambiguous. Velleman also takes Davidson to task for providing merely an analysis of acting rationally, or what Velleman also calls in his 2000 the

"standard model of rational agency." In my opinion, Davidson is rather ambiguous in this regard (and this maybe the biggest failure of the standard model). For example, Davidson does require for intentional agency that "what the agent does is known to him under some description" (1980, 50). He also insists that self-knowledge has to be seen as a constitutive part of linguistic agency. See my 2002b for an explication of this strategy.

9. Agreeing with Korsgaard in this respect, however, does not imply that I also agree with her Kantian conception of morality.

10. I owe the reference to DeBaggio to a conversation with George Graham.

11. Actions, however, are not only criticized as being irrational because the agent acted contrary to what he valued such as in case of an incontinent action. Agents are also criticized because the beliefs that form part of the reasons for the actions are not true or not epistemically justified. It is certainly an act of practical irrationality if a person decides to walk on ice when he is insufficiently epistemically justified in believing that the ice will hold him. From the perspective of folk psychology and the question of agency, the traditional distinction between epistemic and merely practical rationality is thus negligible. See also Baron 2000 in this regard.

12. Gegerly et al. (1995), however, have taken the results of their studies to support Dennett's conception of the intentional stance, according to which agents have to be interpreted to be ideally rational not merely in an objective sense but also in a subjective sense. Such an interpretation of the experiments is certainly too strong. I rather follow Perner (2004), who views these experiments as providing evidence for the claim that rationality in an objective sense is involved early on in our folk-psychological interpretation of other agents.

13. At least, this is how I understand the pragmatist position that Stich is articulating in the last chapter of his 1990.

14. For an extensive analysis of various strategies to save the rationality assumption, see particularly Stein 1996.

15. Nisbett and Ross (1980), however, seem to maintain the weaker position arguing for ameliorative action, despite the earlier "bleak implication" statement. Similarly, Kahneman (2000, 682) states explicitly that he is primarily interested in "understanding the psychology of intuitive judgments and choice" and not in "questioning human rationality" or "demonstrating irrationality." For a seemingly more negative assessment of human rationality, however, see Tversky and Kahneman 1983, 313.

16. Recently, however, Stich has adopted a less pessimistic view regarding the question of how rational human beings are. This is owing particularly to empirical research within the framework of evolutionary psychology. See Samuels and Stich 2003; Samuels, Stich, and Bishop 2002; and Samuels, Stich, and Tremoulet 1999.

Nevertheless, for Stich this does not seem to imply any modification in his position regarding the status of the rationality constraint within folk psychology.

17. Prima facie, Dennett's conception of the intentional stance implies that we have to attribute those beliefs and desires that a system "ought to have" given its "perceptual capacities," its "epistemic" and "biological needs" and "its biography." We have to interpret its behavior as consisting "of those acts that it would be rational for an agent with those beliefs and desires to perform" (Dennett 1987, 49). If this is the case, Dennett is committed to the standard conception of rationality. I would therefore have to conclude that Dennett's conception of the intentional stance cannot be understood as an analysis of our folk-psychological practices or our ordinary commonsensical notions of belief and desires. Dennett, however, has denied the above conclusion explicitly. He suggests that he relies merely on a "flexible," "slippery," or "intuitive" notion of rationality (Dennett 1997, 97–98). Nevertheless, he fails to explain in sufficient detail how we can think of a person as rational who fails to live up to the standard conception of rationality, particularly if the intentional stance is adopted as Dennett suggests from a third-person quasi-scientific perspective. For that purpose, Dennett needs to explain how agents can be regarded as rational animals for whom the principles of our theories of rationality are normatively valid, even though they do not describe the structure of our actual reasoning mechanisms. I suspect that Dennett's difficulty has to do with the fact that he conceives of the intentional stance as a rationalized version of what I have called the detached conception of folk psychology. It conceives of us merely as intentional systems and not as critical reasoners. I also do not understand what exactly Dennett means when he says that we only attribute those beliefs and desires that a system *ought* to have, instead of those belief and desires that would in some sense rationalize its behavior from a subjective perspective. Here Dennett seems to distinguish insufficiently between the subjective and objective notions of rationality, probably owing to his tendency to link the assumption of rationality to evolutionary considerations. I tend to agree with Stich's criticism of Dennett. See Stich 1981 and Nichols and Stich 2003, 142ff. For a persuasive critique of the attempt to justify the standard conception of rationality through evolutionary arguments, see also Stich 1990 and Stein 1996. Notice, however, that showing that Dennett's conception of the intentional stance does not fit well with folk psychology does not imply that folk psychology does not depend on a rationality assumption.

18. I therefore have sympathy for Stich and Nichols' and Goldman's complaint that merely reinterpreting the concept of rationality in a less "narrow and demanding sense" (Heal 2003a, 78) or minimizing the ideal notion of rationality leads to an obscure and vague notion of rationality that has no suitable empirical application (Stich and Nichols 1997, 319; Goldman 1995a, 78). Recently, however, Heal has responded to these complaints and has argued for what she calls a "two-element conception of rationality." Rationality has to be understood "more like a capacity than a particular achievement." According to Heal, the rationality of a person consists in

(i) his grasping that there are "better or worse in inferential transitions between thoughts" and (ii) his "particular inferential outlook," which she understands as transitions of thoughts the person approves of and that are shown in his actual inferences (2003c, 237). I would have preferred if Heal would have distinguished more strictly between the inferences one approves of and the inferences one actually draws. As the psychological literature has shown, the two do not always overlap. Nevertheless, I am very sympathetic to Heal's position that regards the rationality of human beings as primarily "norm-responsive." I regard this indeed as the traditional Aristotelian conception of rationality. See also Føllesdal 1986 (124), where he conceives of man as a "rational animal in the sense that man has rationality as a norm." In criticizing Dennett, however, Heal links this conception of man as rational animal to what one could call a *conversational stance* where we regard each other primarily as partners in a critical dialogue. She seems to distinguish strictly between this conversational stance and the predictive/explanatory stance. It is no longer clear whether in her opinion rationality continues to play a central role to our explanatory and predictive folk-psychological practices, as she maintained earlier on, or whether she now agrees with Stich and others that these folk-psychological practices do not depend on the rationality assumption. In the text I try to show how the traditional assumption of rationality remains central to our explanatory and predictive purposes, since folk psychology conceives of agents primarily as critical reasoners who act for reasons.

Chapter 2

1. I regard my approach as Davidsonian primarily because it is derived from an analysis of radical interpretation. I would, however, like to stress that I do not feel compelled to defend all of Davidson's official doctrines. I am not a great fan of either the doctrine of anomalous monism (see Stueber 2005a), or the doctrine of the inscrutability of reference (see Stueber 1996), or of triangulation, a concept that became important in Davidson's later writings. Indeed I am inclined to argue that the last two theses are not properly Davidsonian, as they are not sufficiently backed by considerations from radical interpretation.

2. For a critique of Davidson along the lines of Chomsky, see also Fodor and Lepore 1992, 72. For a response, see Stueber 1997a. For a comprehensive evaluation of Davidson's philosophy of language, see Stueber 1993. Here I situate Davidson's work also in the context of the philosophical contributions of Quine, Wittgenstein, and Dummett.

3. Proponents of teleofunctional theories of linguistic and mental content, such as Dretske (1988) and Millikan (1993), would certainly object to conceiving of radical interpretation in this manner. For semantic naturalists like them, it is not obvious that the criteria according to which we attribute mental states with certain content to other persons are the criteria that are metaphysically constitutive of mental

content. For them, such identification confuses questions of epistemology with questions of metaphysics. See also McGinn 1989, 164ff., in this respect. I do not have the space in this book to sufficiently discuss such teleofunctional theories. I do, however, want to stress that I am primarily concerned with our folk-psychological practices of explaining the behavior of other agents. Within these practices we are concerned with attributing mental content in the context of determining the reasons agents have for their actions. As far as I can see, teleofunctional theories are concerned with analyzing a much broader notion of mental representation that is at the same time suitable for the explanation of the behavior of animals and artificial systems, as well as other human beings. Millikan (1993, 283), for example, is also quite willing to give up on the assumption that agents know the content of their thoughts in a privileged manner, in light of her account of content. Teleofunctional theories are thus committed to the detached conception of folk psychology. More importantly, I am skeptical that teleofunctional explications of content are able to overcome what I called in my 1997b the problem of conceptual indeterminacy: they do not allow us to identify the content with the specificity required for attributing a *de dicto* belief to the agent. I doubt that teleofunctional theories are able to provide an account of content as we conceive of it within the context of our folk-psychological practices.

4. For a discussion of the differences between Davidson's externalism and Putnam's externalism see Stueber 1993, 149ff.

5. As I show in Stueber 2000, this also implies that the assumption of self-knowledge or knowledge of one's own mental states has to be regarded as a constitutive assumption of folk-psychological interpretation.

6. Insofar as Goldman's argument against charity is concerned, one has to be a bit careful, however. Goldman suggests that the rationality assumption must be wrong because we feel no qualms in not attributing rationality in certain cases of overtly inconsistent behavior—we feel no temptation to deem such behavior rational. In this context it is not clear whether he understands "feeling temptation" in a merely psychological or in a more epistemic sense. The context in which charity has been argued for is primarily an epistemic one. That is, even though we might feel no psychological qualms in attributing irrationality, we still could be epistemically unjustified in doing so. Our psychologically effortless attribution of irrationality could always be challenged by pointing out that such an interpretation of the agent is inconsistent with the rest of our interpretive hypotheses.

7. For that very reason I find McGinn's (1977) critique of Davidson unpersuasive. Similarly, Grandy's (1973) argument against charity and for what he calls the principle of humanity as directing the interpreter to let the interpretee be revealed as similar to us seems to depend on a local conception of charity.

8. Hence Davidson's statement about inconsistencies as mere "perturbations of rationality" can easily be understood as suggesting that interpretation can proceed

only if we conceive of agents as having been programmed according to the ideals of the standard picture of rationality and as implying that we have to conceive of any deviation from such standards as mere performance errors. Given Davidson's reluctance to conceive of an interpretive theory of meaning and action in a psychologically realistic manner, I do not regard this as a very plausible reading of Davidson himself.

9. This tension is best recognized in his short piece "Could There Be a Science of Rationality?" in Davidson 2001.

10. In contrast to Dennett, Davidson has never favored evolutionary considerations for bringing the notion of ideal rationality into the context of interpretation.

11. Fodor and Lepore 1992, x. For further evidence that Fodor and Lepore do not merely set up a straw man, see Stueber 1997 and Devitt 1996, 15–16. Nevertheless as I have argued in my 1997a, Fodor and Lepore are misconstruing the nature of holism that is implied by Davidson's analysis of radical interpretation. As I argue there, they and others do not sufficiently distinguish between Quine's empiricist holism and the holism of radical interpretation. The radical version of holism only follows if like Quine we reject the analytic–synthetic distinction and conceive of unconceptualized sensory experience as the only basis for meaning and content. Under this assumption the meaning of each sentence is fully determined by its logical integration into a theory that confronts sensory experience only as a whole. Every change in the logical structure of the theory therefore has to count as a change of meaning.

12. That we don't worry about attributing a certain amount of irrationality to an agent, as Goldman (1995) suggests, is not an argument against my position. It just shows that we either act epistemically irresponsibly or that we tend to have implicit answers to such questions. My point is that the attribution of irrationality potentially constitutes a reason for questioning the validity of the interpretation. If raised, this question has to be answered.

13. I, however, disagree with Henderson's rejection of the principle of charity as an a priori constraint on interpretation, at least within the context of our folk-psychological practices, and his subsumption of the principle of charity under what he calls the principle of explicability that requires us attributing beliefs and desires only if they can be accounted for by our available psychological theories (Henderson 1993). Part of the disagreement here might have to do with disagreement about what exactly the rationality assumption implies. As I see it, questions of explicability are raised only when the rationality constraint is prima facie violated.

14. Davidson would disagree with this position, since he would suggest that in order to have a belief one also needs to possess the concept of a belief. Ordinary intuitions speak against Davidson. See also Ludwig 2004 for a critique of Davidson's argument in support of this position.

15. I see my considerations here as in general compatible with Pettit's and Koorsgard's positions. In his *Fundamental Prinicples for a Metaphysics of Morals*, Kant suggests that normative questions arise only for creatures for which conformity to the rules of reason is not automatic. Only such creatures are able to recognize the rules of reason as normatively binding; that is, as imperatives. The "Holy Will," on the other hand, is not in such a predicament. Hence God does not conceive of rules of reason as imperatives. If I am right, it is not the ability to conform to rules of reason that raises the question of normativity but the capacity for self-reflection. To be charitable, Kant probably thought that all beings that live up to standards of reason have such an ability. Nevertheless, to engage in some nonempirical metaphysics, one might argue *pace* Kant that even the Holy Will must be able to recognize the rules of reasons as imperatives valid for all rational creatures, since otherwise It would be in no position to judge others accordingly.

16. Dennett had at one point supported the requirement of deductive closure, but he has disavowed it since then. See Dennett 1987, 94. For other references, see Cherniak 1986.

17. Knowledge of the limitations of the human mind is also a prerequisite for devising better strategies for educating ourselves about what we regard as the proper norms of reasoning. Philosophers during the Enlightenment and current researchers in psychology have tended to focus on these potentially positive aspects of their research. It has to be pointed out that such knowledge, as all knowledge, always has potentially negative consequences. It can and certainly has been used to better manipulate the human mind in the public domain. Knowing that the mind tends to disregard abstract statistical information and is much more easily guided or misguided by information presented very vividly allows us also to devise rather devious political advertisements. Here one might want to think, for example, about the infamous Willie Horton ad by the Bush campaign in the presidential election between George Bush Sr. and Michael Dukakis. Nevertheless, since our only other option is to bury our head in the sand, I suggest that the only remedy against the misuse of knowledge is more knowledge in the context of proper moral education and public discussion about appropriate rules of conduct.

18. As Ralph Hertwig has pointed out in conversation, researchers committed to the bounded rationality model are not only interested in cognitive adaptations that are selected for in the evolutionary history of the species. They also apply the evolutionary model to the history of the cognitive development of the individual. For the development of the paradigm in evolutionary psychology, the work of Tooby and Cosmides (1992) has to be acknowledged as ground-breaking. For the purpose of discussing whether such empirical work has normative repercussions, the work of Gigerenzer (1992) is, however, more pertinent. For a discussion of the empirical issues involved in the discussion of rationality within the context of evolutionary psychology, see also Samuels, Stich, and Tremoulet 1999; Samuels, Stich, and Bishop

2002; and Samuels and Stich 2004. Unfortunately these articles only pay attention to the descriptive issues involved and do not sufficiently address the central issue of whether Gigerenzer's suggestions are able to challenge the traditional normative conception of rationality.

19. To be fair to Gigerenzer, one should note that he leaves it to a certain extent open whether cheater detection is indeed the right level of abstraction to characterize the domain of the involved cognitive module or whether it needs to be more abstractly characterized as a module of deontic reasoning (2000, 224). This is in the end an empirical question. For our purposes, however, it is not important to decide this question since even such higher-level abstraction would not endanger his thesis that content-independent norms are the wrong kind of norms.

20. It must be noted, as various authors have pointed out (Kahneman and Tversky 1996; Baron 2000; Samuels, Stich, and Bishop 2002), that ordinarily we do not react to judgments about the probability of single events, such as the likelihood of rain, as if such statements are meaningless.

21. It has to be admitted that the research within the bounded rationality paradigm is ongoing. Researchers within this program still have to determine how they understand the mechanisms that allow organisms to decide which heuristics to follow in specific contexts. Nevertheless, regardless of how this research progresses, the claims implied in the strong reading of the notion of bounded rationality are implausible because they insufficiently take into account the perspective of the agent. On that level, content-independent norms have to be regarded as normatively relevant.

Chapter 3

1. This is particularly true in the writings of Goldman, Stich, and Nichols.

2. For a prime example of epistemological naturalism, see particularly Goldman 1986. I address the relationship between epistemic naturalism and philosophical reflection on the problem of skepticism in Stueber 2001.

3. For examples of this practice see Leslie and German 1995, 124, and Happe and Loth 2002. The examples could be multiplied. Bloom 2002 seems to use the term "theory of mind" ambiguously as referring both to the general mindreading ability and to an account of such ability as involving an underlying theory. For the same ambiguity see also Premack and Woodruff 1978, 518.

4. Within the context of the simulation paradigm, Currie and Ravenscroft (2002) account for autism as a form of "imaginative poverty" (136). For an overview of different theoretical approaches to autism see Baron-Cohen et al. 1993. However, whether autism can be understood primarily as a deficit in mindreading abilities or is rather due to some other more basic mental deficiency is still debated within the relevant literature, since persons with autism are not only deficient in mindreading

but also show weaknesses in other areas. For example, they tend to be impaired in their executive functions. Uta Frith (2003) provides in my opinion the best survey on the broad spectrum of autistic disorders. The only serious shortcoming of her book consists in the fact that she does not consider explanatory accounts from the simulation camp in this context.

5. The boxological manner of representing the various positions in this debate is a favorite method of Stich and Nichols, and it has been very helpful for introducing clarity into a complex debate. But in the development of their own position the postulation of distinct boxes indicating different functional systems seems to be at times psychologically a bit unconstrained. In their 2003, 35, they postulate the existence of a script elaborator, a mechanism or set of mechanisms responsible for the imaginative and creative thinking-through of different possible world scenarios. Certainly we do have that capacity. Normally people refer to it as the capacity of imagination. Yet one wonders what justifies the differentiation between a "possible world box" and a "script elaborator." Such a distinction seems to be justified only if it is possible that one could think about a possible world scenario without imaginatively elaborating on it. Nichols and Stich do not present any evidence for such a scenario. This is important; as it is, I could also postulate a different mechanism for pronouncing each letter of the English alphabet, since everybody who speaks English has that capacity.

6. In contrast to the adult scientist the child is obviously not aware of its theoretical activity and the end result of such theoretical activity can only be conceived of as a tacit theory.

7. Other theory theorists (e.g., Perner 1991) describe the move between stages in different terminology, as a move from a "mentalistic theory of behavior" to a "representational theory of behavior." Only in the last stage is the child able to consider the possibility that the other person has a false belief, because it only now has the capacity for metarepresentation. That is, it understands that another person can subjectively represent or misrepresent an objective state of affairs.

8. Goldman (2000, 178) is quite right to ask whether Leslie can any longer be classified as a theory theorist, since even a simulation theorist could accommodate Leslie's metarepresentations within his framework if the ability to form such data-structures does not imply the possession of a theory.

9. Whether or not these various principles that I use in the schematic representation of possible inferences involved in solving the false-belief task can be attributed to four-year-olds is an empirical question. As far as I know, I am on firm empirical ground (Wellman 1990; Gopnik and Meltzoff 1997).

10. This terminology is due to Davies and Stone (2001, 140). My explication of simulation theory in this paragraph has benefited greatly from this section in Davies and Stone 2001. As they acknowledge, Davies and Stone's distinction goes back to Stich

and Nichols's (1997) distinction between an "actual situation simulation" and "a pretense off-line simulation." The first kind of simulation corresponds to my example of solving a chess problem using actual chess pieces and a chess board. Another example for such simulation is predicting how another person would solve a problem in arithmetic by solving it oneself. In pretense off-line simulation, on the other hand, we feed our cognitive system with pretend beliefs and desires and run it in an off-line manner, that is, without the decision system actually determining our course of action in the real world. Since both simulating processes are very different (only one processes pretend inputs) and since it is to be expected that there will be very different kinds of processes underlying both procedures, Stich and Nichols conclude that it is time to retire the simulation label. This move, however, strikes me as disingenuous and unjustified. The simulation theorist merely claims that the procedures we use for deliberating and arriving at our own decisions are similar to those we use in understanding the states of mind and decisions of other persons. And that still seems to be prima facie plausible. Furthermore, if we understand the simulation proposal as an empirical hypothesis about underlying mechanisms, there certainly will be a myriad of processes underlying our own decision procedures (one of which is a procedure that entertains and draws conclusions from hypothetical assumptions). The simulation theorist merely claims that however many procedures there are, those used in making my own decisions must be the same as those used in understanding other persons. He could leave it up to further empirical research to describe the underlying mechanisms in detail. If I understand him correctly, this is the strategy the Goldman espouses.

11. Although the basic idea of simulation is at times expressed in a terminology that seems to require that the simulator is aware of the fact that he is taking the perspective of the other person, simulation theorists realize that such conscious perspective-taking is rather rare, and that perspective-taking happens most often unconsciously. As an example of such unconscious perspective-taking one might think of the manner in which children and adults seem to process information about stories. As Paul Harris (2000, 49ff.) and others have shown, in processing information about certain story characters, children and adults seem to identify with the perspective of the character in the story and take his or her point of view. Consequently it takes them longer to process information that describes the same event from a different perspective than a description that matches the perspective of the character itself. When hearing the sentence "Bill was sitting in the living room reading the paper," for example, they took longer to process the sentence "when John went into the room" (third-person perspective) than the sentence "when John came into the room" (Bill's perspective). The result is quite suggestive of the thesis that readers do indeed take the perspective of a character at least if that is suggested by the form in which the story is told. Nevertheless, adults and particularly children are very unlikely to be introspectively aware of such perspective-taking.

12. Simulation theorists try to link developmental deficits as observed in autism to a deficit in the autist's imaginative abilities (Gordon and Barker 1994; Currie and Ravenscroft 2002).

13. Note also that even though neuroscientists have come to accept the existence of physical and neuronal resonance phenomena as a necessary precondition for our understanding of other persons, they are quite aware of the fact that there have to be additional neurobiological mechanisms that allow us to differentiate between observed actions, pains, or emotions in others and my experiencing of pain or my executing an action. Hence there has to be a neurobiological mechanism that also underlies our ability to distinguish between ourselves and others. Ruby and Decety (2003, 2004), for example, have found that being asked to take the perspective of another person—in order to consider how that other person would think or feel in that situation—also involves other areas of the brain (particularly the frontalpolar cortex, medial prefrontal cortex, and the posterior cingulated) than when we are asked to imagine how we ourselves would feel or think in that situation (see Decety and Jackson 2004 for a review). How exactly these findings have to be interpreted is still subject to debate and further empirical research.

14. It is also for similar reasons that we should regard folk-psychological explanations to be autonomous from physical and neurobiological explanations of behavior. For a detailed argument for this claim, see Stueber 2005.

15. See also Perner 1996 and Henderson 1995.

16. For a critique of the metaphor of thoughts as "objects in or before the mind," see particularly Davidson, "What Is Present to the Mind," in his 2001.

17. These phenomenological considerations are further supported by a Davidsonian conception of meaning and content based on his analysis of radical interpretation that I outlined in the previous chapter. According to that understanding, our attribution of intentional states such as beliefs and desires to other people proceeds and is epistemically justified independently from an investigation of what goes on in the head of the other person. Within the folk-psychological realm one cannot conceive of such mental states as supervening narrowly on the internal states of a human person; at most they have to be seen as supervening broadly or widely on complex causal relations between a person and his environment. Describing other people in intentional terminology has to be seen as a personal-level characterization or as an attribution of a personal-level property. For an explication of the Davidsonian argument for the nonreducibility of mental content, see also Child 1994. Nevertheless, Child seems to think that Davidsonian considerations are compatible with the idea that mental properties supervene strongly on physical properties relative to particular contexts. For a critique of Child in this regard see Stueber 1997b. The foregoing considerations about the nonreducibility of mental content are certainly discussed controversially within the philosophical community. Unfortunately, they are hardly

discussed at all in the context of this debate. Goldman (2002) explicitly denies that an investigation of our folk-psychological abilities has anything to do with an investigation into the metaphysical issue of the nature of propositional attitudes. Yet in taking the position that simulation theory is principally a theory about subpersonal mechanisms, one adopts implicitly a metaphysical stance regarding the nature of our folk-psychological description of other agents, a stance that at least needs to be clarified within this context.

18. Heal (1995a) also speaks of simulation or what she calls in this article replication as a "process of recentering the world in imagination" (1986, 48). In this context it has to be admitted that it is a bit difficult to pin down Gordon in regard to whether or not he takes the notion of rational agency to be central to our folk-psychological practice and central to simulation. He certainly rejects the idea that understanding action requires finding normatively sanctioned good reasons. Rather, when simulating another person's action we have to understand how another person could be moved to act (Gordon 1995b, 104). More recently, Gordon has elaborated on his understanding of "reasons for action" (Gordon 2000a,b, 2001). Against the mainstream conception in philosophy of mind, Gordon does not conceive of reasons for actions primarily as the beliefs and desires of the agents but understands them as the facts in the world. I am a bit skeptical whether this approach to explicating reasons is viable. First, it is not clear to me how facts in the world as reasons can be conceived of as causes for actions. Facts alone do not cause me to act in a certain manner; rather that I conceive of the world in a certain way in connection with my desire causes me to act. Second, facts alone move me to action only in the context of having certain desires. Gordon's explication of reasons, however, completely disregards the desire component of the traditional conception of reasons.

19. In this context one also has to heed the warnings of hermeneutic philosophers, who in my opinion correctly insist that we can never completely disassociate ourselves from our cognitive, moral, and emotional outlook on the world. Just assume, for example, that I hate Brussels sprouts. How do I transform my egocentric map so that I simulate somebody who likes them? Gordon seems to suggest that I choose an "equivalent replacement" (Gordon 1995b, 109–110), i.e., I assume that this person likes Brussels sprouts as much as I like blueberries. In this case, however, one could not say that the "I" in the simulation refers merely to the simulated person, since my liking blueberries and not Brussels sprouts does all the work in the context of the simulation.

20. Another often mentioned example is the puzzling phenomenon of blindsight, where patients experience damage to part of their visual cortex and report not to see anything in specific areas of their visual field. Yet when asked to guess what objects might be in front of them they perform significantly above chance. This is possible because even though there is damage to the visual cortex, some information is nevertheless processed by other neural pathways of the perceptual system without

the person being conscious of any visual experience. While a phenomenon such as blindsight seems prima facie to be an oxymoron from our ordinary folk-psychological perspective, recognizing that it is a result of the processing of information through some neural pathways that are also normally involved in perception seems to put some pressure on our ordinary way of thinking about perception as a phenomenon that requires some conscious awareness.

Chapter 4

1. Gordon 1995c, 60. Earlier Gordon had claimed that saying that Smith believes that Dewey won the election is the same as saying "let's do a Smith simulation. Ready? *Dewey won the election.*" As Heal remarked this analysis seems to be analogous to speech act accounts of moral concepts and thus faces the same difficulties (Heal 1995b, 43). Gordon's later accounts avoid this objection. Recently Gordon has moved closer to Goldman in agreeing that the mechanism behind our answering a certain object level question might be based on a certain qualitative feeling. See Gordon 1996, 16. But that concession does not really amount to much, since Gordon still rejects Goldman's experientialism as an account of how we come to understand mental concepts.

2. Gordon 1996, 18; 1995c, 61ff. In his 1995c, Gordon seems to suggest that simulation alone can provide us with a complete understanding of the concept of belief. In 1996 he seems to suggest that simulation allows us to form a complete understanding of the concept of belief only if the simulation is guided by certain principles like the rule that facts do not necessarily have to be facts to somebody. Whether or not this constitutes a concession to theory theory I will leave undiscussed here. Gordon denies it because he says it does not mean that simulation is guided by certain generalizations in discursive form. However, this response seems to be insufficient, if one accepts Stich's and Nichol's provision that the theory theorist could accept that the internal theory is implemented in a connectionist framework.

3. Goldman's rejection of a theory-theory or functionalist account of mental concepts is motivated independently of his proposal for simulation theory. As he argues in his 1993 and 2002, if we accept a functionalist account of mental state concepts according to which each type of mental state is defined in terms of its causal relations to other mental states, then knowing that we are in a particular type of mental state presupposes that we are able to detect its relations to other mental states. And detecting that we are in those other mental states requires that we detect their relations to other mental states, and so on. Self-knowledge would thus entail the postulation of an extraordinarily complex internal mechanism, a result that Goldman find utterly implausible. I am not fully persuaded by Goldman's argument. In my opinion it presupposes—as has been pointed out in the discussion about self-knowledge and semantic externalism (Stueber 2000b)—the invalid principle that in order to be aware that one is in a particular mental state one has to know all of the constitutive facts

for that mental state. As an epistemic externalist and reliabilist, however, Goldman does not make this assumption. For me to know that the object in front of me is made of gold I do not have to be aware of the fact that the object in front of me has the chemical structure constitutive for being gold. All that seems required is that my belief that this object is made of gold is formed by a reliable perceptual mechanism. The functionalist can respond to Goldman that in order to explain self-knowledge he merely has to postulate the existence of mechanisms that reliably link a second-order belief state that I believe that I am in a mental state of type m to first-order states of type m. I do not have to detect all the relations that are constitutive for a mental state of type m. Notice also that the functionalist would insist that second-order states are functionally defined. Even though they do not sufficiently answer Goldman's objection, Nichols and Stich's (2003) monitoring account of self-knowledge that goes back to Armstrong (1968) is pointing in that direction.

Another worry, however, looms large over Goldman's proposed account of self-knowledge. He is primarily concerned with accounting for our knowledge of the type of mental state we are in; that is, he wants to explain how we know whether we have a belief or a desire. Yet we not only know that we have beliefs; we also know the contents of our beliefs. According to widespread philosophical opinion, such content is constituted partly by the causal relations between the believer and the world. Thus Goldman has to address the problem of how his inner-feature detection model of self-knowledge can be reconciled with semantic externalism. How is it possible that I recognize that I believe that water is wet by recognizing some internal feature, if the content of my belief is constituted by specific causal relations to the environment? One option would be to argue for a bifurcation of content into narrow and broad content and to suggest that we can directly know only narrow content. I am not a particular fan of the notion of narrow content. It should also be quite unattractive for somebody wanting to provide an account of folk psychology, a context in which we ordinarily assume that we know the truth conditions of our thoughts. Goldman does not seem to have made up his mind regarding semantic externalism. In his 1995a, 92, he emphasizes that his discussion of simulation is not supposed to contradict the idea that the external world partly determines the referent of a thought. In his 1993, 25, Goldman seems to opt for a more internalist approach. In any case, semantic externalism is incompatible with the assumption of self-knowledge only if one accepts the principle that I mention above.

4. Needless to say there is considerable controversy over how exactly to interpret Wittgenstein in this regard. See, e.g., McDowell 1982.

5. As is also well known, Wittgenstein and Wittgensteinians do not conceive of our folk-psychological framework as enabling us to provide causal explanations of behavior. Rather it provides us merely with a framework to interpret behavior as rational action. For Wittgensteinians, however, such reinterpretation has to be strictly distinguished from causal explanation. Following Davidson, I do not believe that Wittgenstein succeeds in arguing for this claim. For a brief discussion of this topic

see the relevant passage of the introduction to Kögler and Stueber 2000. Here I focus on a different strand in Wittgenstein's explication of our folk-psychological practices.

6. See also Wittgenstein 1980, I, 915–916, in regard to one's primitive reactions to the pain of another person. It is also in this context that one has to view Wittgenstein's remarks that terms like "thinking" or "believing" used in the first person are not based on introspection and do not describe particular inner mental experiences. See, e.g., I, 463ff., and II, 183ff.

7. Wittgenstein explicitly rejects the idea that our ability to directly recognize the emotions of another person could be further explained in terms of inner mechanisms of imitation, as Lipps has claimed. See, e.g., I, 1980, 927. I, however, do not know whether Wittgenstein ever read Lipps.

8. Since Hobson's (1991) critique of the theory-theory position is based mainly on Wittgensteinian considerations, his critique suffers from the same shortcomings. I am nevertheless very sympathetic to Hobson's critique of theory theory and the alternative position he hints at toward the end of his article, but I think one needs a different argumentative strategy to reach it.

9. Lipps himself concentrated on our use of terms for emotions. In response to problems similar to those I will diagnose for theory theory, he regarded empathy, conceived of as a noninferential strategy, as basic for our recognition of other minds.

10. This seems to be how Sellars thinks of learning a first-personal use of "I am thinking that p" (Sellars 1963, 189).

11. These Wittgensteinian considerations are supported by empirical evidence that points to the central importance of sociolinguistic conversations about mental topics to the acquisition of folk-psychological categories and the development of folk-psychological abilities. It has for example been found that "profoundly deaf children who grow up in hearing families" (i.e., in families without any member fluent in sign language) "often lag several years behind hearing children in their development of an understanding of false belief" (Peterson and Siegal 2000, 127; see also Garfield, Peterson, and Perry 2001). As one explanation for this fact, Peterson and Siegal mention that such children are less likely than hearing children to talk about matters of mind and to "receive explanations from their parents concerning emotions, reasons for actions, expected roles and the consequences of various behavior." Furthermore, it has also been noticed that "children's early talk about feeling states is significantly correlated to later understanding of belief as measured on false belief tasks" (Bartsch and Wellman 1995). This is certainly a plausible explanation for the observed delay in the mindreading abilities of these deaf children. Whether it is the only possible interpretation of these facts remains to be seen, especially in light of Harris's (2000) suggestion that individual differences in solving the false-belief task is also linked to increased opportunities for engaging in cooperative role play. Yet it should give fur-

ther pause to an empirically minded philosopher like Goldman. If our conception of mental states is indeed based primarily on an understanding of our own mind then it is not clear why deaf children should lag behind in their understanding of other people in this respect, since they presumably have access to their own mind in the same way normal children do. However, these findings are not merely difficult to account for from the perspective of simulation theorists like Goldman but also do not fit well with a certain conception of the theory theory according to which the child is seen as analogous to a scientist engaged in theory construction—especially if the scientist is conceived of as a lonely Cartesian agent trying to investigate the structure of the world, as seems to be the case in Gopnik and Meltzoff 1997. For this reason, theory theorists have to accept mechanisms of empathy since otherwise they are hard pressed to explain how it is possible that science is a social and cooperative enterprise, in which agents—children or adults—are able to learn from each other, particularly if they do not share each other's theoretical perspective. For a critique of Gopnik and Meltzoff's insufficiently social understanding of science and the child-as-scientist metaphor, see Astington 1996; Stich and Nichols 1998; Faucher et al. 2002.

12. Gordon (1996) nevertheless seems to mention the ability of gaze tracking in support of simulation theory.

13. Critical questions by David Henderson and Dan Hutto after hearing presentations of a draft of this chapter have forced me to clarify my position in regard to the question of how much theoretical knowledge is presupposed in assuming conceptual competence.

14. In more technical terms, Heal (2001) suggests that we have to view content expressions as Lagadonian kind terms, that is, we have to conceive of them as essentially "narrowly indexical" expressions. Understanding the reference of such expressions essentially requires the presence of an entity or property referred to by this expression. For our discussion we can abstract from Heal's technical terminology.

15. See, however, Stich and Nichols 1998 in this respect. In the context of philosophy of language, Michael Dummett has used similar considerations to argue that knowledge of a theory of truth à la Davidson cannot be sufficient for an explication of linguistic competence. See Stueber 1993 for a more detailed discussion of Dummett's critique of the Davidsonian program.

16. Similar examples feature prominently in Searle's arguments for the background. See Searle 1983, 145ff., and Searle 1992, 178ff.

17. For a brief suggestion for widening the scope of co-cognition or simulation, see Heal 2003a, 78–79. Similarly, Collingwood has often been thought to limit the scope of reenactment to the level of conscious thought and exclude the realm of other phenomenal states such as feelings and emotions. Reenactment does not allow us to

reconstruct what Collingwood calls the psychology of "blind forces," and "how the flowers smelt in the garden of Epicurus, or how Nietzsche felt the wind in his hair as he walked on the mountains" (Collingwood 1946, 296, 231). Collingwood characterizes the relations between such mental events as blind because it does not make sense to characterize them in normative terms as rational or irrational, right or wrong. They are mere causal associations, such as the association between somebody's hearing a particular piece of music and thinking of his wife because he first met his wife while listening to the same piece of music. There is nothing right or wrong about him making this association. Somebody's listening to a piece of music does not justify thinking of his wife in an intersubjective manner, in the same way that Newton's being hit by the apple does not justify his theory of gravity, even though it might have caused him to think of it. But in the recently discovered and published manuscript, Collingwood (1999, 67–69) clarifies his position to a certain extent. Here he seems to allow that a historian's understanding of another person's thoughts includes the realm of emotions if they are "essentially related" to a certain plan of action. He is also quite explicit about the fact that even thoughts can be related to each other based on mere causal associations grounded in an individual's biography. Such thoughts therefore have to be seen as outside the scope of the method most appropriate for proper historical research. For further discussion of this aspect of Collingwood, see Dray 1995, chap. 4.

18. In the continental tradition of philosophy, Dieter Henrich and Manfred Frank argue similarly. See especially Frank 1991.

19. A word of caution in this context. I do not intend my remarks to constitute an exhaustive interpretation of Kant. But I do think that Kant's remarks on the self and the "I think," especially in the "Paralogism" chapter of the *Critique of Pure Reason*, are compatible with the conception of self-awareness and the irreducible role of the I-concept that is explicated by Castañeda, Perry, and others. In her 2000, Patricia Kitcher takes issue with this interpretation of Kant. She reminds us that Kant's reflections on the "I" have to be situated within his larger epistemic project. Insofar as her critique of McDowell's take on Kant is concerned, her point is well taken. Yet, *pace* Kitcher, I do not think that Perry-like considerations about the "I" are necessarily incompatible with Kant's larger epistemological project. Kitcher argues that Kant could be interpreted in that manner only if he would have asserted a "philosophically interesting asymmetry between first person and third person ascriptions of mental states" (2000, 49). She cites the same passage that I quote, in support of the view that Kant did not acknowledge such an asymmetry. Yet only in the context of a Cartesian conception of the mind, which Kant rejects, does the problem of other minds arise. If we accept instead that other persons share our psychological structure, for either empirical or transcendental reasons, then we can accept simulation as a method of recognizing other minds and at the same time acknowledge the special status of the I-concept. More importantly, if I am right, accepting such special status supports a conception of interpretation favored by Collingwood and simulation theorists.

20. The following considerations are due to pertinent questions raised by Dan Hutto in response to a presentation based on a draft of this chapter at the "Phenomenology, Intersubjectivity, and Theory of Mind" conference at the University of Central Florida, January 2004.

21. Davies and Stone (2001, 136) have suggested that the above argument in favor of what I call reenactive empathy can show only that an alternative to theory theory is available, not that we as a matter of fact use it for understanding other agents. It has to be noted that Davies and Stone do not present Heal's argument in its strongest form as she presents it in her 1996. They do not discuss the frame problem at all in this context. In my opinion the argument at least establishes some involvement of simulation in our folk-psychological interpretations. The question is whether empirical evidence could plausibly make the case that as a matter of fact theoretical inferences are also involved. I am skeptical in this respect.

22. This fact is not sufficiently recognized by Botterill and Carruthers (1999, 84).

23. Collingwood does not address this issue in the context of the ceteris paribus character of psychological generalizations. Furthermore, he does not clearly distinguish between the causal and epistemic contexts of addressing this question; that is, he does not sufficiently distinguish whether appeal to generalizations is causally superfluous from whether it is also superfluous in giving an epistemic justification of a reason explanation.

24. In this context I would like to address briefly the question of whether our systematic inability to predict certain types of behavior as witnessed in some psychological experiments can be used as empirical evidence in favor of theory theory as Stich and Nichols have argued. In the literature this topic has also been discussed under the heading of "cognitive penetrability." According to this line of reasoning, simulation theory requires that we put ourselves in the situation of the targets and simulate their thought processes in order to predict their behavior. On that model we should expect to predict the observed behavior of the target in a variety of experiments in an accurate manner. Yet as experiments in social psychology have shown, we are not able to predict the behavior of subjects in the famous Milgram experiments; we are surprised to learn that subjects persevere in their false beliefs even if they find out that they originally acquired them based on faulty evidence; and we are not able to predict that people tend to grasp the product to their right when they chose among an array of supposedly qualitatively identical products in a supermarket. It has therefore been concluded that the failure to predict people's behavior in such situations speaks for theory theory, since it suggests that in such predictions we use a false or an incomplete folk-psychological theory. Recently, Nichols and Stich are more careful about the conclusion they draw from such evidence. In their 2003 book, they suggest that we have to distinguish between domains where our predictive capacities are relatively accurate from those where they can be rather inaccurate. Our ability to predict another person's inferences accurately is taken as evidence for the use of the

simulation procedure in this area. Evidence for systematic shortcomings in predicting the behavior of another person accurately is interpreted as suggesting that we
use a faulty theory in those domains. Furthermore, Nichols and Stich (2003, 106)
are nowadays careful not to regard the above considerations as constituting a definite
argument against simulation theory. For a restatement of Stich and Nichols's original
line of argument, see Saxe 2005. Unfortunately, Saxe does not sufficiently address
moves within the simulation paradigm to address the above worries. For an excellent
survey of this debate see Ravenscroft 1999. I tend to agree with Ravenscroft's conclusion that prima facie both theories are "compatible with the data on predictive
failure" (1999, 165). More importantly I conceive of reenactive empathy as being primarily concerned with grasping the reasons of another person's actions in order to
understand that person as the author of his or her actions. Following Heal (2003a), I
am inclined to interpret the difficulties in making accurate predictions as being due
to our difficulties in conceiving of aspects of the situation as providing reasons for
the observed behavior. There seems to be no reason for deciding to take the product
on the right after being told that all the products on the shelf are of equal quality. As
I explain in the last chapter, I admit that our empathetic abilities are limited in this
respect. There I also discuss some strategies of how to overcome such limitations. I
am therefore inclined to think that evidence of predictive failure cannot be used to
undermine the arguments for reenactive empathy as I explicate them in the text.

Chapter 5

1. See, e.g., Jackson 1999. Jackson is most plausibly read as raising the epistemic
question. The most extensive discussion of explanation within the context of the
simulation paradigm is Arkway 2000. Arkway's conclusions tend to be mainly negative, yet even she does not sufficiently distinguish between questions of underlying
causal mechanisms and epistemic questions of justification. The debate today is at
times very unclear which question it is addressing. Goldman (1995a) only briefly
alludes to epistemic considerations. He rejects the deductive nomological model of
explanation and opts for a pragmatic account of explanation (1995a, 89) without
providing any account of how simulation would be explanatorily relevant within
the framework of such a pragmatic understanding. Recently, Heal (2003c) has
addressed some of these issues insofar as the question of the justification of folk-
psychological predictions is concerned. But she insufficiently recognizes the epistemic differences between justifying a prediction and providing an explanation.

Robert Gordon's recent work (2000a, 2001) on the nature of reason explanation
constitutes a notable exception in this regard. For him the difference between a reason explanation and causal explanation consists in the differences between the counterfactuals that support such explanations. In interpreting a "causal" counterfactual
such as "If there hadn't been smoke in the kitchen, the smoke alarm would not have
gone off," we use the Ramsey procedure. In interpreting counterfactuals rationally
such as "If there hadn't been smoke in the kitchen, I would not have run into it,"

we use a simulation procedure. Gordon's account of reason explanation continues in the tradition of Dray and Collingwood and their insistence on a distinction between rational and causal necessities. It points in the right direction. Yet Gordon points to the wrong counterfactual and the wrong generalizations as the information that sanctions folk-psychological explanations. In explaining why you ran into the kitchen by pointing to the fact that there was smoke in the kitchen, I certainly presuppose that you believed that there was smoke in the kitchen. If I could change your belief about the kitchen I would thereby also change your behavior. Merely making sure that there is no smoke in the kitchen while letting you continue to believe that there is would not change your behavior. If this is the case then one could argue that explanations of actions in terms of their reasons require appeal to psychological generalizations only for their epistemic justification. If that should turn out to be true, any appeal to empathy seems to be prima facie epistemically irrelevant to folk-psychological explanations. I suspect that Gordon is attracted to his account because it would allow him to explicate how young children could explain actions in terms of their reasons without having a concept of belief. It fits with his general claim that our ability to simulate does not presuppose a possession of psychological concepts.

2. See also Hempel 1965, 239–240, 257–258. Popper argues similarly in his 1957, 138. For the most detailed rejection of empathy along those lines see particularly Abel 1948.

3. I also disagree with Heal's claim that assumptions of psychological similarity are optional in this context and could be replaced with specific principles about rational thought processes. She suggests, for example, that the prediction based on simulation that a person M believes that q should be seen as being supported by the following assumptions:

1. M believes that p_1-p_n and is interested in whether q.
2. That p_1-p_n entail that q.
3. M is such that given the belief in the premises of an entailment and interest in the conclusion, she will come to believe the conclusion. (Heal 2003c, 135)

My objection to Heal rests on two points. First, as I have elaborated, as far as the epistemic justification of simulation as a predictive tool is concerned, it does not necessitate any appeal to psychological generalizations such as (3). Second, and more importantly, as it stands (3) is obviously false, as Heal herself recognizes. Generalizations such as (3) would have to be read as containing a strong ceteris paribus clause and would have to be restricted to entailment relations that are obvious or, as Heal formulates it, are "prima facie" entailment relations. Once one relativizes premises (2) and (3) in this fashion, one implicitly builds in a reference to psychological similarity. The only way to understand prima facie entailment relations as having specific empirical content is to consider them to be entailment relations that I would recognize as such. Yet the only reason for me to suppose that you will recognize such a prima facie entailment relation is that you and I are psychologically similar in the relevant sense. It must be pointed out that Heal's suggestion comes close to Hempel's claim that explanations and predictions of a person's behavior are supported by the assumptions that this person is a rational agent and that the rational thing for him to do in a particular situation is x (see Hempel 1965, 471 ff.).

4. Schiffer (1991) focuses his discussion of ceteris paribus laws on folk-psychological generalizations. He is skeptical about the prospect of folk-psychological ceteris paribus laws because any attempt to make them more precise would lead to formulations of laws in the vocabulary of the more fundamental physical sciences. Such laws would therefore have to exclude any genuinely explanatory role for psychological properties. On the question of the explanatory autonomy of mental properties, see Stueber 2005a.

5. Focusing here on the special sciences, I am obviously assuming that there are strict and exceptionless laws in the basic sciences like physics. As is well known, Nancy Cartwright doubts this assumption. Yet, if one agrees with Cartwright, the assumption that such laws are required in support of our explanatory practices seems even less plausible. See Woodward 2003.

6. For my purposes of explicating the function of empathy within folk-psychological explanations, I could, however, live with a position à la Pietroski and Rey. The position I want to develop could even be adapted to its framework. See Stueber 2003 in this regard.

7. For a brief summary of Woodward, see also Henderson 2005. Henderson uses Woodward's notions to explicate the explanatory role of descriptions of norms in the social sciences. Henderson first made me aware of Woodward's explication of the nature of explanation.

8. It has to be pointed out that the question of how to characterize the domain of a generalization is an empirical one. It is an important question of exactly how one distinguishes between factors that are properly part of the formulation of the invariant generalization and properties that are characterize merely the domain of a generalization. I am not sure that Woodward sufficiently addresses this question. I suspect that one has to admit the relevance of certain pragmatic criteria having to do with the explanatory interest of the various disciplines.

9. Some philosophers, however, have challenged the claim that folk-psychological generalizations have an empirical status. For them such generalizations are more like analytic principles. I have shown in Stueber 2003 that these worries are unfounded. There I argue that we can account for the epistemic intuitions that prima facie support the analytic character of such generalizations by realizing that our understanding of folk-psychological concepts is essentially tied to our reenactive capacities. We cannot imagine that somebody else would not act according to the central action principle of folk psychology, since we cannot imagine that we would act

differently. I am inclined to speak of an "a priori" entitlement to regard intentional generalizations of the above form as a default assumption of psychological interpretation. In doing so, I do not deny that these generalizations are also empirical generalizations that describe the psychological dispositions of specific agents. Moreover, I show that the most explicit argument for the analytic character of folk-psychological considerations (Rosenberg 1985, 1995a) depends on a behaviorist conception of the evidence for the attribution of mental states to others.

10. I base my reconstruction of Dray's argument on his 1957. As his 1995 explication of Collingwood's thesis of reenactment reveals, Dray is still holding onto this position. He speaks of the need for reenactive explanation because of the quasi-normative element involved in action explanations (1995, chap. 3). For my reconstruction of Collingwood within the context of current philosophy of mind see Stueber 2002a.

11. See also Henderson 1993, 177. Dray acknowledges this line of thought indirectly by admitting that rational action explanations require the "standing presumption" that "people act for sufficient reason" (Dray 1957, 137).

Chapter 6

1. It is unimportant that Wittgensteinians—in my opinion wrongly—conceive of mental concepts as playing no role in the causal explanation of behavior. They view them as being used only for redescribing the significance of behavior within the wider public and social realm. For an elaboration of this line of reasoning within the philosophy of social science, see Winch 1958. Besides regarding the arguments for such a noncausal conception of our folk-psychological practices to be lacking, I also find it unsatisfactory that it is not clear what point such a redescription of behavior serves within the Wittgensteinian framework. For a brief discussion of this point, see Stueber 2003.

2. For a brief analysis of Droysen's position, see the relevant sections of Lorenz 1997 and Gadamer 1989.

3. See, e.g., Jane Heal 1995a, 48. Robert Gordon has stressed this fact repeatedly in conversation with me and in his writings. See his 1995b,c and 1996.

4. Bevir agrees with Davidson that our folk-psychological notions are constrained by normative principles of rationality that have no equivalent in the physical sciences. For him this implies only that the folk-psychological idiom is irreducible to the categories of the physical sciences; it has no implications for the structure of justification. See Bevir 1999, 177–187.

5. This is probably because, in emphasizing reenactment as *the* method of the historian, Collingwood focuses on what he perceives as the main difference between the science of history and the natural sciences as positivism conceived of them.

6. Bevir also suggests that there can be no method for understanding human thoughts by pointing to the essential creativity of human thought processes. For that reason we are unable to predict how an agent will respond to an intellectual challenge. We can understand these responses only retrospectively by comparing various interpretative proposals according to the relevant epistemic standards. Here Bevir confuses a number of issues. On the one hand he seems to suggest that the method for understanding thought processes has to be an algorithmic method. But as we have seen, reenactment is necessary because we cannot expect to possess such an algorithmic method for deciding what is relevant in a particular context. Furthermore, reenactment is concerned not with reconstructing all of an agent's mental associations in a particular dilemma but only with his reasons for accepting a particular solution to the dilemma. See Bevir 1999, 249–250.

In the beginning of the book, Bevir (1999) tries to make a similar point by referring to Davidson's claim that our capacity to understand deviant utterances like malapropisms shows that linguistic competence cannot be theoretically explicated. However, Davidson's account of malapropism is an argument only against a theory-theory model of linguistic understanding. *Pace* Bevir, these considerations indeed buttress my position that reenactive empathy is important for understanding rational agency. I understand these utterances because I am able to reconstruct a person's communicative intentions in light of my projective abilities to grasp what would be relevant and appropriate to say in a particular context. Otherwise I could not even understand a linguistic utterance as a deviation. Unfortunately, Davidson draws even stronger conclusions from his considerations about malapropisms. He claims that a language cannot be understood as a system of rules or conventions. See Stueber 1993, 169ff., for a diagnosis of this mistaken conclusion. Nevertheless Davidson's considerations cast doubt on the classification of the rationality approach to interpretation as a version of the theory theory, as Goldman 1995a suggests. See also Stueber 2000 in this regard.

7. See, however, Henderson and Horgan 2000 for a discussion of the limits of simulation within the context of a connectionist conception of the structure of the mind. As I read them, Henderson and Horgan raise similar objections to a strategy of pure simulation from the perspective of current philosophy of mind as those that have been raised from the perspective of traditional philosophy of social science. See also Stueber 2000, sec. 3.

8. Again, I want to stress here that I am not interested in an exegesis of particular authors within this tradition. I am interested in a systematic reconstruction of the line of arguments that have been involved in the critique of empathy.

9. Incidentally, Collingwood—in contrast to current simulation theorists—is quite aware of the fact that historians who have to rely on the method of reenactment cannot find all periods of history intelligible; see Collingwood 1946, 218–219. Collingwood, however, does not sufficiently discuss supplementary strategies to overcome

these limitations. For a discussion of such supplementary strategies, see Stueber 2000, 2002a and Henderson and Horgan 2000.

10. I want to emphasize that the argument so far does not imply that empathy is conceptually impossible. If the thesis about the prejudicial structure of understanding would be understood in this manner, it would be equivalent to the thesis that we are never able to reenact another person's thoughts because we never share the exact same mental states. Understood in this manner the critique of empathy would depend on a radical form of belief holism according to which we can share one belief or thought only if we share all beliefs and thoughts. But as I have argued, such a thesis of holism should be rejected as implausible and as not in any way supported by our interpretive practices within the folk-psychological realm.

It has not always been clear whether the critique of empathy within the hermeneutic tradition has been conceived of as pointing to a conceptual impossibility or a mere practical impossibility. It seems to me that Gadamer at times comes close to making a conceptual point; see Stueber 2002a in this regard. The conceptual point is also often made in another form. Some have objected to empathy because of the fact that in attempting to rethink another person's thoughts we have to be methodologically aware of the relevant differences between us and that person. Winch, for example, claims that the way a historian entertains the thoughts of historical figures "will be coloured by the fact that he has had to employ historiographical method to recapture them. The medieval knight did not have to use those methods in order to view his lady in terms of the notions of courtly love: he just thought of her in those terms" (1958, 132). All of this certainly has to be granted. As a matter of fact, I have already expressed my reservations toward the idea that reenactment requires a complete transformation of the ego-centric map, as has been suggested in some of the remarks of Robert Gordon. As I understand it, proponents of empathy do not have to commit themselves to the claim that in reenacting the thoughts of a medieval knight we have to "become" medieval knights. It just requires us to commit ourselves to the claim that in trying to grasp their reasons for action we have to use ourselves as a model and use our imaginative and deliberative powers to grasp these as reasons that we could have in their situation.

As we have seen, such an empathetic ability is best understood as an extension of our ordinary capacities for counterfactual reasoning. In entertaining a thought whose truth I am not yet committed to, one would nevertheless say that I am thinking the same thought even if I do not believe that it is true. Again, the only reason to deny this conclusion would be to espouse a radical and implausible version of holism according to which any difference in our cognitive attitudes has to count as a difference in thought. Never mind about medieval knights in this case; we could not grasp the thoughts of any other person, since there always will be some cognitive aspects in which we differ. I could not even rethink my thoughts from yesterday, since yesterday I might have been more depressed than today, for example. Even though in attempting to reenact your own thoughts I have to be aware of the differences between you and me—something that you certainly did not necessarily have to be aware of in confronting and reacting to the world in a certain manner—I could still be thought of as reenacting your thoughts even though I do so in a more reflective manner than you.

11. All members of one society certainly do not agree in their emotional attachments regarding various norms, but I would suggest that there has to be some significant overlap in this respect. It is certainly possible and even likely that within the same society somebody might follow certain rules for merely strategic reasons (he conforms to them merely because he fears the ramifications of getting caught) whereas another person might think of them as essential for the well-being of a society.

12. The perspective suggested by the theory theory is not the default mode of ordinary folk. Instead it seems to be the default mode of highly competent autistic persons such as Temple Grandin, who describes herself as an anthropologist from Mars (Sacks 1995).

13. Viewing the interpretive process as open-ended for the above reasons does not imply a position of interpretive relativism. As I have argued in Stueber 1994b, interpretive relativism can be avoided in light of the fact that the open-endedness of the interpretive process does not imply that interpretations cannot be compared with each other and critically evaluated in light of the evidence. In regard to questions about the objectivity of historical narratives, see Stueber 2004.

References

Abel, T. 1948. "The Operation Called *Verstehen.*" *American Journal of Sociology* 54: 211–218. (Reprinted in Fred Dallmayr and Thomas McCarthy, eds., 1977, *Understanding and Social Inquiry*, Notre Dame: Notre Dame University Press.)

Adams, F. 2001. "Empathy, Neural Imaging, and the Theory versus Simulation Debate." *Mind and Language* 16: 368–392.

Alston, William. 1989. *Epistemic Justification*. Ithaca, N.Y.: Cornell University Press.

Aristotle. 1985. *Nicomachean Ethics*. Trans. T. Irwin. Indianapolis: Hackett.

Arkway, A. 2000. "The Simulation Theory, the Theory Theory, and Folk Psychological Explanation." *Philosophical Studies* 98: 115–137.

Armstrong, D. 1968. *A Materialist Theory of Mind*. London: Routledge and Kegan Paul.

Astington, J. 1996. "What Is Theoretical about a Child's Theory of Mind? A Vygotskian view of Its Development." In *Theories of Theories of Mind*, ed. P. Carruthers and P. Smith, 184–199. Cambridge: Cambridge University Press.

Astington, J. W. 2001. "The Paradox of Intention: Assessing Children's Metarepresentational Understanding." In *Intentions and Intentionality*, ed. B. B. Malle, L. J. Moses, and D. A. Baldwin, 85–103. Cambridge, Mass.: MIT Press.

Avenarius, R. 1912 (1891). *Der Menschliche Weltbegriff*. Leipzig: L. O. R. Reisland.

Ayton, P. 2000. "Do Birds and Bees Need Cognitive Reform?" *Behavioral and Brain Sciences* 23: 666–667.

Baker, L. R. 1995. *Explaining Attitudes*. Cambridge: Cambridge University.

Baker, L. R. 1999. "What Is the Thing Called 'Common Sense Psychology'?" *Philosophical Explorations* 1: 3–19.

Baron, J. 2000. *Thinking and Deciding*. Cambridge: Cambridge University Press.

Baron-Cohen, S. 1995. *Mindblindness*. Cambridge, Mass.: MIT Press.

Baron-Cohen, S., H. Tager-Flusberg, and D. J. Cohen, eds. 1993. *Understanding Other Minds*. Oxford: Oxford University Press.

Bartsch, K., and H. Wellman. 1995. *Children Talk about the Mind*. Oxford: Oxford University Press.

Beetz, M. 1981. "Nachgeholte Hermeneutik: Zum Verhältnis von Interpretations-und Logiklehren in Barock und Aufklärung." *Deutsche Vierteljahrsschrift* 55: 591–628.

Bermúdez, J. 2001. "Normativity and Rationality in Delusional Psychiatric Disorders." *Mind and Language* 16: 457–493.

Bevir, M. 1999. *The Logic of the History of Ideas*. Cambridge: Cambridge University Press.

Bevir, M. 2002. "How to Be an Intentionalist." *History and Theory* 41: 209–217.

Bilgrami, A. 1992. *Belief and Meaning*. Oxford. Blackwell.

Blakemore, S., and J. Decety. 2001. "From the Perception of Action to the Understanding of Intention." *Nature Reviews* 2: 561–567.

Bloom, P. 2000. *How Children Learn the Meanings of Words*. Cambridge, Mass.: MIT Press.

Bloom, P. 2002. "Mindreading, Communication, and the Learning of Names for Things." *Mind and Language* 17: 37–54.

Boeckh, A. 1886. *Encyklopädie und Methodologie der Philologischen Wissenschaften*. Leipzig: Teubner Verlag.

Bohman, James. 1991. *New Philosophy of Social Science: Problems of Indeterminacy*. Cambridge, Mass.: MIT Press.

Botterill, G. 1996. "Folk Psychology and Theoretical Status." In *Theories of Theories of Mind*, ed. P. Carruthers and P. Smith, 105–118. Cambridge: Cambridge University Press.

Botterill, G., and P. Carruthers. 1999. *The Philosophy of Psychology*. Cambridge: Cambridge University Press.

Bourdieu, P. 1990. *The Logic of Practice*. Stanford: Stanford University Press.

Browning, C. 1992. *Ordinary Men: Reserve Police Battalion 101 and the Final Solution in Poland*. New York: HarperCollins.

Burge, T. 1998. "Reason and the First Person." In *Knowing Our Own Minds*, ed. C. Wright, B. Smith, and C. MacDonald, 244–264. Oxford: Clarendon Press.

Buss, S., and L. Overton, eds. 2002. *Contours of Agency: Essays on Themes from Harry Frankfurt*. Cambridge, Mass.: MIT Press.

Carey, S. 1985. *Conceptual Change in Childhood*. Cambridge, Mass.: MIT Press.

Carruthers, P., and P. K. Smith, eds. 1996. *Theories of Theories of Mind*. Cambridge: Cambridge University Press.

Cherniak, Christopher. 1986. *Minimal Rationality*. Cambridge, Mass.: MIT Press.

Child, W. 1994. *Causality, Interpretation, and the Mind*. Oxford: Clarendon Press.

Child, W. 2002. "Reply to Goldman." In *Simulation and Knowledge of Action*, ed. J. Dokic and J. Proust, 21–31. Amsterdam: John Benjamins.

Chomsky, N. 2000. "Language and Interpretation: Philosophical Reflections and Empirical Inquiry." In his *New Horizons in the Study of Language and Mind*, 75–105. Cambridge: Cambridge University Press.

Chladenius, J. M. 1742. *Einleitung zur richtigen Auslegung vernünftiger Reden und Schriften*. Leipzig.

Churchland, P. M. 1970. "The Logical Character of Action-Explanations." *Philosophical Review* 79: 214–236.

Churchland, P. M. 1989a. "Eliminativism and the Propositional Attitudes." In his *A Neurocomputational Perspective: The Nature of Mind and the Structure of Science*, 1–22. Cambridge, Mass.: MIT Press.

Churchland, P. M. 1989b. "Folk Psychology and the Explanation of Behavior." In his *A Neurocomputational Perspective: The Nature of Mind and the Structure of Science*, 111–127. Cambridge, Mass.: MIT Press.

Churchland, P. S. 1981. "Is Determinism Self-Refuting?" *Mind* 90: 99–101.

Clark, Andy. 2001. *Mindware: An Introduction to the Philosophy of Cognitive Science*. Oxford: Oxford University Press.

Clements, W., and J. Perner. 1994. "Implicit Understanding of Belief." *Cognitive Development* 9: 377–397.

Cohen, J. 1981. "Can Human Irrationality Be Experimentally Demonstrated?" *Behavioral and Brain Sciences* 4: 317–370.

Collingwood, R. G. 1946. *The Idea of History*. Oxford: Clarendon Press.

Collingwood, R. G. 1999. *The Principles of History*. Ed. W. H. Dray and W. J. van der Dussen. Oxford: Oxford University Press.

Currie, G., and I. Ravenscroft. 2002. *Recreative Minds*. Oxford: Clarendon Press.

Damasio, A. 1994. *Descartes' Error: Emotion, Reason, and the Human Brain*. New York: G. P. Putnam.

Dannhauser, J. C. 1630. *Idea boni interpretis*. Strasbourg.

Danto, Arthur. 1965. *Analytical Philosophy of History*. Cambridge: Cambridge University Press.

Darwin, C. 1998 (1872). *The Expression of the Emotions in Man and Animals*. Edited and commented by P. Ekman. Oxford. Oxford University Press.

Davidson, D. 1963. "Actions, Reasons, and Causes." *Journal of Philosophy* 60: 685–700. Reprinted in Davidson 1980.

Davidson, D. 1980. *Essays on Action and Events*. Oxford: Clarendon Press.

Davidson, D. 1984. *Inquiries into Truth and Interpretation*. Oxford: Clarendon Press.

Davidson, D. 2001. *Subjective, Intersubjective, Objective*. Oxford: Clarendon Press.

Davidson, D. 2004. *Problems of Rationality*. Oxford: Clarendon Press.

Davies, M., and T. Stone, eds. 1995a. *Folk Psychology*. Oxford: Blackwell.

Davies, M., and T. Stone, eds. 1995b. *Mental Simulation*. Oxford: Blackwell.

Davies, M., and T. Stone. 2001. "Mental Simulation, Tacit Theory, and the Threat of Collapse." *Philosophical Topics* 29: 127–173.

Davis, M. 1994. *Empathy: A Social Psychological Approach*. Boulder: Westview Press.

DeBaggio, T. 2002. *Losing My Mind*. New York: Free Press.

Decety, J. 2002. "Is There Such a Thing as Functional Equivalence between Imagined, Observed, and Excecuted Action?" In *The Imitative Mind*, ed. A. Melzoff and W. Prinz, 291–310. Cambridge: Cambridge University Press.

Decety, J., and P. Jackson. 2004. "The Functional Architecture of Human Empathy." *Behavioral and Cognitive Neuroscience Review* 3: 71–100.

Dennett, D. 1981. *Brainstorms*. Cambridge, Mass.: MIT Press.

Dennett, D. 1987. *The Intentional Stance*. Cambridge, Mass.: MIT Press.

Depraz, N. 2001. "The Husserlian Theory of Intersubjectivity as Alterology." *Journal of Consciousness Studies* 8: 169–178.

DeSousa, R. 1987. *The Rationality of Emotions*. Cambridge, Mass.: MIT Press.

Devitt, M. 1996. *Coming to Our Senses: A Naturalistic Program for Semantic Localism*. Cambridge: Cambridge University Press.

Dilthey, W. 1961–. *Gesammelte Schriften*. 15 vols. Leipzig: Teubner Verlagsgesellschaft.

Dilthey, W. 1981. *Der Aufbau der geschichtlichen Welt in den Geisteswissenschaften*. Frankfurt: Suhrkamp Verlag.

Dray, W. 1957. *Laws and Explanation in History*. Oxford: Clarendon Press.

Dray, W. 1995. *History as Re-enactment*. Oxford: Oxford University Press.

Dretske, F. 1988. *Explaining Behavior*. Cambridge, Mass.: MIT Press.

Dreyfus, H. 1972. *What Computers Can't Do: A Critique of Artificial Reason*. New York: Harper and Row.

Dreyfus, H. 1980. "Holism and Hermeneutics." *Review of Metaphysics* 34: 3–23.

Dreyfus, H. 1991. *Being-in-the-World*. Cambridge, Mass.: MIT Press.

Droysen, J. G. 1893. *Outline of the Principles of History*. Trans. E. B. Andrews. Boston: Ginn.

Droysen, J. G. 1977. *Historik*. Stuttgart: Frommann-Holzboog.

Eisenberg, N., and J. Strayer, eds. 1987. *Empathy and Its Develoment*. Cambridge: Cambridge University Press.

Ekman, P., and R. Davidson. 1994. *The Nature of Emotions*. Oxford: Oxford University Press.

Encyclopedia of Human Emotions, vol. 1. 1999. Ed. D. Lewinson et al. New York: Macmillan.

Ermarth, M. 1978. *Wilhelm Dilthey: The Critique of Historical Reason*. Chicago: The University of Chicago Press.

Evans, G. 1982. *The Varieties of Reference*. Ed. John McDowell. Oxford: Oxford University Press.

Evans-Pritchard, E. 1937. *Witchcraft, Oracles, and Magic among the Azande*. Oxford: Oxford University Press.

Fadiga, L., and L. Craighero. 2003. "New Insights on Sensorimotor Integration: From Hand Action to Speech Perception." *Brain and Cognition* 53: 514–524.

Fadiga, L., L. Craighero, G. Buccino, and G. Rizzolatti. 2002. "Speech Listening Specifically Modulates the Excitability of Tongue Muscles: A TMS Study." *European Journal of Neuorsciences* 15: 399–402.

Faucher, L., R. Mallon, D. Nazer, S. Nichols, A. Ruby, S. Stich, and J. Weinberg. 2002. "The Baby in the Lab-Coat: Why Child Development Is Not an Adequate Model for Understanding the Develpoment of Science." In *The Cognitive Basis of Science*, ed. P. Carruthers, S. Stich, and M. Siegal, 335–362. Cambridge: Cambridge University Press.

Fodor, J. 1987. *Psychosemantics*. Cambridge, Mass.: MIT Press.

Fodor, J. 1990. *A Theory of Content and Other Essays*. Cambridge, Mass.: MIT Press.

Fodor, J. 2000. *The Mind Doesn't Work That Way*. Cambridge, Mass.: MIT Press.

Fodor, J., and E. Lepore. 1992. *Holism: A Shopper's Guide*. Oxford: Blackwell.

Fogassi, L., and V. Gallese. 2002. "The Neural Correlates of Action Understanding in Non-Human Primates." In *Mirror Neurons and the Evolution of Brain and Language*, ed. A. Stamenov and V. Gallese, 13–35. Amsterdam: John Benjamins.

Føllesdal, D. 1986. "Intentionality and Rationality." In *Rationality, Relativism, and the Human Sciences*, ed. J. Margolis, M. Krausz, and R. Burian, 109–125. Dordrecht: Kluwer Academic.

Frank, M. 1991. *Selbstbewußtsein und Selbsterkenntnis*. Stuttgart: Reclam.

Frankfurt, H. 1988. *The Importance of What We Care About*. Cambridge: Cambridge University Press.

Frith, U. 2003. *Autism*. Oxford: Blackwell.

Gadamer, H.-G. 1989. *Truth and Method*. New York: Crossroad.

Gallese, V. 2001. "The 'Shared Manifold' Hypothesis: From Mirror Neurons to Empathy." *Journal of Consciousness Studies* 8: 33–50.

Gallese, V. 2003a. "The Roots of Empathy: The Shared Manifold Hypothesis and the Neural Basis of Intersubjectivity." *Psychopathology* 36: 171–180.

Gallese, V. 2003b. "The Manifold Nature of Interpersonal Relations: The Quest for a Common Mechanism." *Philosophical Transactions of the Royal Society* 358: 517–528.

Gallese, V., and A. Goldman. 1998. "Mirror Neurons and the Simulation Theory of Mind-Reading." *Trends in Cogvitive Sciences* 2: 493–501.

Garfield, J., C. Peterson, and T. Perry. 2001. "Social Cognition, Language Acquisition, and the Development of the Theory of Mind." *Mind and Language* 16: 494–541.

Gegerly, G., Z. Nadasdy, G. Csibra, and S. Biro. 1995. "Taking the Intentional Stance at 12 Months of Age." *Cognition* 56: 165–193.

Gegerly, G., H. Bekkering, and I. Király. 2002. "Rational Imitation in Preverbal Infants." *Nature* 415: 755.

Gendler, T. 2000. "The Puzzle of Imaginative Resistance." *Journal of Philosophy* 97: 55–81.

Giddens, A. 1976. *New Rules of Sociological Method*. New York: Basic Books.

Gigerenzer, G. 1996. "On Narrow Norms and Vague Heuristics: A Reply to Kahneman and Tversky." *Psychological Review* 103: 592–596.

Gigerenzer, G. 2000. *Adaptive Thinking*. Oxford: Oxford University Press.

Gigerenzer, G., P. Todd, and the ABC Research Group. 1999. *Simple Heuristics That Make Us Smart*. Oxford: Oxford University Press.

Goldhagen, D. 1996. *Hitler's Willing Executioners: Ordinary Germans and the Holocaust.* New York: Alfred A. Knopf.

Goldie, P. 2000. *The Emotions: A Philosophical Exploration.* Oxford: Oxford University Press.

Goldman, A. 1986. *Epistemology and Cognition.* Cambridge, Mass.: Harvard University Press.

Goldman, A. 1993. "The Psychology of Folk Psychology." *Behavioral and Brain Sciences* 16: 15–28.

Goldman, A. 1995a. "Interpretation Psychologized." In *Folk Psychology,* ed. M. Davies and T. Stone, 74–99. Oxford. Blackwell. (First published in *Mind and Language* 4 [1989]: 161–185.)

Goldman, A. 1995b. "In Defense of Simulation Theory." In *Folk Psychology,* ed. M. Davies and T. Stone, 191–206. Oxford: Blackwell.

Goldman, A. 1995c. "Empathy, Mind, and Morals." In *Mental Simulation,* ed. M. Davies and T. Stone, 185–208. Oxford: Blackwell.

Goldman, A. 2000. "The Mentalizing Folks." In *Metarepresentations: A Multidisciplinary Perspective,* ed. D. Sperber, 171–196. Oxford: Oxford University Press.

Goldman, A. 2001. "Desire, Intention, and Simulation Theory." In *Intentions and Intentionality: Foundations of Social Cognition,* ed. B. F. Malle, L. J. Moses, and D. A. Baldwin, 207–224. Cambridge, Mass.: MIT Press.

Goldman, A. 2002. "Simulation Theory and Mental Concepts." In *Simulation and Knowledge of Action,* ed. J. Dokic and J. Proust, 1–19. Amsterdam: John Benjamins.

Goldman, A., and C. S. Sripada. 2005. "Simulationist Models of Face-based Emotion Recognition." *Cognition* 94: 193–213.

Gopnik, A. 1993. "How We Know Our Minds: The Illusion of First-Person Knowledge of Intentionality." *Behavioral and Brain Sciences* 16: 1–14.

Gopnik, A., and A. N. Meltzoff. 1997. *Words, Thoughts, and Theories.* Cambridge, Mass.: MIT Press.

Gopnik, A., and H. Wellman. 1995. "Why the Child's Theory of Mind Really *Is* a Theory." In *Folk Psychology,* ed. M. Davies and T. Stone, 232–258. Oxford: Blackwell.

Gordon, R. 1995a. "Folk-Psychology as Simulation." In *Folk Psychology,* ed. M. Davies and T. Stone, 60–73. Oxford: Blackwell. (First published in *Mind and Language* 1 [1986]: 158–170.)

Gordon, R. 1995b. "The Simulation Theory: Objections and Misconceptions." In *Folk Psychology,* ed. M. Davies and T. Stone, 100–122. Oxford: Blackwell.

Gordon, R. 1995c. "Simulation Without Introspection from Me to You." In *Mental Simulation*, ed. M. Davies and T. Stone, 53–67. Oxford: Blackwell.

Gordon, R. 1996. "'Radical' Simulationism." In *Theories of Theories of Mind*, ed. P. Carruthers and P. Smith, 11–21. Cambridge: Cambridge University Press.

Gordon, R. 2000a. "Simulation and the Explanation of Action." In *Empathy and Agency: The Problem of Understanding in the Human Sciences*, ed. H. H. Kögler and K. Stueber, 62–82. Boulder: Westview Press.

Gordon, R. 2000b. "Sellars's Rylean Revisited." *Protosoziologie* 14: 102–114.

Gordon, R. 2001. "Simulation and Reason Explanation: The Radical View." *Philosophical Topics* 29: 175–192.

Gordon, R., and J. Barker. 1994. "Autism and the 'Theory of Mind' Debate." In *Philosophical Psychopathology*, ed. G. Graham and G. Lynn Stephens, 163–182. Cambridge, Mass.: MIT Press.

Grandy, R. 1973. "Reference, Meaning, and Belief." *Journal of Philosophy* 70: 439–452.

Grondin, J. 1994. *Introduction to Philosophical Hermeneutics*. New Haven: Yale University Press.

Grundmann, T. 2003. *Der Wahrheit auf der Spur*. Paderborn: Mentis Verlag.

Hahn, L. E. 1997. *The Philosophy of Hans Georg Gadamer*. Chicago: Open Court.

Happe, F., and E. Loth. 2002. "'Theory of Mind' and Tracking Speakers' Intentions." *Mind and Language* 17: 24–36.

Harman, G. 1999. *Reasoning, Meaning, and Mind*. Oxford: Oxford University Press.

Harris, P. 1989. *Children and Emotion*. Oxford: Blackwell.

Harris, P. 1995. "From Simulation to Folk Psychology." In *Folk Psychology*, ed. M. Davies and T. Stone, 207–231. Oxford: Blackwell.

Harris, P. 1996. "Desires, Beliefs, and Language." In *Theories of Theories of Mind*, ed. P. Carruthers and P. Smith, 200–220. Cambridge: Cambridge University Press.

Harris, P. 2000. *The Work of the Imagination*. Oxford: Blackwell.

Heal, J. 1994. "Simulation vs. Theory Theory: What Is at Issue?" In *Objectivity: Simulation and the Unity of Consciousness*, Proceedings of the British Academy 83, ed. C. Peacocke, 129–144. Oxford: Oxford University Press.

Heal, J. 1995a. "Replication and Functionalism." In *Folk Psychology*, ed. M. Davies and T. Stone, 45–59. Oxford: Blackwell. (First published in *Language, Mind, and Logic*, ed. J. Butterfield, 135–150. Cambridge: Cambridge University Press, 1986.)

Heal, J. 1995b. "How to Think about Thinking." In *Mental Simulation*, ed. M. Davies and T. Stone, 33–52. Oxford: Blackwell.

Heal, J. 1996. "Simulation, Theory, and Content." In *Theories of Theories of Mind*, ed. P. Carruthers and P. Smith, 75–89. Cambridge: Cambridge University Press.

Heal, J. 2001. "Lagadonian Kinds and Psychological Concepts." *Philosophical Topics* 29: 193–217.

Heal, J. 2003a. "Simulation and Cognitive Penetrability." In her *Mind, Reason, and Imagination*, 63–88. Cambridge: Cambridge University Press.

Heal, J. 2003b. "Co-cognition and Off-line Simulation." In her *Mind, Reason, and Imagination*, 91–114. Cambridge: Cambridge University Press.

Heal, J. 2003c. "Other Minds, Rationality, and Analogy." In her *Mind, Reason, and Imagination*, 131–150. Cambridge: Cambridge University Press.

Heal, J. 2003d. "What Are Psychological Concepts For?" In her *Mind, Reason, and Imagination*, 225–250. Cambridge: Cambridge University Press.

Hempel, C. 1965. *Aspects of Scientific Explanations*. New York: Free Press.

Henderson, D. 1993. *Interpretation and Explanation in the Human Sciences*. Albany: State University of New York Press.

Henderson, D. 1995. "Simulation Theory versus Theory Theory: A Difference Without a Difference in Explanations." *Southern Journal of Philosophy*, Spindel supplement 34: 65–93.

Henderson, D. 2005. "Norms, Invariance, and Explanatory Relevance." *Philosophy of Social Science* 35: 324–338.

Henderson, D., and T. Horgan. 2000a. "What Is A Priori and What Is It Good For?" *Southern Journal of Philosophy*. Spindel Supplement 38: 51–86.

Henderson, D., and T. Horgan. 2000b. "Simulation and Epistemic Competence." In *Empathy and Agency: The Problem of Understanding in the Human Sciences*, ed. H. H. Kögler and K. Stueber, 119–143. Boulder: Westview Press.

Herder, J. 1774 (1964). "Vom Erkennen und Empfinden der menschlichen Seele." In *Herders Werke*, vol. 3, 7–69. Berlin: Aufbau Verlag.

Hirsch, E. D. 1967. *Validity in Interpretation*. New Haven: Yale University Press.

Hobson, P. 1991. "Against the Theory of 'Theory of Mind.'" *British Journal of Developmental Psychology* 9: 33–51.

Hoffman, M. 2000. *Empathy and Moral Development*. Cambridge: Cambridge University Press.

Holden, C. 2004. "Imaging Studies Showing How Brains Think about Pain." *Science* 303: 1121.

Hollis, M. 1970a. "The Limits of Irrationality." In *Rationality*, ed. Brian Wilson, 214–220. New York: Harper and Row.

Hollis, M. 1970b. "Reason and Ritual." In *Rationality*, ed. Brian Wilson, 221–239. New York: Harper and Row.

Hollis, M., and S. Lukes. 1982. *Rationality and Relativism*. Cambridge, Mass.: MIT Press.

Horgan, T., and J. Woodward. 1991. "Folk Psychology Is Here to Stay." In *Folk Psychology*, ed. J. Greenwood, 149–175. Cambridge: Cambridge University Press.

Hornsby, J. 2000. "Personal and Sub-Personal." *Philosophical Explorations* 1: 6–24.

Hume, D. 1739–1740 (1978). *A Treatise of Human Nature*. Oxford: Clarendon Press.

Hume, D. 1983 (1751). *An Enquiry Concerning the Principles of Morals*. Indianapolis: Hackett.

Hursthouse, R. 1991. "Arational Actions." *Journal of Philosophy* 88: 57–68.

Ickes, W. 1997. *Empathetic Accuracy*. New York: Guilford Press.

Jackson, F. 1999. "All That Can Be at Issue in the Theory Theory–Simulation Debate." *Philosophical Papers* 2: 77–96.

Jackson, F. 2000. "Psychological Theory and Implicit Theory." *Philosophical Explorations* 1: 83–95.

Kahnemann, D. 2000. "A Psychological Point of View: Violations of Rational Rules as a Diagnostic of Mental Processes." *Behavioral and Brain Sciences* 23: 681–683.

Kahnemann, D., and A. Tversky. 1996. "On the Reality of Cognitive Illusions." *Psychological Review* 103: 582–591.

Kain, W., and J. Perner. 2003. "Do Children with ADHD Not Need Their Frontal Lobes for Theory of Mind? A Review of Brain Imaging and Neuropsychological Studies." In *The Social Brain: Evolution and Pathology*, ed. M. Brüne, H. Ribbert, and W. Schiefenhövel, 197–230. Chichester: John Wiley.

Kant, I. 1965. Critique of Pure Reason. Trans. N. Kemp Smith. New York: St. Martin's Press.

Keil, F. 1989. *Concepts, Kinds, and Cognitive Development*. Cambridge, Mass.: MIT Press.

Keyers, C., B. Wicker, V. Gazzola, V. Anton, L. Fogassi, and V. Gallese. 2004. "A Touching Sight: SII/PV Activation during the Observation and Experience of Touch." *Neuron* 42: 335–346.

Kim, J. 1984. "Self-Understanding and Rationalizing Explanations." *Philosophia Naturalis* 21: 309–320.

Kim, J. 1993. *Supervenience and Mind*. Cambridge: Cambridge University Press.

Kim, J. 1996. *Philosophy of Mind*. Boulder: Westview Press.

Kim, J. 1998a. "Reasons and the First Person." In *Human Action, Deliberation, and Causation*, ed. J. Bransen and S. Cuypers, 67–87. Dordrecht: Kluwer Academic.

Kim, J. 1998b. *Mind in a Physical World*. Cambridge, Mass.: MIT Press.

Kim, J. 1999. "Hempel, Explanation, Metaphysics." *Philosophical Studies* 94: 1–20.

Kitcher, P. 2000. "On Interpreting Kant's Thinker as Wittgenstein's 'I.'" *Philosophy and Phenomenological Research* 61: 33–63.

Kögler, H. H. 2000. "Empathy, Dialogical Self, and Reflexive Interpretation: The Symbolic Source of Simulation." In *Empathy and Agency: The Problem of Understanding in the Human Sciences*, ed. H. H. Kögler and K. Stueber, 194–221. Boulder: Westview Press.

Kögler, H. H., and K. Stueber (eds.). 2000. *Empathy and Agency: The Problem of Understanding in the Human Sciences*. Boulder: Westview Press.

Kornblith, H. 1994. *Naturalizing Epistemology*. Cambridge, Mass.: MIT Press.

Korsgaard, C. 1996. *The Sources of Normativity*. Cambridge: Cambridge University Press.

Leslie, A. M. 1987. "Pretense and Representation: The Origins of 'Theory of Mind.'" *Psychological Review* 94: 412–426.

Leslie, A. M., and T. German. 1995. "Knowledge and Ability in 'Theory of Mind': A One-Eyed Overview of a Debate." In *Mental Simulation*, ed. M. Davies and T. Stone, 123–150. Oxford: Blackwell.

Leslie, A. M. 2000. "How to Acquire a Representational Theory of Mind." In *Metarepresentations: A Multidisciplinary Perspective*, ed. D. Sperber, 197–224. Oxford: Oxford University Press.

Lipps, T. 1903a. "Einfühlung, Innere Nachahmung und Organempfindung." *Archiv für gesamte Psychologie* 1: 465–519. (Translated as "Empathy, Inner Imitation, and Sense-Feelings," in *A Modern Book of Esthetics*, 374–382, New York: Holt, Rinehart, and Winston, 1979.)

Lipps, T. 1903b. *Aesthetik*, vol. 1. Hamburg: Voss Verlag.

Lipps, T. 1905. *Aesthetik*, vol. 2. Hamburg: Voss Verlag.

Lipps, T. 1906. "Einfühlung und Ästhetischer Genuß." *Die Zukunft* 16: 100–114.

Lipps, T. 1907. "Das Wissen von Fremden Ichen." *Psychologische Untersuchungen* 1: 694–722.

Lipps, T. 1912–1913. "Zur Einfühlung." *Psychologische Untersuchungen* 2: 111–491.

Lorenz, C. 1997. *Die Konstruktion der Vergangenheit.* Cologne: Böhlau Verlag.

Ludwig, K. 2004. "Rationality, Language, and the Principle of Charity." In *The Oxford Handbook of Rationality,* ed. A. Mele and P. Rawling, 343–362. Oxford: Oxford University Press.

MacDonald, G., and P. Pettit. 1981. *Semantics and Social Science.* London: Routledge and Kegan Paul.

MacIntyre, A. 1986. "The Intelligibility of Action." In *Rationality, Relativism, and the Human Sciences,* ed. J. Margolis, M. Krausz, and R. Burian, 63–80. Dordrecht: Kluwer Academic.

Makkreel, R. 1992. *Dilthey: Philosophy of the Human Studies.* Princeton: Princeton University Press.

Makkreel, R. 1996. "How Is Empathy Related to Understanding?" In *Issues in Husserl's "Ideas II,"* ed. T. Nenon and L. Embree, 199–212. The Hague: Kluwer Academic.

Makkreel, R. 2000. "From Simulation to Structural Transposition: A Diltheyan Critique of Empathy and Defense of *Verstehen.*" In *Empathy and Agency: The Problem of Understanding in the Human Sciences,* ed. H. H. Kögler and K. Stueber, 181–193. Boulder: Westview Press.

Malle, B., L. Moses, and D. Baldwin. 2001. *Intentions and Intentionality.* Cambridge, Mass.: MIT Press.

Malle, B. F., and K. Knobe. 2001. "The Distinction between Desire and Intention: a Folk-Conceptual Analysis." In *Intentions and Intentionality,* ed. B. B. Malle, L. J. Moses, and D. A. Baldwin, 45–67. Cambridge, Mass.: MIT Press.

McDowell, J. 1982. "Criteria, Defeasibility, and Knowledge." *British Academy* 68: 455–479.

McDowell, J. 1985. "Functionalism and Anomalous Monism." In *Actions and Events: Perspectives on the Philosophy of Donald Davidson,* ed. E. LePore and B. McLaughlin, 387–398. Oxford: Blackwell.

McGinn, C. 1977. "Charity, Interpretation, and Belief." *Journal of Philosophy* 74: 521–534.

McGinn, C. 1989. *Mental Content.* Oxford: Blackwell.

Meltzoff, A. 1995. "Understanding the Intentions of Others: Re-Enactment of Intended Acts by 18-Month-Old Children." *Developmental Psychology* 31: 838–850.

Meltzoff, A., and A. Gopnik. 1993. "The Role of Imitation in Understanding Persons and Developing a Theory of Mind." In *Understanding Other Minds: Perspectives from Autism*, ed. S. Baron-Cohen, H. Tager-Flusberg, and D. J. Cohen, 335–366. Oxford: University Press.

Meltzoff, A., and K. Moore. 1983. "Newborn Infants Imitate Adult Facial Gestures." *Child Development* 54: 702–709.

Meltzoff, A., and M. Moore. 1995. "Infants' Understanding of People and Things: From Body Imitation and Folk-Psychology." In *The Body and the Self*, ed. J. L. Bermúdez, A. Marcel, and N. Eilan, 42–69. Cambridge, Mass.: MIT Press.

Meltzoff, A., and R. Brooks. 2001. "'Like Me' as a Building Block for Understanding Other Minds: Bodily Acts, Attention, and Intention." In *Intentions and Intentionality*, ed. B. Malle, L. Moses, and D. Baldwin, 171–191. Cambridge, Mass.: MIT Press.

Meltzoff, A. N., and W. Prinz, eds. 2002. *The Imitative Mind*. Cambridge: Cambridge University Press.

Milgram, S. 1963. "Behavioral Study of Obedience." *Journal of Abnormal and Social Psychology* 67: 371–378.

Millikan, R. 1993. *White Queen Psychology and Other Essays for Alice*. Cambridge, Mass.: MIT Press.

Moran, R. 1994. "Interpretation Theory and the First Person." *Philosophical Quarterly* 44: 154–173.

Moses, L. J. 2001. "Some Thoughts on Ascribing Complex Intentional Concepts to Young Children." In *Intentions and Intentionality*, ed. B. B. Malle, L. J. Moses, and D. A. Baldwin, 69–83. Cambridge, Mass.: MIT Press.

Nadel, J., and G. Butterworth, eds. 1999. *Imitation in Infancy*. Cambridge: Cambridge University Press.

Nagel, T. 1979. *Mortal Questions*. Cambridge: Cambridge University Press.

Nagel, T. 1986. *The View from Nowhere*. Oxford: Oxford University Press.

Neurath, O. 1973. *Empiricism and Sociology*. Dordrecht: D. Reidel.

Nichols, S., and S. Stich. 1998. "Rethinking Co-Cognition." *Mind and Language* 13: 499–512.

Nichols, S., and S. Stich. 2003. *Mindreading*. Oxford: Clarendon Press.

Nisbett, R., and E. Borgida. 1975. "Attribution and the Psychology of Prediction." *Journal of Personal and Social Psychology* 32: 932–943.

Nisbett, R., and L. Ross. 1980. *Human Inferences: Strategies and Shortcomings of Social Judgement*. Englewood Cliffs, N.J.: Prentice Hall.

Novalis. 1981. *Novalis Werke*. Ed. G. Schulz. Munich: Verlag C. H. Beck.

Obeyesekere, G. 1992. *The Apotheosis of Captain Cook*. Princeton: Princeton University Press.

Over, D. 2002. "The Rationality of Evolutionary Psychology." In *Reason and Nature: Essays in the Theory of Rationality*, ed. J. L. Bermúdez and A. Millar, 187–207. Oxford: Oxford University Press.

Perner, J. 1991. *Understanding the Representational Mind*. Cambridge, Mass.: MIT Press.

Perner, J. 1996. "Simulation as Explicitation of Prediction-Implicit Knowledge About the Mind: Arguments for a Simulation-Theory Mix." In *Theories of Theories of Mind*, ed. P. Carruthers and P. Smith, 90–104. Cambridge: Cambridge University Press.

Perner, J. 2004. "Wann verstehen Kinder Handlungen als rational?" In *Der Mensch ein "animal rationale"? Vernunft, Kognition, Intelligenz*, ed. H. Schmidinger and C. Sedmak, 198–215. Darmstadt: Wissenschaftliche Buchgesellschaft.

Perry, J. 1993. *The Problem of the Essential Indexical and Other Essays*. Oxford: Oxford University Press.

Peterson, C. C., and M. Siegal. 1998. "Changing Focus on the Representational Mind: Deaf, Autistic, and Normal Children's Concept of False Photos, False Drawings, and False Beliefs." *British Journal of Developmental Psychology* 16: 301–320.

Peterson, C. C., and M. Siegal. 2000. "Insights into Theory of Mind from Deafness and Autism." *Mind and Language* 15: 123–145.

Pettit, P. 1993. *The Common Mind*. Oxford: Oxford University Press.

Pietrowski, P., and G. Rey. 1995. "When Other Things Aren't Equal: Saving Ceteris Paribus Laws from Vacuity." *British Philosophy for the Philosophy of Science* 46: 81–110.

Poland, J. 1994. *Physicalism: The Philosophical Foundations*. Oxford: Clarendon Press.

Popper, K. 1957. *The Poverty of Historicism*. London: Routledge and Kegan Paul.

Prandtl, A. 1910. *Die Einfühlung*. Leipzig: Verlag von Johann Ambrosius Barth.

Premack, D., and G. Woodruff. 1978. "Does the Chimpanzee Have a Theory of Mind?" *Behavioral and Brain Sciences* 4: 515–526.

Preston, S., and F. de Waal. 2002. "Empathy: Its Ultimate and Proximate Bases." *Behavioral and Brain Sciences* 25: 1–72.

Quine, W. V. O. 1969. "Epistemology Naturalized." In his *Ontological Relativity and Other Essays*, 69–90. New York: Columbia University Press.

Quine, W. V. O. 1960. *Word and Object*. Cambridge, Mass.: MIT Press.

Quine, W. V. O. 1990. *Pursuit of Truth*. Cambridge, Mass.: Harvard University Press.

Ravenscroft, I. 1998. "What Is It Like to Be Someone Else? Simulation and Empathy." *Ratio* 11: 170–185.

Ravenscroft, I. 1999. "Predictive Failure." *Philosophical Papers* 28: 143–168.

Ravenscroft, I. 2003. "Simulation, Collapse, and Humean Motivation." *Mind and Language* 18: 162–174.

Ripstein, A. 1987. "Explanation and Empathy." *Review of Metaphysics* 40: 465–482.

Risjord, M. 2000. *Woodcutters and Witchcraft*. Albany: State University of New York Press.

Rizzolatti, G., and L. Craighero. 2004. "The Mirror Neuron System." *Annual Reviews Neuroscience* 27: 169–192.

Rizzolatti, G., L. Craighero, and L. Fadiga. 2002. "The Mirror System in Humans." In *Mirror Neurons and the Evolution of Brain and Language*, ed. A. Stamenov and V. Gallese, 37–59. Amsterdam: John Benjamins.

Rizzolatti, G., L. Fadiga, L. Fogassi, and V. Gallese. 2002. "From Mirror Neurons to Imitation: Facts and Speculation." In *The Imitative Mind*, ed. A. Melzoff and W. Prinz, 247–266. Cambridge: Cambridge University Press.

Rorty, R. 1970. "In Defense of Eliminative Materialism." *Review of Metaphysics* 24: 112–121.

Rosenberg, A. 1985. "Davidson's Unintended Attack on Psychology." In *Actions and Events*, ed. E. Lepore and B. McLaughlin, 399–407. Oxford: Basil Blackwell.

Rosenberg, A. 1995a. *The Philosophy of Social Science*. Boulder: Westview Press.

Rosenberg, A. 1995b. "Laws, Damn Laws, and Ceteris Paribus Clauses." *Southern Journal of Philosophy*, Spindel supplement 34: 183–204.

Roth, P. A. 1987. *Meaning and Method in the Social Sciences*. Ithaca, N.Y.: Cornell University Press.

Ruben, D.-H. 1990. *Explaining Explanation*. London: Routledge.

Ruby, P., and J. Decety. 2003. "What You Believe versus What You Think They Believe: A Neuroimaging Study of Conceptual Perspective Taking." *European Journal of Neuroscience* 17: 2475–2480.

Ruby, P., and J. Decety. 2004. "How Would You Feel versus How You Think She Would Feel? A Neuroimaging Study of Perspective-Taking with Social Emotions." *Journal of Cognitive Neuroscience* 16: 988–999.

Sacks, O. 1995. *An Anthropologist from Mars*. New York: Alfred A. Knopf.

Sahlins, M. 1995. *How the "Natives" Think about Captain Cook, For Example*. Chicago: University of Chicago Press.

Salmon, W. 1989. "Four Decades of Scientific Explanation." In *Scientific Explanation*, Minnesota Studies in the Philosophy of Science, vol. 13, ed. P. Kitcher and W. Salmon, 3–219. Minneapolis: University of Minnesota Press.

Samuels, R., and S. Stich. 2004. "Rationality and Psychology." In *The Oxford Handbook of Rationality*, ed. A. Mele and P. Rawling, 279–300. Oxford: Oxford University Press.

Samuels, R., S. Stich, and M. Bishop. 2002. "Ending the Rationality Wars: How to Make Disputes about Human Rationality Disappear." In *Common Sense, Reasoning, and Rationality*, ed. R. Elio, 236–268. Oxford: Oxford University Press.

Samuels, R., S. Stich, and P. Tremoulet. 1999. "Rethinking Rationality: From Bleak Implications to Darwinian Modules." In *Cognition, Agency, and Rationality*, ed. K. Korta, E. Sosa, and X. Arrazola, 21–62. Dordrecht: Kluwer Academic.

Saxe, R. 2005. "Against Simulation: The Argument from Error." *Trends in Cognitive Science* 9: 174–179.

Saxe, R., S. Carey, and N. Kanwisher. 2004. "Understanding Other Minds: Linking Developmental Psychology and Functional Neuroimaging." *Annual Review of Psychology* 55: 87–124.

Scheler, M. 1923. *Wesen und Form der Sympathie*. Bern/Munich: Francke Verlag. (Translated as *The Nature of Sympathy*, London: Routledge and Kegan Paul, 1954.)

Schiffer, S. 1991. "Ceteris Paribus Laws." *Mind* 100: 1–17.

Schleiermacher, F. 1998. *Hermeneutics and Criticism*. Edited by A. Bowie. Cambridge: Cambridge University Press.

Scholl, B., and A. M. Leslie. 1999. "Modularity, Development, and 'Theory of Mind.'" *Mind and Language* 14: 131–153.

Searle, J. 1983. *Intentionality*. Cambridge: Cambridge University Press.

Searle, J. 1992. *The Rediscovery of the Mind*. Cambridge, Mass.: MIT Press.

Searle, J. 1995. *The Construction of Social Reality*. New York: Free Press.

Sellars, W. 1963. *Science, Perception, and Reality*. New York: Humanities Press.

Slovic, P., B. Fischhoff, and S. Lichtenstein. 1976. "Cognitive Processes and Societal Risk Taking." In *Cognition and Social Behavior*, ed. J. Carroll and J. Payne. Hillsdale, N.J.: Erlbaum.

Smith, A. 1759 (1966). *The Theory of Moral Sentiments*. New York: August M. Kelley.

Smith, M. 1994. *The Moral Problem*. Oxford: Blackwell.

Spranger, E. 1905. *Die Grundlage der Geschichtswissenschaft*. Berlin: Verlag von Reuther and Reichard.

Spranger, E. 1930. *Lebensformen*. Halle: Max Niemeyer Verlag.

Stamenov, M., and V. Gallese, eds. 2002. *Mirror Neurons and the Evolution of Brain and Language*. Amsterdam: John Benjamins.

Stanovich, K., and R. West. 2000. "Individual Differences in Reasoning: Implications for the Rationality Debate?" *Behavioral and Brain Sciences* 23: 645–726.

Stein, E. 1917 (1980). *Zum Problem der Einfühlung*. Munich: Kaffke Verlag. (Translated as *On the Problem of Empathy*, Washington, D.C.: ICS, 1989.)

Stein, E. 1996. *Without Good Reason*. Oxford: Clarendon Press.

Stern, P. 1898. *Einfühlung und Innere Association in der Neueren Ästhetik*. Hamburg and Leipzig: Verlag von Leopold Voss.

Stich, S. 1981. "Dennett on Intentional Systems." *Philosophical Topics* 12: 39–62.

Stich, S. 1983. *From Folk-Psychology to Cognitive Science*. Cambridge, Mass.: MIT Press.

Stich, S. 1990. *The Fragmentation of Reason*. Cambridge, Mass.: MIT Press.

Stich, S. 1994. "Could Man Be an Irrational Animal? Some Notes on the Epistemology of Rationality." In *Naturalizing Epistemology*, ed. H. Kornblith, 337–357. Cambridge, Mass.: MIT Press.

Stich, S. 1996. *Deconstructing the Mind*. Oxford: Oxford University Press.

Stich, S., and S. Nichols. 1995. "Folk Psychology: Simulation or Tacit Theory?" In *Folk Psychology*, ed. M. Davies and T. Stone, 123–158. Cambridge, Mass.: MIT Press.

Stich, S., and S. Nichols. 1997. "Cognitive Penetrability, Rationality, and Restricted Simulation." *Mind and Language* 12: 297–326.

Stich, S., and S. Nichols. 1998. "Theory Theory to the Max." *Mind and Language* 13: 421–449.

Stich, S., and I. Ravenscroft. 1996. "What Is Folk Psychology?" In S. Stich, *Deconstructing the Mind*, 115–135. Oxford. Oxford University Press.

Stueber, K. 1993. *Donald Davidsons Theorie Sprachlichen Verstehens*. Frankfurt am Main: Anton Hain Verlag.

Stueber, K. 1994a. "Practice Indeterminacy and Private Language: Wittgenstein's Dissolution of Skepticism." *Philosophical Investigations* 17: 15–36.

Stueber, K. 1994b. "Understanding Truth and Objectivity: A Dialogue between Donald Davidson and Hans Georg Gadamer." In *Hermeneutics and Truth*, ed. B. Wachterhauser, 172–189. Chicago: Northwestern University Press.

Stueber, K. 1996. "Indeterminacy and the First Person Perspective." In *Verdad: logica, rerpresentacion y mundo*, ed. C. Martinez Vidal, 333–341. Universidade de Santiago De Compostela.

Stueber, K. 1997a. "Holism and Radical Interpretation: The Limitations of a Formal Theory of Language." In *Analyomen 2*, ed. G. Meggle, 290–298. Berlin and New York: DeGruyter.

Stueber, K. 1997b. "Psychologische Erklärungen im Spannungsfeld des Interpretationismus und Reduktionismus." *Die Philosophische Rundschau* 44: 304–328.

Stueber, K. 2000. "Understanding Other Minds and the Problem of Rationality." In *Empathy and Agency: The Problem of Understanding in the Human Sciences*, ed. H. H. Kögler and K. Stueber, 144–162. Boulder: Westview Press.

Stueber, K. 2001. "Die antiskeptischen Strategien des semantischen und epistemischen Externalismus und ihr Bedeutung für die Erkenntnistheorie." In *Erkenntnistheorie: Positionen zwischen Tradition und Gegenwart*, ed. T. Grundmann, 210–224. Paderborn: Mentis Verlag.

Stueber, K. 2002a. "The Psychological Basis of Historical Explanation: Reenactment, Simulation, and the Fusion of Horizons." *History and Theory* 41: 24–42.

Stueber, K. 2002b. "The Problem of Self-Knowledge." *Erkenntnis* 56: 269–296.

Stueber, K. 2003. "Intentional Explanation, Psychological Laws, and the Irreducibility of the First Person Perspective." In *Monism*, ed. A. Bächli and K. Petrus, 255–278. Frankfurt and London: Ontos Verlag.

Stueber, K. 2004. "Agency and the Objectivity of Historical Narratives." In *Philosophy of History: A Reexamination*, ed. W. Sweet, 197–222. Aldershot: Ashgate Press.

Stueber, K. 2005a. "Mental Causation and the Paradox of Explanation." *Philosophical Studies* 122: 243–277.

Stueber, K. 2005b. "How to Think about Rules and Rule-Following." *Philosophy of Social Science* 35: 307–323.

Sutherland, S. 1994. *Irrationality: Why We Don't Think Straight*. New Brunswick, N.J.: Rutgers University Press.

Thagard, P. 1999. *How Scientists Explain Disease*. Princeton: Princeton University Press.

Thagard, P., and R. Nisbett. 1983. "Rationality and Charity." *Philosophy of Science* 50: 250–267.

Titchener, E. B. 1909a. *Lectures on the Experimental Psychology of Thought-Processes*. New York: Macmillan.

Titchener, E. B. 1909b. *A Textbook of Psychology*, vol. 1. New York: MacMillan.

Todd, P., and G. Gigerenzer. 2000. "Précis of *Simple Heuristics That Make Us Smart.*" *Behavioral and Brain Sciences* 23: 727–780.

Tooby, J., and L. Cosmides. 1992. "The Psychological Foundation of Culture." In *The Adapted Mind: Evolutionary Psychology and the Generation of Culture*, ed. J. Barkow, L. Cosmides, and J. Tooby, 19–136. New York: Oxford University Press.

Tully, J., ed. 1988. *Meaning and Context: Quentin Skinner and His Critics.* Princeton: Princeton University Press.

Turner, S. 1994. *The Social Theory of Practices.* Chicago: University of Chicago Press.

Turner, S. 2000. "Imitation or Internalization of Norms: Is Twentieth-Century Social Theory Based on the Wrong Choice?" In *Empathy and Agency: The Problem of Understanding in the Human Sciences*, ed. H. H. Kögler and K. Stueber, 103–118. Boulder: Westview Press.

Tversky, A., and D. Kahnman. 1983. "Extensional versus Intuitive Reasoning: The Conjunction Fallacy in Probability Judgment." *Psychological Review* 4: 293–315.

Tversky, B., J. Morrison, and J. Zacks. 2002. "On Bodies and Events." In *The Imitative Mind*, ed. A. Melzoff and W. Prinz, 221–232. Cambridge: Cambridge University Press.

Velleman, J. D. 1989. *Practical Reflection.* Princeton: Princeton University Press.

Velleman, J. D. 2000. *The Possibility of Practical Reason.* Oxford: Clarendon Press.

Vischer, R. 1994 (1873). "On the Optical Sense of Form: A Contribution to Aesthetics." In *Empathy, Form, and Space*, ed. H. F. Mallgrave, 89–123. Los Angeles: The Getty Center for the History of Art and the Humanities.

Vogeley, K., and A. Newen. 2002. "Mirror Neurons and the Self Construct." In *Mirror Neurons and the Evolution of Brain and Language*, ed. A. Stamenov and V. Gallese, 135–151. Amsterdam: John Benjamins.

Walton, K. 1997. "Spelunking, Simulation, and Slime." In *Emotions and the Arts*, ed. M. Hjort and S. Laver, 37–49. Oxford: Oxford University Press.

Wason, P. 1968. "Reasoning about a Rule." *Quarterly Journal of Experimental Psychology* 20: 273–281.

Webb, S. 1994. "Witnessed Behavior and Dennett's Intentional Stance." *Philosophical Topics* 22: 457–470.

Wellman, H. M. 1990. *The Child's Theory of Mind.* Cambridge, Mass.: MIT Press.

Wellman, H. M., and A. T. Phillips. 2001. "Developing Intentional Understanding." In *Intentions and Intentionality*, ed. B. B. Malle, L. J. Moses, and D. A. Baldwin, 125–148. Cambridge, Mass.: MIT Press.

Wilkes, K. 1984. "Pragmatics in Science and Theory in Common Sense." *Inquiry* 27: 339–361.

Wilson, B., ed. 1970. *Rationality*. New York: Harper and Row.

Wimmer, H., and J. Perner. 1983. "Beliefs about Beliefs: Representation and Constraining Function of Wrong Beliefs in Young Children's Understanding of Deception." *Cogniton* 13: 103–128.

Winch, P. 1958. *The Idea of a Social Science and Its Relation to Philosophy*. London: Routledge and Kegan Paul.

Winch, P. 1964. "Understanding a Primitive Society." *American Philosophical Quarterly* 1: 307–324. (Reprinted in Wilson 1970, 78–111.)

Wispe, L. 1987. "History of the Concept of Empathy." In *Empathy and Its Development*, ed. N. Eisenberg and J. Strayer, 17–37. Cambridge. Cambridge University Press.

Wispe, L. 1991. *The Psychology of Sympathy*. New York and London: Plenum Press.

Wittgenstein, L. 1958. *Philosophical Investigations*. Englewood Cliffs, N.J.: Prentice Hall.

Wittgenstein, L. 1980. *Remarks on Philosophical Psychology*, 2 vols. Oxford: Blackwell.

Woodward, J. 2000. "Explanation and Invariance in the Special Sciences." *British Journal for the Philosophy of Science* 51: 197–254.

Woodward, J. 2003. *Making Things Happen: A Theory of Causal Explanation*. Oxford: Oxford University Press.

Woodward, J., and C. Hitchcock. 2003: "Explanatory Generalizations, Part I: A Counterfactual Account." *Noûs* 37: 1–24.

Zahavi, D. 2001. "Beyond Empathy: Phenomenological Approaches to Intersubjectivity." *Journal of Consciousness Studies* 8: 151–167.

Zimbardo, P. 1972. "Pathology of Imprisonment." *Society* 9: 4–9.

Index

DATE DUE

Demco, Inc. 38-293